T0329623

RHETORICAL STYLE AND BOURGEOIS VIRTUE

RSA·STR

THE **RSA** SERIES IN TRANSDISCIPLINARY **RHETORIC**

The RSA Series in Transdisciplinary Rhetoric is a collaboration with the Rhetoric Society of America to publish innovative and rigorously argued scholarship on the tremendous disciplinary breadth of rhetoric. Books in the series take a variety of approaches, including theoretical, historical, interpretive, critical, or ethnographic, and will examine rhetorical action in a way that appeals, first, to scholars in communication studies and English or writing, and, second, to at least one other discipline or subject area.

Mark Garrett Longaker

RHETORICAL STYLE AND BOURGEOIS VIRTUE

Capitalism and Civil Society in the
British Enlightenment

THE PENNSYLVANIA STATE UNIVERSITY PRESS
UNIVERSITY PARK, PENNSYLVANIA

Library of Congress Cataloging-in-Publication Data

Longaker, Mark Garrett, 1974– , author.
    Rhetorical style and bourgeois virtue : capitalism and
    civil society in the British Enlightenment / Mark Garrett
    Longaker.
        pages cm — (The RSA series in transdisciplinary rhetoric)
    Summary: "Focuses on the writings of John Locke, Adam
    Smith, Hugh Blair, and Herbert Spencer to explore how the
    discipline of rhetoric connected the economics and ethics
    of capitalism from the British Enlightenment through the
    nineteenth century"—Provided by publisher.
    Includes bibliographical references and index.
    ISBN 978-0-271-07086-5 (cloth : alk. paper)
    1. Capitalism—Moral and ethical aspects—Great
    Britain—History.
    2. Rhetoric—Great Britain—History.
    3. Enlightenment—Great Britain.
    4. Locke, John, 1632–1704.
    5. Smith, Adam, 1723–1790.
    6. Blair, Hugh, 1718–1800.
    7. Spencer, Herbert, 1820–1903.
    I. Title. II. Series: RSA series in transdisciplinary rhetoric.

HC254.5.L745 2015
174'409171241—dc23
2015014592

The Pennsylvania State University Press is a member of the
Association of American University Presses.

It is the policy of The Pennsylvania State University Press to
use acid-free paper. Publications on uncoated stock satisfy
the minimum requirements of American National Standard
for Information Sciences—Permanence of Paper for Printed
Library Material, ANSI Z39.48–1992.

This book is printed on paper that contains
30% post-consumer waste

This is a book about virtue, written in honor of my brother, who embodies fortitude; my father, who practices prudence; and my mother, who exudes benevolence.

Contents

Acknowledgments

This book was initially conceived in a faculty seminar hosted by the Humanities Institute at the University of Texas at Austin. I completed the manuscript while on a faculty research assignment given by the College of Liberal Arts at UT. Publication was assisted by a generous grant from the President's Office of the University of Texas at Austin. Thanks to all of these institutions for their support. Two professional societies provided forums where I could test out these ideas: the Rhetoric Society of America and the International Society for the History of Rhetoric. Thanks to everyone at RSA and ISHR for their erudite company. An earlier version of chapter 3 appeared as "The Political Economy of Rhetorical Style: Hugh Blair's Solution to the Civic-Commercial Dilemma" in the *Quarterly Journal of Speech* 94, no. 2 (2008): 179–99, copyright © 2008 Routledge, and a portion of chapter 2 appeared in "Adam Smith on Rhetoric and Phronesis, Law and Economics," *Philosophy and Rhetoric* 47, no. 1 (2014): 25–47. I am grateful for the editors' permission to reprint these materials.

I owe a great deal to many individuals who contributed their thoughts and insights. I cannot remember what each person offered. They are all equally— inestimably—valuable. Therefore, I choose to present their names in an indecorous list. The manner is no reflection of their importance. Rather, it exhibits my shortcomings. Thanks to Lois Agnew, David Beard, Michael Benedikt, Michael Bernard-Donals, Sarah Canright, Evan Carton, Leah Ceccarelli, Antonio Ceraso, Diane Davis, Diana DiNitto, Oliver Freiberger, David Gore, Daniel Gross, Michael Halloran, Gerard Hauser, Debra Hawhee, Rodney Herring, Neville Hoad, Tim Johnson, Ward Keeler, Nathan Kreuter, John Lucaites, Tracie Matysik, Glen McClish, Stephen McKenna, Julia Mickenberg, Thomas Miller, Patricia Roberts-Miller, Stephen Schneider, Dale Smith, Connie Steel, Nicholas Taylor, Laura Thain, Jay Voss, Art Walzer, and the anonymous reviewers at Penn State Press. Particular thanks are due to Marie Secor and Jeffrey Walker, whose contributions exceed the boundaries of this meager sentence.

I offer the greatest thanks to my wife and two daughters, who remind me that the worst day with family far surpasses the best day with philosophers.

Abbreviations for Frequently Cited Works

Lectures	Hugh Blair. *Lectures on Rhetoric and Belles Lettres*. Edited and introduced by Linda Ferreira-Buckley and S. Michael Halloran. Carbondale: Southern Illinois University Press, 2005.
LJ	Adam Smith. *Lectures on Jurisprudence*. Edited by R. L. Meek, D. D. Raphael, and P. G. Stein. Indianapolis, IN: Liberty Fund Press, 1982.
LRBL	Adam Smith. *Lectures on Rhetoric and Belles Lettres*. Edited by J. C. Bryce. Indianapolis, IN: Liberty Fund Press, 1985.
Sermons	Hugh Blair. *The Sermons of Hugh Blair*. 4 vols. London: Cadell, 1815.
TMS	Adam Smith. *The Theory of Moral Sentiments*. Edited by D. D. Raphael and A. L. Macfie. Indianapolis, IN: Liberty Fund Press, 1984.
WHS	Herbert Spencer. *The Works of Herbert Spencer*. 21 vols. Osnabrück: Otto Zeller, 1966.
WJL	John Locke. *The Works of John Locke*. 9 vols. London: C. and J. Rivington, 1824.
WN	Smith, Adam. *An Inquiry into the Nature and Causes of the Wealth of Nations*. Edited by R. H. Campbell, A. S. Skinner, and W. B. Todd. Indianapolis, IN: Liberty Fund Press, 1979.

Definitions and Introductions

The association between ethics and economics is commonplace. As a result, when supply and demand falter, we appeal to right and wrong. During the last credit crisis, we worried about "moral hazards" and "predatory lending" because we suspected that functional twenty-first-century capitalism depends on people who pursue profit and uphold ethics, people who are greedy but good. The connection between rhetoric and ethics is likewise routine. Therefore, criticism of a person's writing might use words that otherwise describe his character. We might call a phrase "felicitous" or a paragraph "sloppy."

Much less common nowadays is an association between rhetorical style and economics. The political scientist Francis Fukuyama has argued that "capitalism" requires "certain premodern cultural habits" in order to "work properly." Even as he concedes that market societies require ethical behaviors to engender trust, Fukuyama never imagines that linguistic syntax instills a sense of "moral obligation [or] duty toward community."[1] The economist Deirdre McCloskey celebrates the bourgeois virtues because capitalism makes people good and good people make capitalism work: "Virtues support the market . . . [and] the market supports the virtues."[2] But McCloskey makes no mention of metaphors or similes.

Teachers and scholars in the humanities more readily associate rhetorical style with virtue, largely because humanists (especially rhetoric teachers) have long believed that becoming a better writer makes you a better person. This supposition goes back to ancient times. Aelius Theon, probably writing in the first century, described an early exercise that captures the millennia-old association between ethics and rhetoric. Students writing *chreia* read useful sayings (maxims or representative anecdotes) and then briefly embellished, contradicted, or restated them. Through performative repetition they cultivated good habits of speaking (style). Additionally, they reconfigured bits of received wisdom to curate virtue.[3] Roughly a century later, Hermogenes noted that specific stylistic qualities relate to the orator's moral makeup. For example, he said that qualities of the sincere style "are aspects of Simplicity that reveal Character."[4] Aelius Theon's first-century Roman contemporary, Marcus Quintilian, described good rhetorical style using terms that suggest the ideal Roman character: "bold, manly and chaste."[5]

During the English Renaissance, due in large part to Hermogenes's popularity, this ancient association between style and virtue continued.[6] In *The Arte of Rhetorique* (1553), one of the era's most popular manuals, Thomas Wilson associated an appropriate style with an admirable virtue. Lois Agnew paraphrases Wilson: "To develop skill in the appropriate use of language is inherently good because language is the natural and external embodiment of human reason." When the speaker employs an appropriate style, she asks the audience to admire her character. Therefore, according to Wilson, "the way in which an individual uses language has a direct bearing on the life of the community."[7] Despite this long-standing connection between rhetoric and ethics, few today would suggest that good habits of speech sustain a capitalist economy.

Economics is commonly connected to ethics. Ethics is typically associated with rhetoric. Economics and rhetoric seem indirectly linked by their shared affiliation with ethics. This has not always been the case. In the chapters to follow, I argue that the British Enlightenment wove all three disciplines into a cohesive vision of free-market capitalism, rhetorical style, and bourgeois virtue. By returning to and exploring specific writers' connections among these three subjects, I offer rewards to audiences in several disciplines. For those who care about the history of ideas, I demonstrate that during the seventeenth, eighteenth, and nineteenth centuries (and arguably still today) people theorized the virtues of personal liberty and free trade by focusing on the habits of language. To those interested in analyzing and teaching persuasive writing/speech, I explain that the rhetorical tradition has promulgated ethical dispositions that sustain the free market. For those studying the history of economics, I explain that early political economists discussed and disseminated capitalism's excellences by exploring and exhibiting stylistic habits such as clear and honest speech.

To summarize my principal argument, in the late seventeenth, mid-eighteenth, and mid-nineteenth centuries a British philosopher, a political economist, a rhetorical theorist, and a sociologist all tried to cultivate bourgeois virtue by teaching rhetorical style, each building on others' ideas and each addressing a unique stage of capitalist development. Each chapter supports this thesis by exploring the connections among ethics, economics, and rhetoric in the scholarly corpus of one individual while accounting for his intellectual debts and his economic circumstances. Since the argument about rhetorical style and bourgeois virtue is this book's main contribution, the work is arranged into separate essays that make the same point recursively, each time with new evidence and in different circumstances. Four case studies of four people connecting rhetorical style to bourgeois virtue prove that three subjects (ethics, economics, and rhetoric) were interrelated from the late seventeenth through the mid-nineteenth centuries.

The individual chapters are written so that each can be read independently of the rest, but their cohesion into a single argument will not be apparent unless the reader keeps in mind: (1) three key terms (*capitalism, bourgeois,* and *civil society*); (2) a methodological commitment to intellectual history; and (3) a recurring distinction between civil society and civic virtue. The bulk of this introductory chapter is therefore dedicated to defining these terms, to explaining this commitment, and to drawing this distinction.

Capitalism and Intellectual History

In the paragraphs and pages to follow the word *capitalism* refers to the private ownership of wealth and the market distribution of resources. The classical Marxist might say capitalism is characterized by class struggle and the industrial exploitation of labor.[8] The leftist vanguard might say capitalism is a form of (inter)state political organization that enables domination by one governmental institution or one economic class.[9] But since this study focuses on bourgeois thinkers, ideas anathema to their preferred definition are inappropriate. For the bourgeoisie, capitalism features neither exploitation nor the state; rather, capitalism favors freedom from exploitation and absence of the state.

This definition and the above description of this book's principal argument both suppose the value and possibility of an intellectual history that mixes biography, conversational context, and economic circumstance. Each essay aims to fairly present one writer's ideas as they fit in a broader conversation and a wider social situation. The presumptions required to sustain such corpus analysis are themselves questionable. First, I must assume a unified subject (an integral person or author) who writes. Second, I must believe that this presumed author achieved some consistency in his writings. Third, I must accept that some ideas (such as those about rhetorical style and bourgeois virtue) determine others (such as those about political economy or sociology). Finally, I must privilege ideas over institutions, beliefs over actions, individual lives over historical eras, philosophical systems over political movements. Needless to say, though all these presumptions are troubled, they can be defended nonetheless.

The unified subject—the now "dead" author—may be a fiction, but it is an Enlightenment fiction, so we should not be surprised to find people in the British Enlightenment writing as if they were psychically whole. Michel Foucault points out the Enlightenment beliefs in "the public and free use of autonomous reason."[10] Evidence of the era's belief in public reason can be found in the writings of John Locke, Adam Smith, Hugh Blair, and Herbert Spencer, for each discussed liberal civil society, that free space where individuals can rationally pursue their interests and reasonably work out their differences. Evidence of the "author" who possesses autonomous reason can be found in the remarkable philosophical consistency exhibited in each man's intellectual corpus. Most (with only Blair as the exception) revised their earlier works, striving to make them comport with their later beliefs. Some (such as Smith and Spencer) destroyed papers that they could not completely integrate into their philosophical systems. All tried to maintain and apply certain core tenets throughout their lives. Spencer's dedication to a notion of voluntaristic yet biological evolution parodies the Enlightenment "author" struggling for consistency by allowing early principles to determine later ideas. While it is ontologically questionable to assume an autonomous and rational author composing a consistent intellectual corpus, it is historically accurate to say that this questionable notion guided Locke, Smith, Blair, and Spencer.

The final supposition underlying intellectual history—the privileging of ideas over institutions—is difficult to defend, for it touches on a question of value. Feminist histories oppose patriarchy. Microhistories celebrate local actors. Materialist histories endorse economic systems (or their overthrow). Intellectual histories value beliefs, typically an era's "ruling ideas." I cannot say— because I do not believe—that a dominant philosophy deserves more attention than a political program committed to gender equality, a narrative technique dedicated to neglected actors, or a critical inquiry concerned with economic justice. But I nonetheless maintain that historians, economists, rhetoricians, and philosophers can benefit from intellectual history by learning what the dominant class thought, even if we choose to disagree, prefer to value the local actor, or strive to overturn the prevailing mode of production.

While I champion intellectual history, I acknowledge that focusing exclusively on ideas would ignore British capitalism's influential institutions. Locke, Smith, Blair, and Spencer each lived during some stage of capitalism's development. In the late seventeenth century, most of England, arguably all of Scotland, and certainly every square mile of Ireland belonged to what Peter Laslett called a bucolic, feudal, and alien "world we have lost." When John Locke was writing about credit and clear style, he did not imagine himself as bourgeois, nor did he live in a market-oriented society. Nevertheless, he participated in trade and commerce, just as England's turn-of-the-century economy depended on its financial sector. By 1760 when Adam Smith conceived his now-famous free-market apology (*Wealth of Nations*, 1776), urban areas of England, such as Middlesex, did not "belong in the world we have lost."[11] But much of Scotland still did. Christopher Whatley has chronicled dramatic advances in post-Union (1707) Scotland: agricultural improvements, a flourishing financial industry, increased manufacturing. However, Whatley also notes that these developments stumbled due to local recalcitrance. People fought enclosure and commercialization. Demand for luxury items (such as tea, ale, and wigs) increased among the urban middle class but nowhere else. Workers stayed in the fields rather than migrate to the factories.[12] Nonetheless, Adam Smith and Hugh Blair witnessed important developments in marketing and trade. Only Herbert Spencer witnessed the full glory of the English industrial revolution. Capitalism was a frail newborn during England's financial revolution, an unpredictable child during Britain's commercial revolution, and a troubled adolescent during the industrial revolution. The social history of this development explains many British Enlightenment ideas about rhetoric, ethics, and economics.

In the seventeenth, eighteenth, and nineteenth centuries, there was an "apparent [economic] scene" involving factories, governments, capitalists, and workers. Nonetheless, mine is a book about imagination, what Étienne Balibar has called political economy's "other scene." John Locke, Adam Smith, Hugh Blair, and Herbert Spencer all imagined their "material process of history." Accounting for the interaction between their imaginations and their economic circumstances should counter any effort to assert that ideas drive history or that economics determines ideas. As Balibar explained, there is no "absolute 'last instance'" accounting for human history, so we should adopt "a *broad* (hence heterogeneous) concept of materiality."[13] Such a concept must include imaginations and industries, beliefs and institutions, values and policies.

Bourgeois and Civil Society

The word *bourgeois* carries two complementary meanings. A dictionary might present them so:

1. Pertaining or belonging to a modern nonaristocratic subject who freely and rationally debates matters of public importance. Example of *bourgeois* (1): "We conceive bourgeois public sphere as a category that is typical of an epoch. It cannot be abstracted from the unique developmental history of that 'civil society.'" Jürgen Habermas, *The Structural Transformation of the Public Sphere* (1962).[14]
2. Pertaining or belonging to a modern subject who participates in and benefits from free-market capitalism. Example of *bourgeois* (2): "The economists express the relation of bourgeois production, the division of labor, credit, money, &c., as categories fixed, immutable, eternal." Karl Marx, *The Poverty of Philosophy* (1847).[15]

As the above examples suggest, different values adhere to the word depending on its use. Habermas celebrated the public sphere in bourgeois civil society. Marx condemned the exploitative profit justified by bourgeois political economy. Furthermore, the word carries both meanings in every use. The bourgeois subject is both a citizen and a capitalist, speaking freely in the public sphere while trading profitably in the marketplace. In both arenas, the bourgeois subject exhibits the same rhetorical virtues to sustain civil society. She speaks clearly and honestly; she sympathizes with those who do likewise; she embellishes but never obscures meaning; she speaks concisely.

In an older (and distinctly English) usage, the term *civil society* refers to government or the state. When John Locke discussed the transition from the state of nature to "civil society," he meant the formation of government. In the eighteenth century, a new use of the term appeared and found its fullest explication in the political writings of the German philosopher G. W. F. Hegel.[16] Hegel argued that civil society is a free and open arena "between the family and the state." The "creation of civil society," said Hegel, "belongs to the modern world." Civil society is the domain of the bourgeoisie, the place where free people exchange goods and ideas to achieve reasoned cooperation and to pursue personal profit. Their rationally self-interested behavior results in an unintended social good, for "the particular end takes on the form of universality, and gains satisfaction by simultaneously satisfying the welfare of others."[17] Hegel was heavily influenced by English political economy (especially the works of Adam Smith and David Ricardo), so his notion of civil society repeats a basic presumption that Hegel inherited from the British Enlightenment: in bourgeois civil society, social welfare arises from the unintended consequences of rationally selfish behavior. While Hegel imagined it as a place for free trade, Habermas has demonstrated that civil society also featured the free exchange of ideas. Locke, Smith, Blair, and Spencer all believed bourgeois civil society suffers whenever people's speech gets restricted or their wallets constrained. Since states and churches often threaten the public sphere and the marketplace with harmful restraints, civil society depends on a virtuous bourgeoisie to establish its order and to guarantee its stability.

Civil Society Distinguished from Civic Virtue

Ever since J. G. A. Pocock discussed the tension between an ancient belief in "civic virtue" and the bourgeois institution of "civil society," every scholarly use of one term tacitly invokes the other. According to Pocock, "The dominant paradigm for the [eighteenth-century] individual inhabiting the world of value was that of civic man; but the dominant paradigm for the individual as engaged in historic actuality was that of economic and intersubjective man, and it was peculiarly hard to bring the two together."[18] From fourth-century BCE Greece to fifteenth-century CE England, Pocock's "civic man" was imbued with "civic virtue," dedicating his public life to the state. Since the ancient Greek agora and the Renaissance English court were parts of the state, those who deliberated in these arenas studied rhetoric to prepare for civil service. People learned to be good citizens by speaking properly in public situations.

Many late-Renaissance and early-Enlightenment developments led people to interrogate the classical sense of civic virtue. Gerard Hauser has explored two in particular: (1) The Protestant Reformation led to "dissenting" factions. When French Huguenots refused Louis XIV's Catholicism and when English Quakers refused Charles II's Anglicanism, everyone saw that public discourse could defy the state. (2) Town burghers resisted national control of local trade. When English shopkeepers and merchants resisted the Stuarts' mercantilism, people realized that they could publicly associate beyond the state's power. As a result, according to Hauser, the classical belief in civic virtue withered. In its place grew a dedication to civil society, a bourgeois institution whose guiding concept is "a network of associations independent of the state whose members, through social interactions that balance conflict and consensus, seek to regulate themselves in ways consistent with a valuation of difference."[19]

This distinction between civic virtue and civil society separates the modern from the ancient. Furthermore, the difference between the modern and the ancient accounts for two important developments in British Enlightenment rhetoric: belletrism and the plain style. Since the Enlightenment affection for belletrism and the plain style was built on a synthesis of civic virtue and civil society, I will spend a few more paragraphs discussing these terms. The distinction between public virtue and private conscience is a good place to begin exploring the ancient connections among plain writing, stylistic ornamentation, and virtue. Ancient public virtue is a performed quality that infuses any space where people deliberate matters of shared concern. Ancient Greeks did not distinguish a knowing subject from the object known, anymore than they believed in a psyche independent of a society. The classicist Eric Havelock succinctly explained, "Here is a man to whom it has not occurred, and to whom it cannot occur, that he has a personality apart from the pattern of his acts."[20] If performance is not independent of person, if outward demonstration cannot separate from inward virtue, then training a person to speak in a certain fashion will also train her to be a particular(ly good) citizen.

Ancient Greek sophistical education emphasized rhetorical style because the sophists saw the mind as a collection of performed habits patterned after dominant mores. Formal and encyclopedic methods of education focus on the isolated mind receiving information. Sophistical rhetorical education, in contrast, does not separate the individual from the community, nor does it separate knowledge from habit. As a result, ancient sophistical rhetorical education aimed at instilling virtue by teaching values, traditions, and behaviors.[21] Students memorized maxims that encapsulate received wisdom. Proof of their learning—the final exam, so to speak—is a convincing and stylistically appropriate oration.

Modern private virtue is a cloistered quality that suffuses the conscience and guides the individual toward good behavior. The reasons behind the transition from public virtue to private conscience remain disputed. Perhaps the shift from oral to literate culture instigated a simultaneous move from public to private, since orality happens in crowded assemblies whereas literacy happens in lonely libraries.[22] Perhaps the Protestant separation of individual conscience from the congregation triggered the modern separation of psyche from community.

Perhaps squabbles over (city-) state sovereignty led to a belief in political freedom and personal confession. If the state is free, then so must be the citizen; and if the citizen is free, then so must be her conscience.[23] Regardless of the supposed origin, modernity is marked by atrophied publicity and hypertrophied privacy. The sociologist Richard Sennett explained that, in modern times, "the psyche is treated as though it has an inner life of its own."[24]

Belletrism and the plain style are the British Enlightenment's chief rhetorical preoccupations because the bourgeoisie wanted language to reflect private conscience. Bourgeois civil society rests on the supposition that each speaker can freely express her thoughts and sentiments in the public sphere. Richard Lanham once parodied these Enlightenment suppositions about psychology, rhetorical clarity, and the plain style: "I have an idea. I want to present this as a gift to my fellow human beings. I fix this thought clearly in my mind. I follow the rules. Out comes a prose that gift-wraps thought in transparent paper."[25] Lanham's glib summary overlooks the Enlightenment hope that the plain style might allow rational and sincere (nonviolent) communication among diverse people with independent minds. The chapter on Locke explores the psychological assumptions and the political hopes lurking in the British Enlightenment's affection for clear discourse in the public sphere.

The British Enlightenment fascination with aesthetic effect in prose style also recalls the bourgeois hope for civil society. Teaching people to appreciate beautiful discourse makes them into genteel citizens who cooperate through polite habits—kind words, artful sentences, elegant phrases. Contemporary philosopher Mark Kingwell's defense of civility echoes belletrism's promise to improve civil society through gentility: "Civility . . . is a civil goal; it has to do with getting along with one another in society. . . . Civility contributes to smooth social interaction, makes for tolerance of diversity, and conditions a regard for the claims and interests of others."[26] Of course, gentility cannot be rule-bound. If it were, then we would have a series of manners enforced rigidly without awareness of social context or political relevance.[27] The essays on Smith and Blair argue that early British belletrism taught the bourgeoisie's ethical dispositions, not the schoolmarm's stylistic injunctions.

While the separation of civic virtue from civil society helps to explain British Enlightenment rhetoric, this distinction suggests two wholly separate traditions and a clean transition from the ancient to the modern world, from Renaissance civic virtue to bourgeois civil society. Pocock has cautioned against supposing such stark separations. For centuries, even as civil society was emerging, beliefs about civic virtue persisted and sometimes reinforced people's hopes for the bourgeois public sphere. According to Pocock, Scottish intellectuals (such as Smith and Blair) defined "a morality in which virtue might be shown arising from sources in society, culture, and commerce, and existing independently of the practice of autonomous politics." For the Scottish Enlightenment's leading writers (for Smith and Blair) civic virtue arises in civil society.[28] As I argue in the chapters to follow, Smith and Blair also believed that civil society depends on practicing these rhetorical virtues in commerce and conversation. Addressing contemporary criticisms of Enlightenment belletrism allows me to elaborate on this point.

Present-day writers raise two chief arguments when critiquing the British Enlightenment's approach to rhetorical style: (1) Belletrism privileges aesthetic criticism, not civic engagement. (2) Belletrism promotes static and abstract rules rather than flexible principles for good communication.[29] One late nineteenth-century example in the belletristic tradition confirms these claims: Adams Sherman Hill's *Principles of Rhetoric and Their Application* (1878). At the time Boylston Professor of Rhetoric at Harvard and inventor of the U.S. required first-year writing course, Hill discussed three abstract virtues: clearness, force, and elegance. His textbook is peppered with firm rules and literary examples that propose to improve the student's "taste" by exposing her to "the best authors . . . [who] naturally use good language."[30] He told his students, for instance, that "force" can be achieved through personification. He did not explain how the literary trope leads to the aesthetic effect. He illustrated with examples of personification from the writings of Richard Steele, George Eliot, William Shakespeare, Robert Browning, John Milton, William Wordsworth, and Samuel Taylor Coleridge.[31] But we should not expect eighteenth-century belletrism to exhibit Hill's nineteenth-century indifference to civic concerns. The chapters on Blair and Spencer explain how their Enlightenment civic stylistics morphed into Victorian aesthetic preoccupations. Examining textbook abridgments of Blair's rhetorical theory demonstrates that nineteenth-century editors stripped his work of political concerns while inserting literary judgments. Examining Spencer's preoccupation with the social sciences demonstrates that an emphasis on psychology led to dry stylistic rules rather than rich ethical principles. Prior to these developments, however, belletristic and plain-style rhetorics examined rhetorical style in the public sphere.

Before defining *capitalism*, *bourgeois*, and *civil society* in such detail, I stated this book's principal argument: in the late seventeenth, mid-eighteenth, and mid-nineteenth centuries a British philosopher, a political economist, a rhetorical theorist, and a sociologist all tried to cultivate bourgeois virtue by teaching rhetorical style, each building on others' ideas and each addressing a unique stage of capitalist development. The above discussion of civic virtue suggests a second contribution to intellectual history, a narrative about the introduction of civic virtue into civil society. Each chapter in this book explains how one British Enlightenment intellectual wove civic (bourgeois) virtue into civil society by promoting clarity and gentility in rhetorical style.

So far, I have introduced my principal argument, its key terms, my methodology, and the argument's relevance to a range of scholarly conversations. In what's left of this introduction, I gesture toward a broader claim that each chapter pursues and to which the conclusion returns.

Nowadays, it is common to hear descriptions of our newly stylish and exceptionally rhetorical postindustrial economy. At the dawn of the twenty-first century, as the NASDAQ reached its zenith, new economy acolytes rhapsodized: "Markets are conversations."[32] Glory in the "aesthetic" economy.[33] At the nadir of the new economy's collapse, its detractors bemoaned an information age that "takes the mind, language and creativity as its primary tools for the production of value"[34] and that applies the "standards of a finance- and consumption-driven entertainment culture" to "democratic governance."[35] Altogether, celebrants and critics sing a common fugue about the information economy, the rhetorical worker, and the age of style. My study of capitalism and civil society in the British Enlightenment reveals that our age is not exceptional. From its seventeenth-century financial beginning through its nineteenth-century industrial episode to its twenty-first-century digital projection, capitalism has been thoroughly rhetorical. John Locke obsessed over discursive clarity and its role in commercial contracts. Adam Smith agonized about sincerity and its necessity in free-market commerce. Hugh Blair believed that the bourgeois consumer's affection for fashion and the bourgeois speaker's attention to figuration could improve commerce. Finally, Herbert Spencer insisted that a free industrial nation needs poetry to foster bourgeois sympathy. It may tickle our present-day fancy to imagine capitalism's past as a series of cinematic vignettes from the age of mechanical reproduction: colorless and silent. But a glance back at the British Enlightenment reminds us that the earliest bourgeois citizens adorned themselves and their language because they believed that capitalism (postindustrial or otherwise) requires rhetorical style and bourgois virtue.

1

John Locke on Clarity

Everyone has listened and not understood. We can all differentiate the indecipherable from the disagreeable.[1] Despite a common experience of clear communication, efforts to explain clarity vary. Aristotle, for instance, called it the most important virtue (*arête* or excellence) of an effective style. He suggested that the rhetor speak to the audience in familiar terms, using expressions that are appropriate (*prepon*) to the subject.[2] Aristotle saw clarity as a functional relationship between rhetor and audience. Many hundreds of years later, Western thinkers began to conceptualize clarity as a relationship between discourse and its object.[3] The change happened sometime in the seventeenth and eighteenth centuries. It is especially prevalent in the writings of John Locke.

The differences between these contrasting theories of clarity depend on historical circumstance. Appropriately clear, conciliatory discourse in the democratic Greek agora would encourage *homonoia* (harmony among citizens), allowing lively debate without ideological faction.[4] Clarity-as-transparency appealed to those invested in three interrelated social, political, and economic developments: the rise of the British empirical sciences, the evolution of English parliamentary democracy, and the invention of English commercial society. Past historians of rhetoric have emphasized the empirical sciences and parliamentary democracy, but none has sufficiently addressed commercial society. In order to understand Locke's approach to stylistic clarity as an effort at disseminating bourgeois virtue, we must pay special attention to the commercial dimension of late seventeenth-century England. As this chapter explains, Locke believed that clear-spoken Englishmen would maintain vibrant debate in the public sphere and profitable exchange in the marketplace while accommodating a weakened English monarch, an empowered group of Whig parliamentarians (many of them merchants and sovereign creditors), and a quickly developing English financial sector.

While making this argument about the bourgeois quality to Lockean clarity-as-transparency, this chapter emphasizes intellectual developments that contributed substantially to Locke's rhetorical theory—the English scientific revolution and Continental theories of natural law. Before addressing any such intellectual context and before arguing that Locke was the arch-bourgeois theorist of stylistic clarity, I first review Locke's basic approach to rhetoric and stylistic clarity. This exploration begins with his reservations about language and its abuses.

The Rhetorical Disease and the Physician's Cure

In book 3, chapter 9 of the *Essay concerning Human Understanding* (1689), Locke attributed all of language's problems to seven "abuses of words," which he presented in chapter 10. To summarize: (1) people use words without referencing clear and distinct ideas; (2) people use words inconsistently; (3) people use old words to reference new meanings; (4) people mistake words for things; (5) people use words to mean things that words cannot signify; (6) people suppose that commonly used words have an apparent signification when they do not; (7) people use words figuratively (*WJL* 2:22–42). Locke, the physician, diagnosed discourse's disease. In chapter 11, he presented "remedies" for the aforementioned "abuses." His prescription opens with a modest concession that language's ailments are terminal. Locke said, "I am not so vain to think, that any one can pretend to attempt the perfect reforming the languages of the world" (*WJL* 2:42). The malady may be incurable. But it is not fatal. And it is nonetheless treatable. Locke suggested five palliatives: (1) do not use words without referencing specific ideas; (2) especially when expressing particular thoughts ("mixed modes"), annex "simple," "clear," and "distinct" ideas to your words (*WJL* 2:46); (3) use words in the most commonly accepted signification; (4) declare the meaning of your words; (5) always use the same word in the same sense.

Locke's recommendations deserve to be reshuffled for a few reasons. Remedies 1, 2, and 5 prescribe essentially the same thing. In addition, Locke emphasized some prescriptions by discussing them at greater length. Recommendations 1, 2, and 5 get a single paragraph each. Recommendation 4 is explicated for thirteen paragraphs. Finally, Locke's enumerated recommendations exclude his strong admonition against disputation. Echoing Locke's *Some Thoughts concerning Education* (1693), sections of chapter 11 harangue against disputation. As he explained in *Some Thoughts*, continually arguing for and against a proposition simply produces "a poor baffled wretch" who cannot "maintain whatever he has once affirmed." The disputant is thus an "insignificant wrangler" with no regard for "truth" (*WJL* 8:178). In chapter 11 of the *Essay*, Locke expressed a similar sentiment, dedicating five of the seven introductory paragraphs to a diatribe against "wrangling" over "obscure, unsteady or equivocal terms" (*WJL* 2:44). He especially calumniated the "great mint-masters" of equivocal terms, the "school-men and metaphysicians" (*WJL* 2:23). These scholastics promoted disputation exercises that Locke disliked while himself a student and a tutor of rhetoric at Christ Church.[5] Though he did not label it a separate recommendation, Locke's injunction against disputation deserves notice. After all, he believed that "the admired art of disputing" contributed significantly "to the natural imperfection of languages, whilst it has been made use of and fitted to perplex the significa-tion of words" (*WJL* 2:25).

To emphasize Locke's warnings against disputation, to give each recommen-dation its due attention, and to collapse similar prescriptions, I recast Locke's "recommendations" as four rules to remedy language's infirmity: (1) The Rule against Vague or Absent Signification: *Do not use words that fail to reference clear ideas, or words that only vaguely reference their ideas, or words that cannot possibly reference any ideas* (a recasting of Locke's first, second, and fifth recommenda-tions). (2) The Rule of Propriety: *Use words in their most common significations* (a recasting of Locke's third recommendation). (3) The Rule of Definition: *When using an uncommon word or when using a common word in an uncommon way, define your terms* (a recasting of Locke's fourth recommendation). (4) The Rule against Disputation: *Do not wrangle over important or vaguely defined terms* (a recasting of similarly themed passages in the *Essay* and *Some Thoughts*).

Each rule recalls ideas that Locke expressed elsewhere: in his writings on politics, economics, religion, culture, and natural science. In the 1680s, Locke concomitantly wrote his principal works on education, epistemology, econom-ics, and politics. He often revised one work in light of another. His efforts toward consistency warrant a synthetic reading of this material—rhetorical, economic, epistemological, and political—as a coherent intellectual corpus.[6] Rule 1 relates to Locke's writings on empirical science. Rule 2 recalls ideas explored in his eco-nomic pamphlets. Rules 3 and 4 echo Locke's political musings. Furthermore, Locke drew on conversations about commercial contracts and English finance to fashion his sense of a clear commercial style.

The Scientific Revolution and the Rule against
Vague or Absent Signification

Without a doubt, Locke's notion of clarity resulted from his participation in the English scientific revolution. Scientists of the era wanted language that would clearly represent the things observed in their experiments. In the introduction to his great philosophical work, Locke said that the *Essay* was written at the request of the English Royal Society of London for the Pursuit of Natural Knowledge. For this reason, Hans Aarsleff stated that the *Essay* and especially book 3, "On Words," should be understood as "a manual in the epistemology of the Royal Society, whose aim was the promotion of natural knowledge."[7] But this connection between Lockean clarity and British empiricism overlooks a few factors. To begin with, Locke's vehement denunciation of rhetorical obscurity seems inappropriate to the subject. In addition, Locke said that language's scientific application is less important than its moral and political uses. Finally, the scientific revolution only accounts for the rule against vague or absent signification. The remaining three rules must be explained with reference to early-Enlightenment legal theory and economic circumstance.

A quick survey of seventeenth-century English empirical science and its accompanying philosophy of language explains much about Locke's first rule. Robert Boyle—Locke's friend, correspondent, and fellow experimental scientist—exemplified the Royal Society view of language. Boyle wanted science to replicate rhetorically what the scientist experienced directly. When experimenting with his air pump, Boyle did not suppose direct knowledge of causal relationships because causal force cannot be witnessed. Instead, Boyle believed that the scientist must play a language game, separating "facts" from their connecting causes. When discussing a "spring of the air" that affects objects situated in an atmosphere, Boyle imagined the spring as something evinced by his experiments. He treated the cause as a fiction supposed but never witnessed.[8] Boyle's example illustrates language's important and troubling place in the seventeenth-century British empirical sciences. Boyle needed the "spring" metaphor to describe what he witnessed, but the term implied a cause that Boyle assumed only for explanation's sake.

Language's imperfection led many in the Royal Society to initiate a program of rhetorical reform. They took their cue from Francis Bacon, who said that the "first distemper of learning" appears "when men study words and not matter."[9] Bacon's view of language was conflicted. On the one hand, he subscribed to the Renaissance view of stylistic copiousness as an intellectual resource. From this perspective, figurative language seems to promote new ideas. On the other hand, he praised the empiricist's plain style. From this perspective figurative language seems to hinder the search for objective truth.[10] Bacon's Royal Society followers focused on the plain style alone, pursuing what their chronicler Thomas Sprat called "not the Artifice of Words, but a bare knowledge of things."[11] Their hope for clear rhetorical reference is best exhibited in John Wilkins's *Essay towards a Real Character and a Philosophical Language* (1668), which put forward an artificial language of signs perfectly referencing ideas. Wilkins promised that "if men should generally consent upon the same way or manner of *Expression*, as they do agree in the same *Notion*, we should then be freed from that Curse in the Confusion of Tongues, with all the unhappy consequences of it."[12]

Locke echoed Sprat and Wilkins. He separated words from things. In *Some Thoughts*, he insisted that "truth is to be found and supported by a mature and due consideration of *things themselves*, and not by *artificial terms and ways of arguing*" (*WJL* 8:178, emphasis added). In the *Essay*, he proposed that "truth" be found in the "consideration of things themselves" (*WJL* 1:74). Furthermore, like Boyle and other Royal Society participants, Locke incorporated a religious argument into his apology for linguistic perspicuity.[13] In *The Reasonableness of Christianity* (1695) he said, "The works of nature, in every part of them, sufficiently evidence a deity; yet [prior to the development of the natural sciences] the world made so little use of their reason, that they saw him not, where, even by the impressions of himself, he was easy to be found" (*WJL* 6:135). Locke's epistemological writings reinforce the scholarly connection between the Royal Society and his language philosophy.[14] Like Boyle, Locke insisted that all human knowledge begins with experience and particularly with sensation. Objects outside of consciousness impress themselves on the senses. The mind represents these impressions as referentially reliable, simple ideas (*WJL* 1:79). The mind can compound and arrange such simple ideas in a variety of ways, but these resulting "complex ideas" are only clear "when the ideas that go to their composition are clear" (*WJL* 1:384). When Locke railed against the imperfection of words and particularly against words that do not reference clear ideas, he assured his reader that "the names of simple ideas are, of all others, the least liable to mistakes" (*WJL* 2:18). When Locke enjoined his reader to "use no word without a signification," he wanted the most referentially stable signification of distinct simple ideas (*WJL* 2:46).

However, other evidence cautions against wholly attributing Locke's language philosophy to Royal Society empiricism. To begin with, Locke did not hew closely to the Royal Society's language philosophy. As Rhodri Lewis has recently explained, Locke believed "thought was neither uniform nor able to mirror the order of the world."[15] Wilkins's artificial language movement assumed a consistency of human thought; if perfected, such regular thought could represent nature. Locke disagreed on both points. Even more important, as Lewis remarks, Locke did not believe that any language could perfectly convey knowledge, though he did think language could be improved to "ameliorate the potential for communicative misunderstanding."[16] According to Locke, words interrupt intuitive knowledge by encasing transparent ideas in foggy terms: "[Words] interpose themselves so much between our understandings and the truth which it would contemplate and apprehend, that like the medium through which visible objects pass, their obscurity and disorder do not seldom cast a mist before our eyes, and impose upon our understandings" (*WJL* 2:20). He worried about "students being lost in the great wood of words" (*WJL* 2:125). Language, a fallen medium, obscures. Rhetorical clarity, an endless crusade, construes.

While ignoring Locke's disagreements with Royal Society language philosophy, attributing his rhetorical theory to British empiricism's influence also leaves two glaring remainders, one affective and the other analogical. First, the affective remainder: the vitriolic quality of Locke's attack on "rhetoric." In contrast to language's important "civil use," little harm comes from rhetorical malfeasance in the natural sciences, for the "philosophical use" of language among those investigating the natural world is not terribly important (*WJL* 2:7). Because he found verbal imprecision in the natural sciences inconsequential, Locke professed greater hope for progress in the moral sciences: "Morality is the proper science and business of mankind in general" (*WJL* 2:216). Some of Locke's vitriol might be traced back to the Royal Society campaign against religious enthusiasm. Sprat and his cohort criticized rhetoric while launching a broader attack on religious nonconformists who marshaled mysticism and rhetorical flourish to weaken the Restoration alliance among the Crown, the Anglican Church, and the Royal Society intelligentsia. Like Sprat, Locke likely associated the pursuit of alchemy with religious enthusiasm. Like Sprat, Locke probably believed that seventeenth-century mystics assaulted science, reason, rational religion, and rhetorical clarity with unceasing volleys of mysticism, hermeticism, pathetic revelation, and verbal obscurity.[17] Seen in this context, Locke's attack on rhetoric sounds like a Royal Society screed against "occult" beliefs and "magical" practices—an association of rhetorical obscurity with "mystical word plays, anagrams, cryptograms, and other rhetorical accoutrements of the charmed Renaissance cosmos."[18]

But to put Locke in Sprat's political company we must ignore certain historical facts, such as his sympathy for religious dissenters. During the 1680s, Locke
sided with religious radicals who opposed the Crown and the Anglican clergy.[19]
Locke was no high-flying Charles II sympathizer, so mystical rhetoric undercut-
ting monarchical and ecclesiastical authority would not drive him into a frenzy.
Moreover, as the Restoration exited and the Glorious Revolution took the historical stage, Locke held onto his ire. He remained angry about stylistic obscurity after the political forces prompting the Royal Society's disdain for "rhetoric"
had dissolved. As religious enthusiasm became less threatening, Locke's anger
toward rhetoric increased. In the *Essay*'s earliest extant iteration, probably composed in the late 1660s, Locke bludgeoned those who abused words. In the first
draft, he said that rhetoric teaches us to wrangle over empty sounds.[20] In a later
draft, he contended that the scholar does not improve the world; he merely
coins new words.[21] This slander expands in the *Essay*'s published editions, where
Locke insisted that rhetoric's teachers and practitioners destroy "the instruments
and means of discourse, conversation, instruction, and society." In the 1690s,
with William on the throne and Catholic mysticism a forgotten menace, Locke
declared that rhetorical figures render "useless" the "two great rules, religion and
justice" (*WJL* 2:28). Tying Locke's growing hatred for obscurity to his participation in a Royal Society battle against enthusiasm may explain the affective
remainder in the 1660s, when he began writing the *Essay*, but not in 1690, when
he published it. His growing ire seems more striking when we see it alongside a
favorite Lockean analogy. In one of his most oft-quoted lines, Locke declared "all
the art of rhetorick, besides order and clearness . . . perfect cheats" (*WJL* 2:41).

Of course, during the early decades of the Restoration, Royal Society members regularly used the same analogy when attacking religious enthusiasts.
Samuel Parker, for instance, called dissenting enthusiasts "*Pedantick Cheats*."[22]
Thomas Sprat, in an especially emotional moment, proposed to "abolish all *Holy
Cheats*" who abuse rhetoric to deceive.[23] In the 1660s, Locke sympathized with
many of Parker's political commitments, including his support of the Crown
and the Church. But by the 1680s, Locke was composing some of the most effective attacks on Parker's ideas.[24] Therefore, it seems strange to say that Locke
shared an analogy with Parker and Sprat because he shared their political an-
tipathy toward religious radicals. By 1680, Locke had become a religious radical. Additionally, unlike Sprat or Parker, Locke did not analogize sophists to
scholarly or ministerial cheats. He compared the rhetorically obscure to another
species of villain altogether, the commercial cheat.

Going back to the earliest manuscript draft of the *Essay*, we can see Locke placing the verbal equivocator in a criminal pantheon next to the dissembler who uses coins that do not contain the promised silver.[25] In the *Essay's* published version, he said the sophist shares company with those who "in the affairs and business of the world . . . [would] call 8 sometimes seven, and sometimes nine, as best served his advantage" (*WJL* 2:25). Locke's proclivity for the money/language analogy has been well documented.[26] I will not draw grand conclusions from the scant evidence of a favored trope. Locke's repeated analogy between argumentative and commercial dissembling, between the sophist and the cheat, may have been illustrative. Or he may have parroted a comparison that can be found in the writings of Aristotle and Francis Bacon.[27] Alone, Locke's vitriol against rhetorical cheats and his money/language analogy explain very little. They seem like spare parts left in the box after we have bolted Locke's rule against vague or absent signification to the scientific revolution. However, another, much larger remainder suggests reconsidering the affective and the analogical extras. Locke offered three other prescriptions to cure linguistic obscurity, and none of them relates directly to the scientific revolution or the Royal Society campaign against mysticism. The real remainders are neither affective nor analogical. The real remainders are the rules of propriety, of definition, and against disputation. These can only be explained by attending to Locke's political and economic writings in the context of the English financial revolution, the Glorious Revolution, and the Continental conversation about natural law.

The Financial Revolution and the Rule of Propriety

In this section, I argue that late seventeenth-century anxieties about financial institutions and monetary stability account for Locke's desire to use words in their most common or "vulgar" significations. Locke's responses to credit and monetary crises repeat anxieties about referential instability, worries similar to those he expressed when extolling stylistic propriety. He exhibited a commonplace bourgeois longing for money whose value everyone can agree on and words whose meaning all can recognize. He proposed that propriety in credit and conversation can obviate confusion, prevent fraud, and allow exchange.

Locke's dedication to stylistic propriety was a response to the rapid emergence of high finance in London, so before diving into seventeenth-century discourse on political economy and its connection to Locke's theory of clarity, we should wade through the social history of late seventeenth-century English capitalism. Some historical accounts give the impression that English high finance burst forth once the ink on the Bank of England's charter (1694) had dried. It is more accurate to say that banks, bills, notes, and loans grew rapidly from diffuse roots set deep in the sixteenth century. By the late seventeenth century, England was more commercially advanced than its Continental contemporaries (excepting France and Holland). To begin with, strict Tudor control weakened or crippled municipal authority. Outside England, strong municipal governments prevented consistent laws and interrupted their enforcement. Inside England, uniform standards of currency and measurement, as well as reliable communication and transportation systems, all resulted both directly and indirectly from strict Tudor rule. All yielded a hospitable trade environment. The internal English economy benefited from a national customs system. Merchants moved goods from one town to another without having to worry about multiple and uneven fees. England also had a developed system of roads and waterways, complemented by a tradition of not tolling for profit. Merchants trafficking in the former German empire had to contend with a surfeit of levies charged anywhere a territory, an imperial city, or a strong military band decided to demand payment. English merchants had no such difficulty.[28] Additionally, English merchants benefited from a publicly financed commercial fleet. Stuart support for colonial expansion extended Elizabethan maritime supremacy.

Though the Tudors did establish strict economic control, their successors were less effective. The Labor Law of 1565, attempting to fix wages, still stands as one of the most thorough efforts at state control of the English economy. When the Stuart kings attempted to exercise similar economic authority, they met resistance. The English people distrusted government and chartered monopolies alike. The English courts ruled that restraining trade was harmful. After the Glorious Revolution, anything resembling the early Stuart meddling in internal economic affairs disappeared.[29] Thereafter, William and Mary focused on external expansion through colonial development. A favorable environment for international and colonial trade shifted English agriculture toward commercial profit. Large landholders consumed or consolidated small estates. Enclosure and engrossment allowed estates to grow large, generate surplus, and compete. Soon, efficient agro-commercial enterprise dominated the south and the east, using wage labor, reinvesting profits ("improving the land"), and circulating produce to distant markets.

In the late seventeenth century, just as merchants and commercial farmers hungered for stable credit, the English financial sector erupted. Curiously enough, large-scale banking did not initially serve commerce. Instead, English finance catalyzed in a political dispute between Parliament and the Crown. Before the Civil War, the king called English Parliament to do his bidding. Under Charles II, Parliament regularly refused to supplement the king's inadequate rents. Though Parliament did raise taxes to support Charles II's military endeavors, they did not collect sufficient revenue, leading the Crown to depend heavily on creditors. Charles II worked himself into such debt that in 1672 he had to stop payment of £1.2 million from the Exchequer. This episode prompted English government to improve tax collection and to dedicate funds specifically to ensure the payment of public debts. Tax farming was replaced by direct government collection. In order to preserve a steady line of low-interest private credit for public debt, the administration increased efficiency and abolished unpopular taxes. Once a stable market for public debt was established, under William and Mary, a similarly stable market for private debt quickly developed.

The market for public debt contributed to a range of important developments. New financial instruments (such as the £1 million tontine sold in 1693 to finance William's War) became commonplace. The Bank of England was chartered in exchange for a £1.2 million loan to the government. Later subscriptions to the Bank would expand this public debt. Parliament sold incorporation charters to raise public revenue. The South Sea Company and the East India Company were both born to England's new financial age. Though founded to sell public debt, banks offered other services: underwriting notes, taking deposits, making loans for private use. In short, after Charles II's disastrous handling of public debt, Parliament colluded with the Crown. Committed to costly martial endeavors, William happily conspired with Whig financier-parliamentarians. Their legislation allowed the king to borrow from a range of wealthy and otherwise marginalized capitalists, including Jews, Huguenots, foreigners, and dissenters. This borrowed money bolstered English military power abroad and coddled a fast-growing financial sector at home. An alliance between capitalism and monarchy allowed a meager island—once home to a bankrupt and militarily weak king—to defeat the largest and most centralized state on the Continent: William beat France on the battlefield by outspending his opponent two to one on a per-capita basis. He flexed absolutist muscles abroad while kowtowing to, borrowing in, and enabling a financial industry at home.[30]

John Locke had dealings in all three sectors: commerce, agriculture, and finance. He was an agrarian capitalist himself (on a small scale) and became intimately familiar with agricultural commerce. He grew up in the country, was an absentee landlord, and wrote brief technical works on efficient husbandry, all promoting commercial improvement.[31] He also worked as the physician and sometimes adviser on economic policy to the famous Whig agrarian capitalist Anthony Ashley Cooper, 1st Earl of Shaftesbury. Between 1669 and 1670, at Shaftesbury's request, Locke served as secretary to the Council for Trade and Plantations. He listened as the proprietors of the Carolina colony deliberated their new acquisition's commercial potential. He even wrote their constitution. Locke's association with Shaftesbury put him in the company of Whig merchants, shopkeepers, and landed gentry, all anxious to take advantage of enclosure and improvement. Whigs pandered to the economic interests of the nascent English bourgeoisie because many of them were personally invested in commerce.[32] Locke spent the 1680s in the company of men like his good friend Robert Pawling, both a radical Whig and a tradesman.[33] Locke's association with English commerce continued after his life as a radical politico ended. In May 1689 he accepted a post as Commissioner of Appeals for Excise. He wrote about and directly advised Parliament on issues such as bank formation and currency reform.

Though Locke was a rhetoric teacher first and tutored a range of wealthy young men, he dedicated much of his adult life to English commerce. While his writings on husbandry demonstrate an affiliation with agricultural capitalism, his writings on money demonstrate his attention to the English financial revolution. Locke's writings on money show that his language philosophy incorporated a concern for propriety that he simultaneously theorized in economic terms. The rule of propriety is not just a stylistic guideline, nor is it principally a political suggestion. Locke believed that propriety in currency and language preserves commercial stability, since propriety depends on consent, and consent to a common medium permits financial and conversational exchange.

Locke's theory of stylistic and monetary propriety presents the bourgeois public sphere and the capitalist free market as symbiotic halves of civil society, both depending on the shared virtue of rhetorical clarity. In the *Second Treatise of Government* (1689), a text composed at the same time as the *Essay*, Locke most fully explored the importance of consent when writing about the invention of currency and of language. The quotidian exchange of words requires consent to language's most common uses: "Words, especially of languages already framed, being no man's private possession, but the common measure of commerce and communication, it is not for any one, at pleasure, to change the stamp they are current in, or alter the ideas they are affixed to" (*WJL* 2:47–48). Since the "gaining of a social consensus depends upon linguistic clarity," civil society requires stylistic propriety.[34] To argue his case, Locke narrated the transition from primitive subsistence in the state of nature to commercial civilization.

As Locke explained, the state of nature ends when people agree to a common language and a common money. The state of nature begins to end when people abandon barter in favor of a market economy. Money catalyzes a shift from "natural law" to "positive law" by overcoming two natural restrictions: spoilage and sufficiency. Together, these restrictions curtail the production and exchange of property. In the state of nature, people could not appropriate more than they could immediately use. If a person accumulated property beyond what was sufficient to his use, then he would "intrench upon the right of another, or acquire . . . to the prejudice of his neighbor." As a result, the state of nature allowed individuals a "very moderate Proportion." The overproducing individual "offended against the common law of nature . . . for he had no right, farther than his use called for any of them, and they might serve to afford him conveniences of life" (*WJL* 4:358–60).

Money's innovation superannuated spoilage by allowing people to exchange their surplus. As Locke says, "Thus came in the use of money, some lasting thing that men keep without spoiling, and that by mutual consent men would take in exchange for the truly useful, but perishable supports of Life" (*WJL* 4:365). In a barter economy, every economic transaction happens in a tense and trembling moment of disagreement. Locke believed that commercial stability depends on consent, a peri-social development occurring somewhere in the passage from a delimited subsistence in the state of nature to the satisfying surplus of a commercial economy.[35] In their transition, people agreed to a universal equivalent, silver. Locke was an unusual proponent of "intrinsic" value in precious metals. He did not believe that the precious metal contains or embodies value. Rather, Locke favored silver because he believed that people had agreed on it.[36] As he wrote in *Some Considerations of the Consequences of Lowering of Interest and Raising the Value of Money* (1691): "Mankind, having consented to put an imaginary value upon gold and silver by reason of their durableness, scarcity, and not being very liable to be counterfeited, have made them, by general consent, the common pledges, whereby men are assured, in exchange for them, to receive equally valuable things, to those they parted with, for any quantity of those metals" (*WJL* 4:22).

Close analysis of Locke's approach to monetary propriety exhibits a powerful idea that he extended to every corner of English capitalism. He believed that a free commercial society depends on practical but by no means guaranteed actions and institutions.[37] The early consent to monetary propriety (silver) is one such practice. Coins must symbolize silver in their stamp and contain silver in their alloy. If the stamp does not correspond to the metallic content, then the entire monetary system shudders. If monetary reference shakes to the point of collapse, then civil society loses a foundational pillar. If the rumblings of monetary collapse commence, then their low murmur soon drowns in civil society's roaring failure. Locke's responses to two developments in late seventeenth-century England demonstrate how much he valued consent to a clear unit of monetary exchange. These are the clipping crisis and the introduction of bank notes. Close analysis of Locke's responses to these episodes illuminates his affection for clarity. This analysis also explains why he adored the rule of propriety and why he called those who abuse language "cheats."

In 1695 influential parliamentarians and property-holders began to worry about their currency. Several developments stoked this anxiety. In 1694 the newly founded Bank of England widely circulated notes. People unfamiliar with banking remained wary of the novel asset. They also became skeptical of their familiar coins. They learned that English money traded for less abroad (probably because William's soldiers fought the Nine Years' War in French territory but were paid in light English specie). Finally, there is evidence to indicate that, after a slight drop in domestic commodity prices between 1694 and 1695, English citizens experienced a large inflationary spike in 1695–96. (The inflation may have been caused by mounting government debt and a shortage of privately offered commercial capital in finance and trade.)

Regardless of the many villains, government officials quickly found a culprit in the coins themselves. The average weight of silver in English coins had fallen roughly 50 percent, though the stamp remained unchanged. This reduction was due partly to regular wear and partly to an ineffective system of guaranteeing metallic content. But friction and poor oversight proved unsatisfying rogues. Clippers, on the other hand, had hands to shackle and necks to hang. For well over one hundred years, individuals shaved the edges off hammered coins and reminted the clipped silver. Clipping probably accelerated in the mid-1690s due to a 24 percent rise in the value of bullion, but the increased activity could not have caused the mid-decade inflation, nor should it have warranted the fury directed toward clippers. After all, most English "moneyed men" did their business on the domestic market, where light specie traded at full value.[38]

In a now-famous vitriolic sputter, which sounds hyperbolic to the modern ear, John Locke earnestly labeled clipping the equivalent of "treason," a hanging offense (*WJL* 4:144). He furthermore insisted that light English coin be recalled and reminted. His proposal was catastrophic. The amount of English currency in circulation reduced dramatically, causing rampant deflation, which disproportionately affected wage earners and the poor. Without warning, many found that the local shopkeeper would no longer accept their light coins. Failing to exchange their debased currency with the Exchequer and suffering at the limited mercy of goldsmith bankers who bought old currency at a severe discount, people rioted in Halifax and Kendal, petitioned the government in Norwich, and threatened revolt in Derbyshire.[39] Prior to reminting (1695), Locke believed the debased condition of English specie was a "crisis," even if the clippers did nothing harmful and even if the debased currency had no severe or long-standing effects. He worried that commerce would stall as participants refused to trade silver for commodities at an agreed-on parity.[40]

In the clipping crisis Locke saw a failure of consent. He derided clippers because these nefarious individuals damaged "the public faith": "Men in their bargains contract not for denominations or sounds but for intrinsic value; which is the quantity of silver, by public authority warranted to be in pieces of such denominations" (*WJL* 4:144). Passing a light for a weighty coin is the equivalent of fraud: "arbitrarily to give one man's right and possession to another" (*WJL* 4:145). By misrepresenting the amount of silver in English coins, the clipper "is robbing the honest man who receives clipped money." Those who would raise the value of silver in English coins proposed to cheat everyone "by public authority" (*WJL* 4:146). Clippers violated ordinary commercial contracts. Tudor kings, who devalued specie to pay for wars, and William Lowndes, the Secretary to the Treasury who suggested reminting at a reduced silver content, violated the social contract.[41] Locke reasoned that reminting at actual weight would restore order by reestablishing a trustworthy standard. His response to another financial development shows a similar deference to propriety, a similar desire to preserve the peri-social consent that stabilizes social and commercial contracts.

As hinted earlier, Locke had reservations about the nascent English banking industry. He opposed neither banks nor credit. He supported and owned shares in the Bank of England. In fact, he conceded that, when the money supply could not meet commercial demands, credit could briefly fill the gap (*WJL* 4:178–79). Nevertheless, Locke questioned the effort to found the Bank of England in part because he feared such an institution might gain a monopoly control over the English money supply by issuing notes that did not rely on the peri-social and therefore stable consent to silver.[42] Fear of monopoly control and suspicion of

notes were not uncommon in Locke's era. Bank notes were fairly new instruments. For several decades prior to the 1690s, goldsmith bankers accepted deposits and tendered receipts, which were established and often accepted as "cash
notes" or "bills." The Bank of England issued similar paper. But anxiety about
the notes' references (to the bearer, the owner, and the capital) made English
citizens reluctant to experiment with anything more exotic. Checks with spaces
for the names of the payee and the bearer were not introduced until Child's
Bank did so in 1729. Notes simply payable to the bearer would not be available
until the late eighteenth century.[43] English commerce needed banks to provide
credit, just as English merchants needed notes to transfer capital. Nonetheless,
like Locke, most believed that purchasing power inhered in silver. This consent
to a metallic unit of currency made notes a monetary impropriety.[44] As Locke
said, "A law cannot give to bills that intrinsic value, which the universal consent
of mankind has annexed to silver and gold" (WJL 4:22).

The above review of Locke's economic writings reveals that his affection for
propriety marks him as bourgeois in the capitalist sense of the term. He wanted
to stabilize markets by avoiding monetary impropriety. Quick comparison to
his writings on propriety in public discourse demonstrates that he appreciated
the public sphere as much as he did the market. While he wanted government
to institute monetary propriety by enforcing statutes against light specie, he
wanted free citizens to institute conversational propriety by speaking clearly.
According to Locke, clarity in commerce is a legal matter; clarity in conversation
is an ethical practice.

Like notes and coins, words should follow common use. For this reason,
Locke worried about improper discourse and its destructive potential.[45] Ironi-
cally, Locke's bourgeois justification for rhetorical clarity led him to a quasi-
Aristotelian standard of propriety—the audience's agreement about a term's
use. As he explained in the *Essay*, God made "a sociable creature . . . furnished . . .
with language, which was to be the great instrument and common tie of society"
(WJL 1:427). In the *Second Treatise*, he further explained that God put us "under
strong obligations of necessity, convenience, and inclination" to form communities bound by "understanding and language" (WJL 4:383). Conversational stability allows "comfortable, safe, and peaceable living one amongst another, in a
secure enjoyment of their properties, and a greater security against any, that are
not of it" (WJL 4:394). Conversational stability protects the rights to secure
property and its free pursuit. Though he had great faith in simple ideas as well
as their names and though he suggested that people compose their complex

notions out of clear and simple ideas, he also believed that many ideas derive from reflection. Some are abstract generalizations, such as "whiteness," drawn from simple and specific experiences, such as the color "white" in a specific spring flower (*WJL* 1:138–39). Some are amalgams of ideas, both simple and complex (*WJL* 2:4–6). All such "complex" ideas interested Locke because they are most likely to misrepresent the world. Since they are manufactured in order to facilitate thought, complex ideas can veer away from the objective "things" impinging on our senses. Each person's free formation of complex ideas may careen into referential instability, for "the same liberty also that Adam had of affixing any new name to any new idea, the same has anyone still" (*WJL* 1:509).

Affronted by the libertine use of language, the instability that it can produce, and the impotence of his first rule to address the problem, Locke relied on common consent to prevent discursive anarchy. Adam may have had complete liberty to form complex ideas, but "in places where men in society have already established a language amongst them, the significations of words are wearily and sparingly to be altered" (*WJL* 1:509). The bonds of "common use . . . [and] consent" restrain each person's "inviolable . . . liberty to make words stand for what ideas he pleases." These bonds also facilitate cooperation by allowing us to speak to one another properly and "intelligibly" (*WJL* 1:434). Locke's faith in propriety was no philosophical latecomer. In the earliest extant version of the *Essay* (1660), he wrote that someone can judge an ambiguous assertion by considering "common consent of the country & those men whose language we use."[46] This is the rule of propriety in its earliest formulation. Despite its potential, this solution never completely satisfied Locke.

From the early drafts of the *Essay* through its most refined iterations, Locke worried that an assumed consensus about a complex idea will permit confusion and invite disagreement.[47] Though people may have agreed long ago to a word and its related idea, a "change of customs and opinions bringing with it new combinations of ideas" can easily upset this stability (*WJL* 1:278). Since Locke steadfastly believed that customs vary across geography and history, he worried about consensus maintained by common use.[48] Moreover, "common use, being but a very uncertain rule . . . proves often a very variable standard" (*WJL* 2:57). At best, common use delivers a "tolerable latitude" of "agreement in the signification of common words" (*WJL* 2:56). Since they can wantonly form ideas and follow personal whimsy, people will inevitably violate the standard of "proper speaking." Just as the clipper calls a light coin heavy or a banker calls a baseless note valuable, so can any disputant call property a "privilege" and not a "right."

More troubling still is the human ability to learn words without acquiring any ideas. The "sounds are usually learned first," but "in the search of the true and precise meanings of names," people often fail to develop their ideas for want of "observation," "explication," or "industry." As a result, words "are in most men's mouths little more than bare sounds" (*WJL* 2:11). Troubled by these possibilities, Locke settled into an imperfect solution: "Propriety of speech is that which gives our thoughts entrance into other men's minds with the greatest ease and advantage." He labeled propriety the "common measure of commerce and communication" because he believed it could address civil society's economic and rhetorical ills (*WJL* 2:48).

Locke's affection for discursive and monetary propriety illuminates another facet of his rhetorical theory: his suspicion of stylistic figuration. As he explained, the "figurative application of words" can "insinuate wrong ideas." Both the rhetorical figure and the spurious note deviate from an established proper use (*WJL* 2:41). If "silver, and not names . . . pays debts and purchases commodities" (*WJL* 4:89), then terms in their common use, not rhetorical figures, convey meaning. Locke even accused some economists of confusing the nature of "money" with their "mystical, obscure, and unintelligible way of talking." His rejoinder, "expressed in ordinary and direct language," promises to alleviate the negative effects of such stylistic impropriety (*WJL* 4:103–4). Locke defended the proper metal of commercial exchange in a proper manner of unornamented prose. In the public sphere where bourgeois subjects debated policy without state censorship, Locke's "clear" arguments about monetary policy metonymically captured the relationship he imagined between the market and the public sphere, two institutions conjoined since humankind left the state of nature, two institutions bound by the stylistic virtue of clarity and the rhetorical rule of propriety.

The Glorious Revolution and the Rules concerning Definition and Disputation

Like present-day political theorists, historians of rhetoric tend to read Locke's writings through the guiding lens of his *Essay*: claiming that epistemology explains political and rhetorical theory; believing that Locke's skepticism led to his political radicalism; averring that Locke's realism underpinned his commitment to clarity.[49] While I question the decision to subordinate economic to political factors when discussing Locke's work, I wholly agree with Richard Ashcraft's effort to take Locke's emphasis on moral philosophy and practical reasoning as the "hermeneutic guide" to the *Essay*.[50] Locke was a political dissident pledged to religious toleration, constitutional government, and free trade. As Ashcraft ably demonstrated, Locke's political commitments best explain his writings on government and economics.[51] Building on Ashcraft's argument, I contend that Locke's writings on government and economics best explain his affinity for rhetorical clarity. While the previous section relies mostly on the social history of English finance to explain Locke's rule of propriety, this section emphasizes the intellectual history of natural-law theory to account for Locke's remaining two rules: the rule of definition and the rule against disputation.

Early-Enlightenment natural-law theorists obliquely referenced church fathers, such as St. Augustine and Thomas Aquinas. Like their Christian predecessors, Enlightenment jurists believed that "positive" (or human) law should be built on "natural" (or divine) law. Continental natural-law theorists typically explained the natural laws themselves and then derived the positive laws most in line with these divine ordinances. English natural-law theorists differed from those on the Continent in one important regard. Continental theorists, mostly living in the areas affected by the Thirty Years' War, sought to establish a rational system of jurisprudence independent of religious doctrine. Ravaged by confessional strife, writers such as Hugo Grotius and Samuel Pufendorf hoped to situate jurisprudence atop reason while affirming some vague divine origin. English theorists similarly sought a rational basis for jurisprudence but did not shy away from emphasizing the divine origin of natural law or human reason.

In his published writings, Locke only cited one natural-law theorist. As a result, an effort to situate his work in this conversation should begin with Richard Hooker, who professed a typical belief in a divinely granted system of laws, which itself laid the groundwork for human law. From Hooker, Locke learned that a person using "right reason" could intimate natural law, from which she could derive positive law, a flawed human approximation of divine mandate.[52] In the *Essay*, Locke explained that we arrive at the "innate principles" that guide our thought and action by way of reason: "There is no knowledge of these general and self-evident maxims in the mind, till it comes to the exercise of reason" (*WJL* 1:20). In the *Second Treatise*, he insisted that natural law binds people to certain behaviors, such as the preservation of self and society: "The state of nature has a law of nature to govern it" (*WJL* 4:341). Writing at a time when English politicians were questioning the monarch's reach, Locke borrowed Hooker's ideas to speculate about a legal grounding independent of the Crown.

Locke opined that natural law holds firm in the state of nature, but early social stability is continuously threatened as people try, without "right," to "take away the freedom" that God affords all rational creatures. Positive law aims to avoid this "state of war" (*WJL* 4:348). While transitioning from the state of nature, people agreed to mediate their grievances through a legal apparatus. Among other things, they invented "positive" criminal law to protect their "natural" rights. In order to assert the natural right to property, a citizen must appeal to the magistrate, instead of directly violating another's freedom by confiscating stolen goods (even if that confiscation be justified by "right"). The magistrate's mediation and the legal system protecting the natural right to property both ensure stable property ownership, which motivates people to generate and to exchange wealth. Needless to say, the magistrate's authority depends on a higher standard in God's law. But it also depends on the original social contract to obey the magistrate and to respect property. This original agreement provided a behavioral consistency that both Pufendorf and Locke thought necessary to commerce.[53] Stability required for commerce comes first from people's rational consent to the social contract and second from their consent to the magistrate. Nonetheless, though civil society depends on the magistrate's authority, the marketplace and public sphere are otherwise free from the magistrate's influence.

To further illustrate the limitations that Locke put on the Crown, I will put him in conversation with Thomas Hobbes and Ralph Cudworth, two seventeenth-century English natural-law theorists. Locke knew both men's works, so there is good reason to compare his writings to theirs. Additionally, like Locke, Hobbes worried about language (and clarity) when discussing the necessary conditions for functional government and profitable commerce. Hobbes's political and rhetorical theories are comparable to Locke's for a number of reasons. First, Hobbes discussed language's misuse in ways remarkably analogous to the "abuses" Locke mentioned in book 3 of the *Essay*.[54] Second, Hobbes believed that language laid the foundation for human association. For both Hobbes and Locke, without language, there would be no community, no state, and no civil society.[55] Finally, language troubled Hobbes in the same way it troubled Locke. According to Hobbes, eloquence could dissolve, just as it had constituted, social stability.[56] Hobbes's deep-seated belief in language's political importance and his abiding concern about language's stability exhibited themselves in a feverish hostility toward rhetoric.[57]

Hobbes prescribed a defining sovereign to secure the social contract, a monarch who writes and enforces positive law. Unlike Locke, Hobbes did not allow civil society an expanded purview. Civil society should remain independent of the state, but it should not be a place to debate matters of state. Under the sovereign and in civil society, citizens may exchange goods and enjoy entertainments, but they may not dispute governmental policy. The individual citizen, according to Hobbes, should not debate "*good* and *evil*" and therefore "must accept what the legislator enjoins as *good*, and what he forbids as *evil*."[58] In addition to the definitional authority, the sovereign needs military authority because "covenants without the sword are but words." We cannot expect "a great multitude of men to consent in the observation of justice and other laws of nature without a common power to keep them all in awe."[59] Hobbes's Leviathan wears the miter, carries the scepter, and wields the sword because, under the threat of violence, the magistrate dictates public religion and governmental policy. Locke, of course, would never publicly agree with the Malmesbury monster. (He often disavowed anything but passing familiarity with Hobbes's work.)[60] Nonetheless, the two men shared a belief that the social contract depends on language, and they likewise shared a fear that rhetoric can destabilize civil society.

In the mid-1660s, while Reader in Rhetoric and Censor of Moral Philosophy at Christ Church, Locke criticized the English Revolution and pledged loyalty to Charles II. Though his political alliances affirmed Hobbes's support of the sovereign, Locke nonetheless contested many of Hobbes's beliefs.[61] Locke's experiences before the Glorious Revolution soured him on monarchical power. He supported Charles II, while allying with the 1st Earl of Shaftesbury, cultivating liberal political theories, and worrying about James II. By the 1680s Locke was writing his *Two Treatises*, which questioned the divine rights of kings and championed the right to revolt, he was consorting with libertines, and he was probably conspiring to overthrow Charles's brother. Shaftesbury's "Protestant plot" to replace James II with James Scott, the 1st Duke of Monmouth, landed Shaftesbury and Monmouth in prison. Locke fled to Rotterdam, where he wrote his three great works: the *Essay*, the *Two Treatises*, and the essays on money and interest.[62] By the end of this affair, Locke was no monarchist, neither theoretically nor politically. Authority had to be located elsewhere. Locke found it in reason, law, and language.

Locke followed a course similar to that traced by Ralph Cudworth, whose work he likely knew and whose family he befriended.[63] Cudworth believed that Hobbes's defining sovereign would do nothing but assert arbitrary positive law.[64] Arguing against Hobbes, Cudworth demarcated natural from positive law. Cudworth claimed that individuals exercising their "Rational or Intellectual

Nature" could determine whether the magistrate's positive law comports with natural law.[65] Though he championed reason, Cudworth never asserted a right to revolt when the magistrate's positive law deviates from natural law. In his celebrated *Second Treatise*, however, Locke rushed in where Cudworth dared not tread. Locke's defense of the right to revolt supposes that individual citizens can learn natural law and can judge positive law by the divine standard. Citizens' apprehension and judgment of natural and positive law, their public use of reason, depends on clear communication.

Like Cudworth, Locke maintained that God had given people the faculty to discover the natural laws of association: the principles of good government and the guide to harmonious community. Though we have no divinely implanted "innate ideas," we are blessed with the light of reason, "since the wise and considerate men of the world, by a right and careful employment of their thoughts and reason, attained true notions" (*WJL* 1:66). Some of these truths are readily apparent, some require formulation as propositions, and some require a "train of ideas placed in order, a due comparing of them, and deductions made with attention" (*WJL* 1:75). By comparing ideas in the moral sciences, we can search after truths and thus "come nearer perfect demonstration than is commonly imagined" (*WJL* 2:115). Words allow abstraction and relation, but they also "interpose themselves . . . between our understandings and the truth which it would contemplate and apprehend" (*WJL* 2:20).[66] Reason depends on language. Discourse perpetuates civil society, provided that people do not abuse rhetoric. Locke's faith in divine reason and proper language allowed hope for stable positive law (a social contract) without the sovereign's arbitrary proclamations or his bloody sword. Since God allowed people to learn and to communicate, a rationally deduced and clearly communicated divine standard will lead us away from amphiboly's wide gate: "Where God, or any other law-maker, hath defined any moral names, there they have made the essence of that species to which that name belongs; and there it is not safe to apply or use them otherwise" (*WJL* 2:132).

Locke's writings on natural law and the social contract explain his vitriolic denunciation of rhetorical abuse. He needed to reconcile his belief in language's instability and his dedication to civil society without reaffirming the sovereign's absolute control over positive law. Therefore, he argued vehemently for rhetorical reform. Particularly, he argued for the rules concerning definition and disputation. My strict attention, so far, to Locke's political theory overlooks an important commercial dimension. Like many of his contemporaries, Locke did not strictly differentiate *social-contract theory* (an explanation of distributive and contributive justice, the rights and obligations of the sovereign and the citizen as established in some agreement, tacit or explicit) from *ordinary contract theory* (an explanation of commutative justice, the rights and obligations between independent parties agreeing to a some mutually beneficial arrangement).[67] This easy conflation of an agreement between sovereign and citizen and an agreement between buyer and seller allowed Locke to presume that a stable social contract will ensure a stable commercial contract, and a stable civil society will host a stable capitalist economy, since both public discourse and private exchange require rhetorical clarity.

Continental natural-law theorists similarly presumed that commerce depends on a stable legal system and vice versa. They additionally presumed that language could provide such stability in social and commercial contracts. For instance, Pufendorf extended the essentially Christian notion of natural law into a treatment of various duties that arise from natural rights. Civil law must present such duties clearly: "For the meaning of the law to be correctly grasped, those who promulgate it have a duty to be as perspicuous as possible."[68] Duties, according to Pufendorf, include not only the magistrate's clearly phrased laws but also the individual's private contracts. To exemplify contracts necessitating clear and settled language, Pufendorf listed typically commercial agreements, such as "loan for use," "deposit," "sale," "lease," "contract of partnership," "surety" (loan security/collateral), and "mortgage."[69] Grotius contended that the most "ancient" and "simple" contract was "the Contract of Sale," which facilitates "an Exchange . . . the most antient Method . . . of Trading and Commerce."[70] Grotius also focused on commercial contracts, such as agreements to exchange labor for capital, interest-bearing loans, and business partnerships such as joint-stock corporations.[71] Locke did not simply study the interrelation between social and commercial contracts. Like his Continental predecessors, he witnessed the connection between stable law and functional capitalism.

In late seventeenth-century England, Locke saw firsthand that the incentive to commercial contract diminishes when the sovereign breaks the social contract. In 1672 Charles II violated goldsmith bankers' property rights by refusing to pay a sovereign debt. As a result, these same bankers could not repay debts owed to private citizens. A violation of the social contract rippled out into a series of violated commercial contracts. Charles II's decision led to intense legal wrangling and an eventual petition of right. The plaintiffs had little hope for repayment, since the Crown controlled the courts. When the petition eventually failed in 1699, the bankers petitioned the House of Lords, where they received a favorable ruling in 1701. This suit established a satisfactory procedure for sovereign creditors to enforce their debt contracts.[72]

Seventeenth-century England's private capital market would never have flourished without a legal framework guaranteeing that the government would honor its debts.[73] Similar developments in the English legal system resulted from commercial efforts to ensure that property rights would be upheld. Disputes over bills of exchange, for instance, were traditionally handled in slow and capricious admiralty courts. In the late seventeenth century, common-law courts took a larger role. As a result, adjudication became much more predictable and expedient.[74] Late seventeenth-century suspicion of notes ebbed as the common-law courts handled more commercial disagreements. An increased volume of stable notes contributed to liquidity and thereby to trade. Locke not only witnessed these developments, but also was directly involved in them. In the 1690s, after being denied payment for his work as secretary of the Privy Council Committee for Plantations under Charles II, Locke petitioned the Crown, directly asking that the contract be honored. Of course the petition was denied. When Locke theorized natural law, stability of contract, and the right to revolt, he wrote about his own rights as a citizen and his own welfare as a capitalist.

Locke offered two rhetorical rules to stabilize contracts, allowing a weakened monarch and an expanded civil society by promising an empowered legal system. The rule of definition ensures that everyone involved can understand the contract, thus providing the informational "Exactness" that Hugo Grotius wanted to see in "a Contract being contrived for the mutual Advantage of the contracting Parties."[75] From other natural-law theorists Locke learned about language's paramount role in the social contract. Richard Hooker, for instance, taught Locke that the "chiefest instrument of human communion . . . is speech."[76] Locke echoed Continental natural-law theory when stressing the importance of commercial contracts. He began his *Second Treatise* by explaining that, in the state of nature, where people are free of positive law but nonetheless governed by natural law, certain rights (such as the rights to property and liberty) persist. Individuals can engage in "promises and bargains for truck, &c . . . for truth and keeping of faith belongs to men as men, and not as members of society" (*WJL* 4:346). To prevent anyone from exercising force without right, people pledge obedience to a magistrate who establishes and enforces positive law, which ensures that commercial compacts will be honored and liberties preserved (*WJL*

4:348–50). Individual contract becomes a foundational civil right manufactured to preserve certain natural rights (such as property and liberty) without risking descent into a state of war and without bowing to the whims of a defining sovereign.

The commercial importance that Locke afforded the right to contract becomes evident in his writings on property. He explained that the right to possess anything to which a person contributes labor exists in the state of nature, but its exercise is limited. People can only own what they can consume. Upon leaving the state of nature, people agree to a system of commercial exchange (facilitated by money), which allows acquisition of wealth and leads to an overall social benefit: labor divided according to talent, people pursued excellence and bounty, industry flourished, civilization improved. "This partage of things in an inequality of private possessions, men have made practicable out of the bounds of society, and without [individual] compact; only by putting a value on gold and silver, and tacitly agreeing in the use of money: for in governments, the laws regulate the right of property, and the possession of land is determined by positive constitutions" (*WJL* 4:367). Such a legal system depends on rhetorical clarity, for vague or obscure laws cannot be enforced or adjudicated, and heedless disputation hampers commerce by rending contracts with honed terminological parsing. Locke even applied the principle of clarity to divine contracts. Distributive, commutative, and heavenly justice all depend on stylistic clarity. According to Locke, God hands down "by plain and direct words" the contract regarding salvation (*WJL* 6:34). In a pamphlet war with the Puritan divine John Edwards, Locke insisted that the good Christian need only obey clearly expressed divine laws: "Where it is spoken plainly, we cannot miss it; and it is evident he [God] requires our assent: where there is obscurity . . . a fair endeavor [at understanding and obedience] as much as our circumstances will permit, secures us from a guilty disobedience of his will, or a sinful errour in faith" (*WJL* 6:228).

Locke insisted on the rule of definition because he thought that the discursive precision and the neologisms required in stable contracts will follow no standard of common use. When there is neither natural archetype nor vulgar definition (no simple ideas or common use), the speaker must declare what she means by a specific term. But "those [terms] belonging to morality, being most of them combinations of ideas, as the mind puts together of its own choice, and whereof there are not always standing patterns to be found existing; the signification of their names cannot be made known, as those of simple ideas, by any showing; but, in recompense thereof, may be perfectly and exactly defined"

(*WJL* 2:49). In one of his more extended examples, Locke defined "stealing" as the "taking from another what is his, without his knowledge or allowance." Separating the behavior of "stealing" from an idea of "the moral pravity of the action" will help juries with difficult cases, such as "the private taking away his sword from a madman, to prevent his doing mischief." The clear definition allows a rational jurist to see that "when compared to the law of God, and considered in its relation to that supreme rule . . . [taking away the madman's sword] is no sin or transgression" (*WJL* 1:379–80).

After explaining the political and commercial importance of clear definition, Locke gave advice about how to define. The first suggestion has already been covered. He wanted people to list all the ideas relating to a concept. "Stealing," for instance, includes an idea of an action and an evaluation of moral quality (*WJL* 1:379). Second, Locke counseled against defining "by genus and differentia," which leads to characterizing a general term by "the next general term." To classify "man" as a "rational animal" does not help the person seeking to understand (*WJL* 1:439–40). Finally, Locke warned against defining by simile, a practice that replaces "fancy" with knowledge. The definition by simile (or metaphor or allegory) gives no information about "the inside and reality of the thing," since comparative definitions encourage us to "content ourselves with what our imaginations, not things themselves, furnish us with" (*WJL* 2:378).

If the rule of definition serves commutative justice and sustains civil society, then the practice of disputation hampers both. The "peripatetic philosophy" that dominated English higher education in the late seventeenth century did not teach "the world any thing but the art of wrangling" (*WJL* 2:169), which itself would not be a problem if such wrangling did not disrupt an orderly public sphere or a profitable marketplace. But when interlocutors "are not agreed in the signification of those words, nor have in their minds the same complex ideas which they make them stand for . . . all the contests that follow thereupon, are only about the meaning of a sound." Because of such wrangling, "in the interpretation of laws, whether divine or human, there is no end" (*WJL* 2.11). One particular thread in Locke's writings illustrates the importance that he afforded both the rule of definition and the rule against disputation. Toward the end of his chapter "On the Idea of Personal Identity," Locke conceded that a satisfactory definition of "person" may forever elude us, since the composite ideas (body, soul, consciousness, self) are themselves often abstract and indefinable. Nonetheless, he put forward such a definition because on "this personal identity is founded all the right and justice of reward and punishment" (*WJL* 1:340).

Locke opted for a fabricated bit of nomenclature, a "forensick term," to allow free discussion of actions and their merit. Such a definition permits rational discussion about "intelligent agents, capable of law, and happiness and misery" (*WJL* 1:346). Judges can hold accountable, people can contract with, and citizens can debate about a "conscious thinking thing" (*WJL* 1:340). The definition serves in the court, in the market, and in the public sphere.

In public debates, Locke chastised others for using the term ("person") in a "vulgar" or "common" way because such usage could "puzzle and mislead, rather than enlighten and instruct." In a heated pamphlet debate about religion with Edward Stillingfleet, Bishop of Worcester, for instance, Locke chided the Anglican prelate for his "figurative and common [expressions] . . . where inaccurate thoughts allow inaccurate ways of speaking." Weighty philosophical matters with immediate moral and legal implications, such as the nature of a "person," demand specific, philosophical definitions. According to Locke, Stillingfleet refused to substitute "metaphorical expressions (which seldom terminate in precise truth)" for "clear and distinct apprehensions" (*WJL* 3:175). In his reply, Stillingfleet reproached Locke for abandoning "old Words."[77] Stillingfleet, in essence, said that Locke refused to follow the rule of propriety. Locke countered that Stillingfleet violated the rule of definition. Worse still, Stillingfleet violated the rule against disputation by quibbling over such important terms.

Locke's Rhetorical Regimen

Since Locke never wrote a formal treatise on rhetoric, in order to understand his expectations for the proper practice and study of appropriately "clear" discourse this section analyzes Locke's public arguments and his educational writings. Locke's public arguments exemplify the stylistic clarity that he theorized in his writings on epistemology, politics, and economics. After exploring his public arguments, I analyze Locke's writings on education to show that he developed a rhetorical pedagogy of clarity. As already mentioned, Locke did not trust language. Like semantic universalists, such as John Wilkins, he worried about rhetorical instability yet insisted that it was avoidable. Like natural-law theorists, such as Samuel Pufendorf, he thought language's poly-vocality threatened contractual stability.[78] Unlike his predecessors, Locke did not retreat into a safe grove of mono-vocal clarity. He maintained that "semantic instability is *endemic* to language."[79] His philosophy of language promotes a uniquely modern refusal to assert any ultimate escape from tropological slippage. Locke attempted to avoid language's slide into obfuscation by speaking clearly and by teaching others to do likewise.

While arguing about metaphysics and theology, Locke linked his words to specific and clear ideas, thus following his own rule against absent or vague signification. When discussing "liberty," for instance, he insisted on tying the abstract term to a clear idea of a particular experience: "having the power of doing, or forebearing to do, according as the mind shall choose or direct" (*WJL* 1:226). Locke also abstemiously used figurative language to illustrate particular concepts. He especially avoided conflating the figure for the concept embellished. Consider the following example: "To think often, and never to retain it so much as one moment, is a very useless sort of thinking: and the soul, in such a state of thinking, does very little, if at all, excel that of a looking-glass, which constantly receives variety of images, or ideas, but retains none; they disappear and vanish, and there remain no footsteps of them; the looking-glass is never the better for such ideas, nor the soul for such thoughts" (*WJL* 1:85–86). In this sentence, we see him choosing the humble simile rather than the striking metaphor to ensure clarity.

When possible, he elected the most common usage, thus following the rule of propriety. When discussing a particular idea derived from sensation—"That which thus hinders the approach of two bodies"—Locke opted for the common term, "solidity," even as he confessed that another term, "impenetrability," might be more exact. The common term is best because clearest, and its clarity derives from "its vulgar use" (*WJL* 1:99). When deviating from common use, Locke clearly defined his potentially "improper" terms, thus following the rule of definition. When he could not define clearly, he openly admitted this inability and chose, instead, a flawed though functional term. In one of the most celebrated passages of the *Essay*, Locke declared that he had no clear idea of what "substance" is and thus could only reference "what it does." A "substance" is defined as "that which supports accidents" (*WJL* 1:156). Locke presented his reader with a model of clear public argument, yet in his later years he stumbled over the rule against disputation, for he engaged a series of protracted pamphlet wars about heresy and toleration. He did not regard these debates as wrangling, though he did accuse his interlocutors of obscure discourse and unnecessary disputation. At one point in a heated argument with John Edwards, Locke sought to separate himself from his disputant, who had no "real concern for truth and religion" and whose arguments presented little "reasoning" and less "clearness" (*WJL* 6:184).

Other comical moments feature Locke's adversaries accusing him of rhetori-cal obscurity. According to Bishop Stillingfleet, Locke used empty *"Scholastick Language,* which is always most proper when there is nothing under it."[80] In another charge, Stillingfleet teased Locke with his own monetary metaphor: "It seems our old Words must not now pass in the current Sense; but then it is fit they to be *called in,* and *new stampt,* that we may have none but *New Milled Words."* Recalling Locke's disastrous proposals to remint English coins, Stillingfleet chided, "I am utterly against any *Private Mints of Words;* and think those Persons assume too much Authority to themselves, who will not suf-fer common Words to pass in their general Acceptation."[81] Stillingfleet risibly crammed Locke's discourse into the Procrustean bed of bourgeois clarity. Locke humorlessly conceded that language is slippery. He confessed that any effort to follow all his rules will ultimately lead to failure. Nevertheless, people must rely on common usage when it serves, and they must invent new uses when the rule of propriety falls short: "Till public mints of words are erected, I know of no remedy for it, but that you must patiently suffer this matter to go on in the same course, that I think it has gone in ever since language has been in use" (*WJL* 3:279).

Locke constructed an elaborate ethical defense of clarity along with a pre-scription for its rhetorical achievement. Moreover, he followed his own regimen. He also provided instructions for the would-be bourgeois rhetorical pedagogue. Locke's writings on rhetorical education blend a quasi-classical notion of civic virtue into a pedagogy that serves capitalist society. Locke's program for rhe-torical education begins with a distinctly Aristotelian assumption about civic virtue: moral education happens through the steady inculcation of habit.[82] Even as he railed against syllogistic disputation and topical argumentation, Locke ad-opted an Aristotelian approach to education, saying that children learn by ha-bitual repetition of virtuous behavior. Children "entertain and submit to [these habituated behaviors], as many do to their parents, with veneration; not because it is natural: nor do children do it, where they are not so taught: but because, having been always so educated, and having no remembrance of the beginning of this respect, they think it natural." According to Locke (and Aristotle), "Cus-tom [is] a greater power than nature" (*WJL* 1:51–52). Education introduces chil-dren to custom by way of habit. Both Locke and Aristotle believed that people could train themselves. As Locke explained, "Pains should be taken to rectify these [bad habits]; and contrary habits change our pleasures, and give relish to that which is necessary or conducive to our happiness" (*WJL* 1:267).

Locke conceded that "the heathen philosophers . . . well understood wherein their notions of virtue and vice consisted" (*WJL* 1:374), and he expanded on these ancient ideas by advocating a moral education in virtuous habits that uphold natural law. He admitted that most people are guided not by their regard for "the laws of God, or the magistrate," but rather by the "law of fashion . . . which keeps them in reputation with their company" (*WJL* 1:376). He believed that "custom settles habits of thinking in the understanding." He further believed that people's customs are guided by praise and blame in public as well as pedagogical circumstances. Therefore, Locke concluded that moral pontificating is futile (*WJL* 1:420). Rather, the educator must encourage customs that uphold natural law: "Those who have children, or the charge of their education, would think it worth their while diligently to watch, and carefully to prevent the undue connexion of ideas in the minds of young people" (*WJL* 1:422). Nearly two millennia prior, Aristotle had insisted that the "citizen should be moulded to suit the form of government under which he lives."[83] In the late seventeenth century Locke agreed, suggesting that students be shaped for bourgeois civil society.

When addressing religious toleration, Locke contributed to the modern liberal political tradition by separating civil society from the state. He insisted that the commonwealth should have no influence over a "voluntary society of men joining themselves together of their own accord in order to the public worshiping of God, in such a manner as they judge acceptable to him, and effectual to the salvation of their souls" (*WJL* 5:13). While he completely separated religion from the state, Locke put education in the commonwealth's service. To be fair, Locke never advocated state-funded or -regulated education. Neither did Aristotle. But Locke did want education to impart civic virtue. Religion remains a private concern left to free worship in civil society because religion attends to personal matters of salvation. Education is a public concern because bourgeois character affects political stability and commercial possibility.

Some Thoughts concerning Education, which began as a series of letters about Locke's tutoring of Sir John Banks's son, offers glimpses into how Locke wanted the rhetoric teacher to impart the virtuous habits of stylistic clarity. The book opens by declaring that the "great thing to be minded in education is, what habits you settle: and therefore in this, as all other things, do not begin to make any thing customary, the practice whereof you would not have continue and increase" (*WJL* 8:18–19). Education should train "men of business," not grammarians or scholastics (*WJL* 8:162). Locke cautioned against two mainstays in rhetorical education: disputation and practice in stylistic figuration. Both lead to the "captious and fallacious use of doubtful words" (*WJL* 8:179). He advised the would-be rhetoric teacher to offer examples of stylistic clarity. The tutor should praise "things that are well writ in English, to perfect his [the student's] style in the purity of our language" (*WJL* 8:178).

At the earliest possible age, students should "tell a story of any thing they know." In order to promote good habits of clear style, the tutor should "correct at the first the most remarkable fault . . . [students] are guilty of" (*WJL* 8:179). Once students are comfortable narrating, they should imitate a laudable example, such as a translation of Aesop's fables. Locke promoted other exercises to generate prose for the tutor's correcting gaze. Reading Cicero's *De Inventione* could teach students to write narrative arguments. When a student's stories display sufficient skill and clarity, she should write letters, following examples, such as "Voiture's, for the entertainment of friends at a distance, with letters of compliment, mirth, raillery, or diversion; and Tully's epistles, as the best pattern, whether for business or conversation" (*WJL* 8:180). Locke concluded these reflections with an apology for education in English composition rather than in Latin or Greek.

Two points about Locke's advice deserve notice. First, he encouraged students to write in English, the "language of business." Second, he encouraged students to master the art of letter writing. Epistolary correspondence in the vernacular facilitated both domestic and interstate trade during the seventeenth and eighteenth centuries. Letters were to Enlightenment commerce what the telegraph was to nineteenth-century industrial distribution, what radio and television have been to twentieth-century marketing, and what the Internet has become for electronic retail.[84] It is no wonder, then, that Daniel Defoe in his *Complete English Tradesman* (1726) advised the aspirant merchant to "indite his letters in a tradesman's style, and correspond like a man of business."[85] But Locke's affection for epistles should not outshine the most important element of his proposed rhetorical pedagogy. In every effort, from storytelling to letter writing, he wanted students to discourse clearly. Leveraging examples of clear discourse and the tutor's carefully inserted evaluation, Locke hoped that rhetorical education would carve the habits of virtuously clear discourse into each student's character.

When Defoe described and exemplified the style of writing most appropriate to English commerce, he echoed Locke, saying that the tradesman should write in "an easy concise way," should avoid "flourishes," and "should be plain, concise, and to the purpose." The merchant should clearly transfer information from one mind to another, "that men may understand one another's meaning."[86] Defoe, of course, was not the only bourgeois gentleman to take up Locke's crusade for perspicuous prose. Across the Atlantic, another famous tradesman read Locke, labored to develop a more "perspicuous" style, and advanced a very Lockean program of education. Influenced by Locke's *Essay* and *Some Thoughts*, Benjamin Franklin put himself through a program of rhetorical education to learn the stylistic virtue of "Perspicuity."[87] Later in life, Franklin devised a curriculum for the Academy of Philadelphia. Conceived as an effort to train young merchants, Franklin's curriculum included instruction in clear prose, a sustained effort to teach epistolary correspondence, and a distinct derision of disputation exercises.[88] Ever since Max Weber famously declared that Franklin embodied the capitalist ethos, the American paragon has stood as a bourgeois archetype.[89] In rhetorical pedagogy, Franklin was following Locke's lead.

Locke himself tried to write in the clear manner that he advanced and that his followers appreciated. He explained and defended clarity's epistemological, economic, and political value. In his rhetorical theory and in his public debates, Locke celebrated liberal civil society marked by stylistic clarity. In rhetorical education, however, Locke saw the greatest potential for instilling bourgeois virtue. He could philosophize about clarity's importance and practice its presentation, but he believed that he would have his most significant social impact by carefully instilling in students the unthinking yet virtuous reflex of a humble figure, a defined term, a popular usage, or a reluctant refutation.

2

Adam Smith on Probity

The art trader transforms beauty into a commodity. The communications consultant turns conversation into information. The commercial lawyer writes friendship into a contract. Such are common allegations that the bourgeoisie debases noble endeavors. From such a perspective, Adam Smith stands forth as the bourgeois-ethicist par excellence, for Smith suggested that commercial society had set aside the classical virtue of bravery and the Christian virtue of benevolence to favor "prudence only . . . the habits of caution, vigilance, sobriety and judicious moderation." Seeing Smith in this way requires willful ignorance. For just a few short words after handing down the ethic of prudence only, Smith conceded that "prudence only . . . seems to degrade equally both the amiable and respectable virtues, and to strip the former of all their beauty, and the latter of all their grandeur" (*TMS* 307). According to Smith, prudence may be capitalism's signature virtue, but if prudence is the only virtue, then civil society suffers.[1] Furthermore, Smith complicated prudence itself by saying that it brings forth a rhetorical virtue, probity.[2]

Smith's ethics may seem narrow to contemporary philosophers and literary critics who make grand claims about sincerity.[3] He said that the "prudent man is always sincere, and feels horror at the very thought of exposing himself to the disgrace which attends upon the detection of falsehood" (*TMS* 214). He referred to clear honest "Prose" as "the Language of Business" (*LRBL* 137). Honesty arises largely because a "dealer is afraid of losing his character, and is scrupulous in observing every engagement. When a person makes perhaps 20 contracts in a day, he cannot gain so much by endeavouring to impose on his neighbors, as the very appearance of a cheat would make him lose." As a result, "whenever commerce is introduced into any country, probity and punctuality always accompany it" (*LJ* 538). "When the greater part of people are merchants they always bring probity and punctuality into fashion, and these therefore are the principal virtues of a commercial nation" (*LJ* 538–39). We might conclude that Smith traced honesty to a calculation of utility: "It is not from the benevolence of the butcher, the baker, or the brewer that we expect [their probity] . . . but from their regard to their own interest" (*WN* 26–27). A more extended analysis reveals, however, that, according to Smith, the ruthless calculation of interest does not lead to bourgeois probity. Honesty may be prudent, and the prudent man may be honest, but he is not honest because he is prudent. Probity comes from a felt sense of right, which leads to an honest rhetorical style.

Probity's commercial importance and its rhetorical manifestation were key themes not only in Smith's lectures on rhetoric but also in his writings on ethics, his lectures on jurisprudence, and his opus on political economy. Understanding Smith's appreciation of bourgeois probity requires first exploring his lectures on rhetoric, which relied on Enlightenment psychology and classical philosophy; examination of his later works (the lectures on jurisprudence and *The Wealth of Nations* in particular) reveals the commercial importance he afforded the stylistic virtue. Finally, his efforts at promoting rhetorical criticism of imaginative literature illustrate how he wanted students to study, discern, and produce honest discourse in the free arenas of civil society: the literary salon, the commodities exchange, and the rhetoric classroom.

Enlightenment Psychology and Pathetic Probity

Smith relied on Enlightenment psychology when explaining how language can convey sentiment. The early editions of *The Theory of Moral Sentiments* (1759) provide an explanation of moral judgment premised on psychological mechanisms, such as sympathy and imagination.[4] Similarly, Smith's lectures on rhetoric and belles lettres (as recorded in a student's 1762–63 notebook) posited psychological mechanisms, such as sympathy and ideational association, to account for stylistic probity. As a result, his theory of stylistic probity can be described as a "rhetorical psychology of sympathetic figuration." As recent scholarship explains, Smith drew on French sources when arguing that certain figures of language are naturally associated with and call forth certain psychological states.[5] But the French had no monopoly on eighteenth-century naturalistic psychology. The Enlightenment entertained a transnational conversation about the human mind, including English, German, Dutch, and French voices.[6] Smith's psychology especially echoes British (English, Irish, and Scottish) writings. His notion of stylistic probity invokes two psychological mechanisms (sympathy and the association of ideas) popular among his British predecessors.[7]

The first mechanism that Smith discussed in relation to rhetorical probity is sympathy, the ability of one person to feel in mind and body as does another. Sympathy relates to rhetorical style because "when the sentiment of the speaker is expressed in a neat, clear, plain and clever manner, and the passion or affection he is possessed of and intends *by sympathy*, to communicate to his hearer, then and then only the expression has all the force and beauty that language can give it" (*LRBL* 25). Smith elaborated on this point much later in the lectures when ridiculing artificial sentiment among "Romance writers of the middle age" who expressed love using "Amplicatives and Superlatives," modifiers that more naturally "express our admiration and respect." Such puffed-up diction "is not the Genuine and natural language of Love." A naturally affectionate style should feature "Diminutives and such-like . . . terms" (*LRBL* 131).

Smith's understanding of emotional transference was not unique. Many of Smith's contemporaries celebrated an emotional faculty of judgment, for they believed this faculty would encourage gentility in the public sphere. The English moralist Anthony Ashley Cooper, 3rd Earl of Shaftesbury, and Smith's Scottish mentor Francis Hutcheson both theorized a moral sense that can detect people's sentiments and a language that can express their feelings.[8] Influenced by Shaftesbury and Hutcheson, the Anglican Bishop Joseph Butler preached several sermons that trace human morality to our natural ability to sympathize with others. Sympathy, according to Shaftesbury, Hutcheson, and Butler, is the universal, psychological basis for human cooperation. In the second half of the eighteenth century, Scottish writers incorporated this notion of sympathy into their disquisitions on topics outside of psychology. David Hume built sympathy into a political philosophy by arguing that fellow feeling allows for pride and humility, which themselves lead to community, status, and education.[9] Henry Home, Lord Kames, echoed Hume's characterization of sympathy, tying it into his language philosophy: "Sympathy invites a communication of joys and sorrows, hopes and fears: such exercise . . . is necessarily productive of mutual good-will and affection."[10] Hume and Kames placed sympathy at the core of a naturally (and possibly divinely) implanted conscience, what Butler called "the rule of right within."[11] Discussing moral philosophy, they set sentiment over reason.[12] Only occasionally did they venture into the realm of rhetoric.

In the early eighteenth century, many writings on rhetoric focused on a Lockean sense of reason and promoted a "rational" civil society where "legislation" influenced by free public debate would "result not of a political will, but of a rational agreement."[13] Those who championed reason over sentiment regularly spoke ill of rhetoric largely because of long-standing associations among stylistic flourish, passionate indulgence, and imaginative flight. Ralph Cudworth, for instance, worried that anything other than a "plain" style would pander to our weaker faculties and hinder moral improvement: "Speech, Metaphors, and Allegories do so exceedingly please, because they highly gratify this Phantastical Power of Passive and Corporeal Cogitation in the Soul."[14] When Thomas Sprat insisted that "*eloquence* ought to be banish'd out of all *civil Societies*," he affiliated rhetoric with passion and imagination.[15] He insisted that the bourgeois public sphere (and its enclave of scientific debate) should redound with rational, plain-style speech. But the rationalist's hostility toward sentimental rhetoric did not go unanswered. Like Shaftesbury, Hutcheson, Butler, Hume, and Kames, many favored sympathy over reason. The rhetorical-stylistic corollary to this celebration of sympathy was the belletristic movement: theorizing and praising imaginative figuration and sentimental syntax. Thomas Sheridan, Smith's Irish elocutionist contemporary, directly rebutted the rational-critical, plain-style ideal. According to Sheridan, "there are two other parts of the human mind," both ignored by "Mr. Locke's Essay: the one the seat of the passions . . . the other the seat of the fancy; which is called the imagination."[16] The apt rhetor should remember that "the passions and the fancy have a language of their own."[17]

Sheridan believed that, by natural gift, people can encode and decode their emotions in language: "We find, that man, in his animal capacity, is furnished, like all other animals, by nature herself, with a language which requires neither study, art, nor imitation; which spontaneously breaks out in the exactest expressions, nicely proportioned to the degrees of the inward emotions."[18] Edmund Burke, Smith's English contemporary, found his way from a psychology of sympathy to a theory of poetry.[19] While Sheridan wanted students to express emotion naturally in sentimental delivery, Burke wanted them to interpret emotion properly in literary art. Together, they capture the British Enlightenment preoccupation with sentiment (and sincerity) rather than reason (and clarity).[20] Adam Smith belongs in Sheridan's company, for Smith's interest in rhetoric fit hand-in-glove with his affection for the British sentimentalist philosophy. When Smith told his students that "as the sentiment will be different, so will the stile also" (*LRBL* 40), he followed a long line of British writers who believed that sympathy enables language to convey genuine emotion in honest discourse. Smith countered Locke's (and Cudworth's) rational-critical model of bourgeois civil society. He suggested that, in addition to reasoned clarity, liberal civil society also requires sympathetic honesty. Belletrism and the plain style constitute two opposing sides to an argument about how best to engage public discourse in a free commercial nation. Locke told bourgeois citizens to speak clearly. Smith told them to listen sympathetically.

Smith's discussion of syntax drew on another psychological principle widely accepted during the British Enlightenment: the association of ideas. Once again, Smith wrote in conversation with his English forebear. John Locke explored cognitive association when reflecting on the mind's natural tendency to connect concomitantly conceived notions (*WJL* 1:419–27). Others, such as David Hartley and David Hume, elaborated on Locke's philosophy.[21] Locke (and Hartley) advocated clear prose that connects ideas syntactically as they are connected cognitively: to speak clearly, one should connect ideas in a sentence as they are connected in the mind. Smith knew and admired Locke's work, but he most likely and most directly inherited associational psychology from his Edinburgh mentor Lord Kames, whose aesthetic theory and critical practice referenced associational psychology.[22]

Smith wove associational psychology into his reflections on syntax. In his fourth and fifth lectures on rhetoric, Smith explained how syntactic order affects a sentence's emphasis and thus shapes its pathetic content. He began by discussing the "arrangement of words" with reference to the natural "Judgement of the humane mind [which] must comprehend two Ideas between which we declare that relation subsists or does not subsist." According to Smith, each basic syntactic unit contains three elements, which associate concepts in a linear chain linked by presentational order. The first "subjective" element determines the matter. The second "attributive" element determines the feeling associated with the matter as well as its connection to the third "objective" element. Since the mind seeks to associate a subject with an affect and then with an object, the writer should follow a certain syntactic order: first the subject, then the affectively freighted attributive (including modifiers and verbs that apply to the subject), and finally the object. As Smith explained, "These three must generally be placed in the order we have mentioned as otherwise the meaning of the sentence would become ambiguous" (*LRBL* 16–17).

Smith elaborated on this basic three-part syntax by exploring two other syntactic components: the "conjunctive" and the "adjunctive." Though lacking particular location, conjunctives and adjunctives perform specific syntactic-affective functions. Conjunctives associate ideas by connecting "different terms of a sentence or period together." Adjunctives associate the speaker's feelings with these ideas by expressing "what particular opinion the speaker has of it, the person to whom it is addressed, and such like." Smith elaborated on the adjunctive's pathetic function: "The adjunctive is that which expresses the Habit of the Speakers mind with regard to what he speaks off or the sentiment it excites, as, tis strange, alas, etc. Sir is an adjunctive which denotes your addressing yourself to a particular person; all Interjections are adjunctives" (*LRBL* 17).

By theorizing syntactic order, conjunctives, and adjunctives, Smith offered a pathetic syntax to ensure proper emotional transference. The optimal syntactic order "most naturally occurs to the mind and best expresses the sense of the speaker concerning what he speaks." Only the mentally addled speaker will slavishly follow rudimentary syntactic order: subjective, attributive, objective. "Thus would a man speak who felt no passions, but when we are affected with anything some one or other of the Ideas will thrust itself forward and we will be most eager to utter what we feel Strongest" (*LRBL* 18). Smith further explained that the order in literary translation should reflect the speaker's emphasis, not her foreign-language syntax. He cautioned against any stylistic figuration that inverts the natural syntactic order without reflecting some sentiment. Supplanting the subjective for the attributive should express something about the "spirit and mind of the author." If such a hyperbaton has no sentimental purpose, then it will come across as "unsufferably Languid and tedious" (*LRBL* 19). In his fifth lecture, Smith extended this sentimental grammar into a discussion of the unfortunate sentence that has "a tail coming after it, that is when the sense appears to be concluded when it is not really so." Smith offered some direct advice in this case: "This is always to be avoided by placing the terminative and circumstantiall term before the attributive." Many writers (including Isocrates and Shaftesbury) produced syntactic "tails" to preserve "the agreable cadence of periods." Ending "the different . . . [sentences] nearly with the same number of words" violates the natural sentimental order, which "often hurts the propriety and perspicuity of the sentence, which are still more to be regarded" (*LRBL* 21). He concluded the lecture with further aesthetic criticism of writing style.

In all, Smith's treatment of figuration and syntax amount to a psychological belletrism. I have focused on Smith's commitment to Enlightenment psychology because his theory of stylistic probity cannot be understood without placing it in this intellectual conversation. Nevertheless, most important for this chapter's purposes is Smith's advice about how sentimentally to produce and how sympathetically to interpret genuine prose. This advice aims to instill the habits of genteel cooperation, habits that sustain productive and free debate in the bourgeois public sphere. According to Smith, speaking clearly will help bourgeois civil society—but so will speaking sentimentally and listening sympathetically.

Stoic Philosophy and Ethotic Probity

Smith's approach to bourgeois gentility did not rely strictly on Enlightenment psychology. In his eighth lecture on rhetoric, not long after attributing the "beauties of stile" to the author's "sentiment," Smith explained that style should also reflect the author's "naturall character" (*LRBL* 40). His attempt to theorize sentimental transference (drawing on psychology) is distinctly modern, but Smith's lectures about the stylistically honest display of personal character (drawing on Stoic philosophy) is notably classical.[23] Accounting for Smith's Stoic inheritance allows a deeper understanding of his belletristic theory of rhetorical probity.

As Lois Agnew explains, both ancient Greek and Roman Stoics sought to understand, without recourse to superstition or transcendental explanation, how "individuals are naturally bound to other people and to the universe as a whole."[24] This effort often led to ancient theories of sympathy and common sense, attempts to understand what allows people to relate to the community and to the natural world. For the Stoic philosopher, sympathy and common sense both exist independent of politics and the state. Before becoming socialized, people can understand one another's feelings, and they can furthermore judge right and wrong by a common standard.[25] Eighteenth-century English thinkers, such as Shaftesbury and Thomas Reid (who succeeded Smith as the Chair of Moral Philosophy at the University of Glasgow), revived these ancient ideas when discussing a natural capacity for sociability and benevolence.[26] This brand of classical philosophy is good fodder for anyone contemplating cooperation independent of the state, for inborn natural sympathy and common sense make a free civil society possible.

Stoicism, a classical and distinctly pagan system of ethics, bequeathed the eighteenth century a useful past that many wielded for "modern" purposes. However, continuous allusion to Roman and Greek forebears should not lead us to label the British Enlightenment (or Smith in particular) "neo-classical."[27] Shaftesbury revived Stoic notions of order and harmony to counter Hobbes's depiction of "Men as . . . *Wolves*."[28] Reid appropriated the Stoic notion of common sense to combat Cartesian (and Humean) skepticism.[29] However classical their references, Shaftesbury and Reid adapted ancient philosophy to Enlightenment ends. Smith, likewise, took up ancient ideas when they served his theory of an honest rhetorical style.

Atop the Stoic notions of "order," "propriety," and "harmony," Smith erected a critical-rhetorical practice of stylistic honesty. An honest style should display the orator's character and should reflect the era's mores. The critic should judge the composition by attending to the rhetor and to his society. Lectures 26 and 30 most fully explore this quasi-Stoic belief that the rhetor's character should reflect the interpenetration of rhetorical style, individual character, and social-historical ethos. Lecture 26 does so by comparing Cicero to Demosthenes, a popular eighteenth-century exercise. Cicero's oratorical style—which Smith described as having "a certain Gravity and affection of dignity"—reflects his patrician character. According to Smith, in pre-Christian Rome two classes dominated and opposed each other: "Optimates" were led by elite senators, and "Populares" followed demagogues who promised "equall division of Lands and the distributing of Corn at the Publick charge" (*LRBL* 156–57). Cicero exhibited his patrician character in a rhetorical mode that recalls the "Nobleman of Rome," in a style "pompous and ornate" (*LRBL* 158).

Demosthenes, on the other hand, lived in a much more egalitarian age. According to Smith, the ancient Greek audience included Athenian citizens "on equall footing," a group who "lived and talkd together with the greatest familiarity." Ancient Greece eschewed the "Pomp and air of those who speak with authority" and favored a language marked by "freedom, ease and familiarity" (*LRBL* 158). Cicero's style is spotted by "figures of speech" and an aversion to "Idiomatical turns or other Vulgar expressions." This style would be inappropriate in Demosthenes's Greece, even if the oration adequately expressed Cicero's aristocratic ethos. Demosthenes's rhetorical propriety, in this circumstance, depended on an everyman ethos, stylistically captured by "Common phrases and Idioms, and Proverbs" (*LRBL* 159). While Smith conceded that "the tempers of men had no doubt . . . their effects," he attributed these contrasting styles mostly to "the different conditions of the countries." Their improprieties stemmed not from idiosyncratic shortcomings but from national qualities taken to an extreme. At times Cicero was "more ornate and pompous than the temper of his audience would have required," and occasionally Demosthenes was "more bare and careless than even the familiarity and equallity of his countrymen would have required" (*LRBL* 160–61).

When he discussed the honest expression of an orator's character, Smith focused almost exclusively on critical evaluation. Lecture 30 returned to Demosthenes and Cicero in order to expand on the practical judgment of rhetorical propriety. This time, Smith examined style to determine whether an entire era deserves praise. He moved past the simple judgment of individual character and toward the complex judgment of a national ethos. Cicero's rhetorical ethos exhibits admirable qualities, including "a very high degree of Sensibility," which the great orator acquired through elite Roman education in the liberal arts. In Demosthenes's rhetorical ethos, Smith noticed "an austere temper," comporting with the "free and easy manner of the Greeks [who] would not admit of any such perroration designed to move the passions as those we meet with in Cicero." Coming from different societies, these men exhibited different *ethe*, each admirable in its own regard, and each manifested in different kinds of rhetoric: "Upon the whole Cicero is more apt to draw our Pity and love and Demosthenes to raise our Indignation. The one is strong and commanding, the other persuasive and moving" (*LRBL* 192–95).

Had the lecture ended there, students would have arrived at a kind of critical relativism: all styles are good in their own rights, since each sincerely and appropriately expresses personal character and national ethos. But Smith added eighteenth-century England as a third point of historical comparison. He told his students that English oratory displayed a "plain, distinct, and perspicuous Stile without any of the Floridity or other ornamentall parts of the Old Eloquence," and he attributed this national ethos to the English legal system, populated by those "who have been bred to the law" (*LRBL* 196). According to Smith, experienced jurists attend to the legal details, not the pathetic appeals. In the English court system, "the pleader therefore can do no more than tell over what facts he is to prove." Though Smith attributed the characteristically unemotional English ethos to the English court system, and particularly to the removal of "Judges" who display their "innatention and ignorance" (*LRBL* 197), he nevertheless maintained that all English society exhibited the same "order and Decorum of Behavior," which he described as "a calm, composed, unpassionate serenity." He contrasted this ethos with the Spanish "Majestick Proud and overbearing philosophical Gravity" and the French "gaiety, affableness, and Sensibility" (*LRBL* 198). When noticing cultural differences, Smith admired England's stable judicial system and its ordered legislative process, where "nothing will be receivd . . . which is not or at least appears not to be a plain, just and exact account" (*LRBL* 199).

Smith justified his admiration for the English character and its reserved style in lecture 20 and in his "Considerations concerning the First Formation of Languages," an essay he probably began composing to earn the Chair of Logic and Rhetoric at the University of Glasgow (1751). In lecture 20, Smith speculated that the history of language reflects the progress of human society. Specifically, he maintained that "primitive" societies brimmed with "Rude and Ignorant people" who delight in strong emotional appeal and imaginative flight. In more

developed societies, where people enjoy "greater internall Tranquility and Security," they consider "the motions of the human mind, and those events that
were accounted for by the different internall affections." In advanced societies,
the "Refinement of manners" leads to an expository plain style and away from
evocative rhetorical flourish. Such rhetorical refinement accounts for the classical turn away from fable and toward history, away from imaginative superstition and toward rational explanation. Tacitus, for instance, favored "narrating
the more important facts and those which were most concerned in the bringing
about great revolutions, and unfolding their causes, to instruct their readers in
what manner such events might be brought about or avoided" (*LRBL* iii–12). In
sum, Smith narrated the progress of civilization as a progress of rhetorical style.
Against this diachronic backdrop, students learned to judge stylistic qualities
based on their appropriateness to various historical stages. The plain English
essay follows and surpasses the ornate Greek fable.

In his "Considerations," Smith elaborated even further on this notion of linguistic progress. He said that poetic (imaginative and affective) styles are the
most primitive, because ancient peoples invented new words, expressions, and
syntactical patterns to capture the new experiences raining upon them. Prolixity
suits poetic expression, fashions emotional appeal, and expresses a fantastic culture. As society progressed, people developed abstract terms, and they reduced
syntactic complexity by agreeing to the most versatile forms. A modern style
features less poetic vocabulary and reduced syntactic complexity; these qualities
hinder poetic expression but help expository ratiocination. Smith explained the
principle behind linguistic progress by analogizing language to a machine: "All
machines are generally, when first invented, extremely complex in their principles, and there is often a particular principle of motion for every particular movement which it is intended they should perform. Succeeding improvers observe,
that one principle may be so applied as to produce several of those movements;
and thus the machine becomes gradually more and more simple, and produces
its effects with fewer wheels, and fewer principles of motion."[30] Of the modern
idioms, English is the most developed and the least poetic. English abandoned
declensions, distinctions of gender, and unnecessary verb conjugations.[31]

By holding them against the backdrop of historical progress, Smith positively
evaluated the English language as well as the dispassionate English ethos, placing
both at the apex of Western civilization—and he was neither the only nor the
first Scotsman to do so. In 1742, Smith's closest friend, David Hume, published
his ironic essay "Of Eloquence," in which he confessed that eighteenth-century

England was "inferior [to the ancients] in eloquence."[32] Hume also noted that dry English prose reflected certain modern advances, such as an admirable "multiplicity and intricacy of laws" and "the superior good sense of the moderns," which both are "a discouragement to eloquence."[33] Tongue-in-cheek, Hume praised English character and eloquence. Dryly, Smith celebrated English stylistic accomplishment. Both held up the dispassionate English ethos and unornamented rhetorical style as paragons of good sense and virtue.

In addition to national ethos, Smith also connected style to the rhetor's idiosyncratic personality. In his seventh lecture on rhetoric, he expounded on a series of moral characters and the styles appropriate to them. The "Plain man," Smith explained, "pays no regard to common civilities and forms of good breeding." He manifests this temperament in a style that refuses to conform to "manners" and that avoids "Wit" and "Antithesis or Such like expressions." The "Simple man," by comparison, still refuses to don "the outward marks of civility and breeding that he sees others of a more disingenuous temper generally put on; but then, when . . . [these figures of language] naturally express his real sentiments, and do'nt appear constrained, he readily uses them." Smith labeled Jonathan Swift a plain stylist "so far from studying the ornaments of language that he affects to leave them out even when naturall," and he called Sir William Temple a simple man "not anxious about ornament but when they are naturall he does not reject them" (*LRBL* 36–38).

In Smith's review, neither Swift nor Temple seems morally corrupt, nor do their styles invite disapproval. Smith encouraged his students to judge the individual rhetor based on a single criterion: an honest display of character in rhetorical style. In *The Theory of Moral Sentiments*, Smith criticized Swift for setting a "pernicious example" by demonstrating an imprudent, "improper and even insolent contempt of all the ordinary decorums of life and conversation" (*TMS* 215). In the lectures on rhetoric, however, Smith presented Swift as a fine example of stylistic honesty. When discussing Swift's "common" manner of writing, Smith praised not the style itself but rather its relation to Swift's "generall character as a plain man" (*LRBL* 42). He even defended Swift against critics who faulted him for a lack of abstract reasoning or uncommon figuration. Smith granted that Swift never displayed "levity of mind as well as freedom of thought." His prose lacks some fashionable "warmer and more earnest expressions" (*LRBL* 41), but at least he spoke his mind.

Smith compared Swift to another humorist—Lucian. Swift's "naturall moroseness" led him to a characteristic contempt and an austere style. Swift's

"Language is always correct and Proper and no ornaments are ever introduced nor does he ever write but in a manner most suitable to the Nature of the Subject" (*LRBL* 48). Lucian, on the other hand, possessed a "merry gay and jovial temper," allowing for a witty style, "surprising and diverting his reader." Lucian occasionally indulged what seems like a digression only to "return to his Subject after keeping one in suspense." Smith ladled equal praise upon the two authors, despite their contrasting rhetorical styles and moral constitutions. They complement one another, forming "a complete system of ridicule" (*LRBL* 49–50). Smith next discussed the writings of Joseph Addison, famed author of the *Spectator* essays. Addison's modest character displayed itself in "flowryness" and in the "frequent use of figures," chiefly "metaphors, similes and Allegories." Though the genteel essayist differed from the dour Irish satirist (Swift) and the gay Roman humorist (Lucian), Smith admired Addison because his "modesty . . . causes him likewise [to] deliver his sentiments in the least assuming manner." As a result, Addison's "similes are always represented as naturally presenting themselves." Addison's figuration projects the "character of a most polite and elegant writer," a man rhetorically in sync with his times (*LRBL* 52–54).

Smith roundly and continuously condemned one writer throughout his lectures, balancing a dark antithesis against Swift's and Addison's shining examples: he denounced the stylistically disingenuous and ethically ambiguous writings of Anthony Ashley Cooper, 3rd Earl of Shaftesbury. At numerous points in his lectures on rhetoric, Smith digressed to abuse Shaftesbury for creating a "dungeon of metaphorical obscurity" (*LRBL* 8), preserving a "uniformity of cadence" (*LRBL* 38) even though it results in "many superfluous words," and keeping "at a vast distance from the language we commonly meet with" (*LRBL* 42). Smith especially criticized *The Moralists* (1711), a stylistically insincere treatise. According to Smith, Shaftesbury's teacher (John Locke) lacked a "very strong affection to any particular sect or tenets in Religion, who cried up freedom of thought and . . . Liberty of Conscience in all matters religious or philosophicall without being attached to any particular men or opinions" (*LRBL* 56). As a result of Shaftesbury's libertine proclivities, he never developed a stable or admirable character. In Smith's words, "The author seems not at all to have acted agreably to the Rule we have given . . . but to have formed to himself an idea of beauty of Stile abstracted from his own character, by which he proposed to regulate his Stile" (*LRBL* 56).

What resulted, according to Smith, was a buffoonish attempt at "polite dignity," a tawdry "grand and pompous diction" (*LRBL* 59). Smith lauded Shaftesbury's

Inquiry concerning Virtue or Merit for its genuinely direct style. Irony and ridicule mark Shaftesbury's other writings (such as *The Moralists, Soliloquy*, and *Sensus Communis*). Smith spent most of his time calumniating *The Moralists*. Unlike the *Inquiry, The Moralists* appeals to an ideal audience of polite, Whiggish young men with the dazzlingly witty repartee of two interlocutors (Philemon and Palemon). Shaftesbury stylistically seduced his intended audience into a skeptical philosophy by troubling the direct and plain style of the *Inquiry* and by smuggling (under the cloak of ironic dialogue) suggestions like Philocles's flippant praise of skeptical over rational foundations for religious faith.[34]

Despite his concerns about an absent moral compass, Smith found Shaftesbury's stylistic disingenuousness most troubling. While criticizing *The Moralists*, Smith recounted in dispassionate terms Shaftesbury's crusade to "overturn the Old Systems of Religion and Philosophy" (*LRBL* 58), but he vehemently condemned Shaftesbury's elegant yet ethically vapid figures. Even Shaftesbury's attempts at humor (a signature trope in his writings) fail because they improperly express the polite moral character he wanted to fashion for himself: "This species of Ridicule is always buffoonish and he surely falls greatly off from the Polite dignity he studies to maintain, when he allows himself a species of wit that is greatly beneath the character of a gentleman" (*LRBL* 60–61). Next to Shaftesbury's darkly duplicitous example, the prudent rhetor shines. Smith attributed a range of qualities to the prudent style. He admired English judges' "unpassionate serenity" (*LRBL* 198). He adored "Men of the greatest Calmeness and Prudence" (*LRBL* 192), such as Cicero. Smith's honorific aside to the Roman Republic's great orator anticipated an encomium (in *The Theory of Moral Sentiments*) to "the middling and inferior professions, real and solid professional abilities, joined to prudent, just, firm, and temperate conduct" (*TMS* 63).

Attending to Smith's lectures on rhetoric in the context of Enlightenment psychology and Stoic philosophy explains the rhetorical theory itself. This intellectual history also showcases the connection between Smith's rhetorical theory and bourgeois gentility. In the section that immediately follows, I focus on the relation between Smith's theory of rhetorical probity and his dedication to free commerce. As this essay's introduction explains, Smith associated capitalist prudence with probity.[35] To better understand how he associated the rhetorical virtue to capitalism, we must look to Smith's later writings on ethics, jurisprudence, and commerce. Evidence indicates that Smith's lectures on rhetoric and belles lettres remained more or less the same from the late 1740s (when he began declaiming on the topic) until the early 1760s (when a student penned the notebook that now shapes our scholarly remembrance of Smith's rhetorical theory).[36] Even if Smith never returned to revise his lectures on rhetoric and belles lettres after delivering his lectures on jurisprudence (ca. 1754–64) or authoring *The Wealth of Nations* (1776), my analysis of his lectures on rhetoric proves that he began reflecting on probity early in his career. He later elaborated on these rhetorical reflections in legal and economic registers. The lectures on rhetoric and belles lettres, therefore, stand as an important ur-document in Smith's intellectual corpus.

Probity's Utility

Understanding probity's role in commerce requires initial exploration of two foundational assumptions: first Smith believed that every system of law rests on a universal psychological foundation, and second he believed that history progresses in distinct stages. Smith did not assume God's natural law and then reason deductively. Instead, he rested natural law on the universal ability to sympathize. He assumed that positive law includes historically developed rules built on this psychological foundation and suited to the era's economy. In this regard, Smith was more Hume's than Locke's disciple, more a sentimentalist than a rationalist, and more a belletrist than a plain-stylist.[37] Toward the end of this section, I will connect Smith's economic writings to his theory of rhetorical probity. But first, I address Smith's writings on capitalism and jurisprudence with specific focus on his theory of commercial contract and with particular attention to his naturalistic psychology and his stadial theory of history. Without this intellectual history, Smith's rhetorical theory appears distinct from his economic writings. Placed against the backdrop of his writings on law and commerce, however, Smith's rhetorical theory looks like an effort to promote a rhetorical virtue that can sustain order and trust when commercial society's laws cannot yet guarantee stable and enforceable contracts.

Smith's naturalistic treatment of psychology allowed him to reject a great deal of the natural-law theory that Samuel Pufendorf and Hugo Grotius had contributed to the Western legal tradition. For instance, he could jettison the cherished Lockean notion that "property" is a natural right existing before the state. Instead, Smith posited the psychological mechanism of sympathy (and the judgment such sympathy allows) as the basis for property rights. Smith revisited Locke's example of a person picking an apple and described a right to possession based on sympathy with the person who had first harvested the fruit. He asked his students, "How is it that a man by pulling an apple should be imagined to have a right to that apple and a power of excluding all others from it—and that an injury should be conceived to be done when such a subject is taken for the possessor?" No rational arguments appealing to divine mandate will convince the spectator that the apple-picker has a right to the fruit, or that the apple-grabber has committed a crime. Rather, judgment arises pathetically from the spectator's sympathy with the apple-picker's resentment: "The cause of this sympathy or concurrence betwixt the spectator and the possessor is, that he enters into his thoughts and concurrs in his opinion that he may form a reasonable expectation of using the fruit or whatever it is in what manner he pleases" (*LJ* 16–17).

Smith similarly explained that people judge contract violation by exercising their sympathetic faculties. To illustrate, he offered another hypothetical example: "If I should say that I intend to give you voluntarily £100 next new years day, but make this declaration in such a manner as plainly shews I don't intend you should depend upon it, and expressly say, 'You need not depend upon it, but this is my present design,' the spectator could not here imagine that he to whom I made the promise would have any reasonable expectation; but this without doubt he would, if I should plainly declare that I meant that he should depend upon it." The spectator sympathizes with the aggrieved party's expectations and feels her resentment. As Smith put the matter, "The expectation and dependence of the promittee that he shall obtain what was promised is hear [*sic*] altogether reasonable, and such as an impartial spectator would readily go along with" (*LJ* 87). According to Smith, sympathy accounts for capitalism's two legal pillars, property and contract. As he later told his students, the "whole of criminal law is founded on the fellow feeling we have with the resentment of the injured person" (*LJ* 277).

Though Smith planted the legal foundation of commercial society on sympathy's terra firma, he did not imagine law or commerce as static architectures. Smith approached law, like many other Scottish legal theorists and social scientists, by empirically observing the stages of human development alongside the legal statutes and ethical principles corresponding to each stage.[38] Sympathy underlies all human history, but the laws and mores sitting atop its foundation change. He arrived at this stadial theory of history by following the worn path of his mentor, the renowned Scottish jurist Henry Home, Lord Kames, who believed that "population made a rapid progress, and government became an art;

for agriculture and commerce cannot flourish without salutary laws."[39] Smith elaborated, saying that laws change as society develops from hunter-gatherer tribes, to shepherd confederations, to agricultural kingdoms, and finally to commercial empires. Though immediately inherited from Kames, Smith's progressive view of history can be traced to the late seventeenth-century Whig distinction between primitive society (before commerce) and advanced society (after commerce).[40]

Further discussion of his approach to property law illustrates Smith's stadial theory of history and his belief that laws change when economic modes of production are altered. What began as a right to things immediately held or occupied (in an age of shepherds and clan government) changed into an individual right to land (in an age of agriculture and allodial government) and then changed further into an ancestral right to land (in an age of limited commerce and feudal government). Laws of accession proliferated when the agricultural era introduced a sense of ownership extending beyond the hunter's carcasses or the shepherd's milk. Laws of prescription and succession became important as more elaborate agricultural economies developed. Families wanted to maintain land, and governments aimed to reduce squabbling over ownership. Statutes regarding succession achieved the former end, statutes regarding prescription, the latter (LJ 27–37). Smith assumed that economic progress had caused legal reform.

Smith believed that laws regarding the voluntary transfer of property (contract laws especially) did not multiply until commerce usurped agriculture. Commercial contract laws offer no right to the property itself; rather, they present the recipient a right to "demand and compel him [the proprietor] to fulfill the engagement he has come under" (LJ 71). Thus, early capitalists invented expectation rights—the right to expect timely and complete fulfillment of a contract. As a result, commercial societies teem with laws and lawsuits regarding "servitudes and pledges" (LJ 85). The highest form of commercial organization also possesses the greatest statutory plenty, for "the more improved any society is and the greater length the severall means of supporting the inhabitants are carried, the greater will be the number of their laws and regulations necessary to maintain justice, and prevent infringements of the right of property" (LJ 16).

In The Wealth of Nations, Smith wrote extensively about such expectation rights in one particular commercial arena—finance. These laws permit simple commercial credit (bills) by providing a system of enforceable contracts that protects the expectation of timely and full payment to recipients who hold such promissory paper. "When the barbarous laws of Europe did not enforce the performance of contracts," merchants had to rely on customs of timely repayment in exchange for commercial paper. To remedy this situation, "the laws of all European nations, have given such extraordinary privileges to bills of exchange, that money is more readily advanced upon them, than upon any other species of obligation" (WN 309). With such a legal framework in place, eighteenth-century bills could make a complete circuit through several hands and return to the original possessor with interest attached, allowing the relatively new practice of "raising money by circulation" (WN 310). According to Smith, no market—not the bond market, not the commodities exchange, not the stock exchange—can function without government providing the basic security to own and profit.

Smith's stadial theory of history fit with his lived experience in Scotland. He imagined Scotland as a nation in transition, leaving the agrarian life that still characterized the Highlands and entering the commercial economy that burgeoned in the Lowlands (LJ 540–41). Glasgow was transitioning to the nineteenth-century manufacturing center it would become.[41] Merchants, retailers, and professional men (lawyers, physicians, and so forth) filled Edinburgh, but it was not a wholly commercial urban center. James Craig's plan for an orderly mecca of bourgeois living (New Town) was approved in 1767, but the city did not begin construction until 1800. In the meantime, Edinburgh's merchants and shopkeepers tolerated disorderly streets, unsanitary living conditions, regular riots, corrupt municipal government, and shoddy law enforcement.[42] Glasgow lagged further behind. Smith witnessed national and municipal shifts away from agriculture and toward commerce, away from anarchy and toward law, away from property rights (which would still be maintained) and toward expectation rights (which were not fully enshrined in the common law or enforced by the courts).

When Smith surveyed history at a distance, he saw the smooth progress of economic and legal institutions in tandem, but when he closely regarded his own era, he saw a legal system out of step with the commercial demands of eighteenth-century Scotland. Common-law courts "imperfectly recognized and enforced" executory contracts (contracts not yet fully realized) because, as one historian of jurisprudence explains, "such contracts were not then . . . thought to be generally actionable until the act has been performed."[43] Commercial litigants sought the stability to plan future endeavors based on their expectations of revenues, services, and goods. English law eventually changed to accommodate these pressures.[44] In the nineteenth century, English judges began to attach an "increasing importance" to "promise, agreement, and intention as the basis of legal liabilities."[45] In the 1760s, as Smith delivered his lectures on jurisprudence, he saw no such advances: "Another thing which greatly retarded commerce was the imperfection of the law with regard to contracts, which were the last species of rights that sustained action, for originaly the law gave no redress for any but those concluded on the spot." Only the most basic and earliest form of agreement, the simple market exchange, could benefit from legal action. At midcentury, Smith said that the law had not advanced much past this rudimentary stage: "At present all considerable commerce is carried on by commissions, and unless these sustained action little could be done" (*LJ* 528). Along with others (such as David Hume and Jeremy Bentham), Smith led the intellectual brigade to fight for expectation rights.[46]

Abstruse legal arguments about expectation rights cannot wholly account for Smith's indignation. The failure to recognize or enforce expectation rights truly threatened local merchant economies. In large part thanks to Locke's monetary policy, eighteenth-century England continually hungered for specie and particularly starved for coins of small denomination. As a result, commerce depended on informal credit networks: customers owed shopkeepers; shopkeepers owed merchants; merchants owed jobbers; jobbers owed manufacturers. Tenuously built on trust, this system of credits and debits scrawled in ledger books sufficed but also produced regular and often calamitous credit crises. If one debtor defaulted, or if one creditor refused payment, the entire regional network shook.[47] As early as 1711, the renowned essayist Joseph Addison allegorized "Lady Credit" as a figure who showed "a very particular Uneasiness" and who could quickly become "infinitely timorous in all her Behavior."[48] When Lady Credit swooned, Addison witnessed "Mony Bags . . . shrinking."[49]

A credit crisis could ruin any British merchant, for the laws enforcing debt obligations allowed creditors extraordinary access to debtors' property and freedom.[50] Moreover, the poor debtor would be hard-pressed to enforce payment on the bills and contracts he possessed. Though British citizens regularly alleged breach of contract and petitioned the courts for reward, judges typically rebuffed them. If a contract did not stipulate any penalty for overdue payment, the debtor had no incentive to pay on time. Acting out of self-interest, many simply fulfilled their contracts in an untimely manner.[51] Even if British courts regularly awarded damages based on the violation of expectation rights, enforcement would depend on either private initiative or a patchy police system.

Smith bemoaned the law's inability to advance alongside commerce. He believed Scotland had a legal problem, but he proposed an ethical solution, saying that the age of commerce encourages laws to protect expectation rights and ethical norms to prevent their violation: "It is commerce that introduces probity and punctuality" (*LJ* 528).

Economic progress of civilization brings legal developments and ethical advances. In his *Theory of Moral Sentiments*, Smith noted a stark difference between ancient and modern ethical systems. The ancients praised the "great, awful, and respectable virtues," while moderns admire "the soft, amiable, the gentle virtues." Modern citizens adulate the prudent merchant more than they do the brave warrior. According to Smith, the progress from an agricultural (and warlike) society to a commercial (and peaceable) society catalyzed a philosophical affection for "prudence only . . . the highest encouragement to the habits of caution, vigilance, sobriety, and judicious moderation" (*TMS* 306–7). Most important for the purposes of my argument, Smith insisted that the "prudent man is always sincere, and feels horror at the very thought of exposing himself to the disgrace which attends upon the detection of falsehood" (*TMS* 214). Smith elaborated on the commercial utility of bourgeois probity when discussing contract law with his students in the 1760s.

Like Locke, Smith insisted that plain-style clarity is a sine qua non of commercial contract: "The first contracts which were binding were those wherein the intention of the contractor was plain and uncontroverted; that is, such as were conceived in a certain set form of words which it was agreed expressed the design of the contracter that the other should depend on the performance of what was contracted" (*LJ* 89). In addition to clearly conveying the promised action (a payment, service, etc.), the contract also had to express "his intention at that time to do as he said." Said Smith, "All that is required . . . to make such a declaration lawfull is sincerity" (*LJ* 87). The spectator judges the sincerity of the contracting parties based on whether the promising party offers "an open and plain declaration that he desires the person to whom he makes the declaration to have a dependence on what he promises. . . . I promise to do so and so, you may depend upon it" (*LJ* 87). Only a barrister imagining the rarified circumstances of a courtroom or the stilted language of a contract could expect such a ham-fisted rhetorical display of sincerity. In the commercial world, where business often relies on handshakes and other such informal agreements, participants cannot rely on legal language's clarity nor can they rely on the lawyer's declaration of honesty.

Smith knew that different social situations call forward different standards of judgment. In *The Theory of Moral Sentiments*, he said that a person could judge legal matters by the "rules of grammar." Smith discussed a debt obligation to exemplify a case wherein the "rules of justice are accurate in the highest degree, and admit of no exceptions or modifications." In the debt contract, intention is openly declared and honestly professed: "If I owe a man ten pounds, justice requires that I should precisely pay him ten pounds, either at the time agreed upon, or when he demands it." The circumstances are "precisely fixt and determined." But many situations defy clear guidelines and unequivocal categories, so they call forth "a certain idea of propriety, by a certain taste for a particular tenor of conduct" (*TMS* 175). In *The Wealth of Nations*, Smith presented two cases that defy the fixed and grammatical standard of legal judgment: (1) merchant-sophists mask their interests when advocating policies that will grant them monopolies; (2) bankers fail to judge the honesty of their debtors. In each case, commercial probity gets violated to the detriment of the participants and of society. Each case requires that people apply "a certain idea of propriety" to judge probity's rhetorical manifestation in commercial transactions.

According to Smith, the merchant-sophist hides emotion to persuade the audience. He wins a temporary profit but ultimately diminishes opportunity. With fewer chances to "truck, barter, and exchange," everyone loses (*WN* 25).[52] When criticizing the mercantile system (especially in books 1 and 4 of the *Wealth of Nations*), Smith presented two characters: the dishonest merchant and the ignorant parliamentarian. Occasionally, he trotted the dishonest merchant alone onto the stage to showcase his duplicity. Merchants conceal a difference between a commodity's "natural price" (the cost of producing and bringing the good to market) and its "market price" (the amount most consumers will pay). But this benign duplicity cannot last since "their great profit would tempt so many new rivals to employ their stocks in the same way, that, the effectual demand being supplied, the market price would soon be reduced to the natural price" (*WN* 77). Similarly, manufacturers often collude to suppress workers' wages and increase profit. Their combination requires "the utmost silence and secrecy" (*WN* 84) as well as some false claims about "the bad effects of high wages." Meanwhile, manufacturers must hide the "pernicious effects of their own gains" (*WN* 115). Though Smith painted an ugly picture of manufacturers' collusion and the dishonest rhetoric defending their combination, he trusted that natural forces would correct this behavior: "Such combinations . . . are frequently resisted by contrary defensive combination of the workmen" (*WN* 84).

More important, since workers must afford necessities to support themselves and their families, wages must exceed "a certain rate below which it seems impossible to reduce, for any considerable time" (*WN* 85). The free market for labor and for goods disciplines dishonest merchants and manufacturers. When they collude with politicians, however, insincere capitalists wreak havoc that the free market cannot rectify.

Smith thought that Britain had an alarming history of trade restrictions and monopoly privileges imposed under the banner of public benefit. Politicians granted privileges in exchange for discounted loans or direct payments: "In England, indeed, a charter from the king is likewise necessary [to incorporate for commercial purposes]. But this prerogative of the crown seems reserved ... for extorting money from the subject, than for the defence of the common liberty against such oppressive monopolies" (*WN* 140). Town burghers, likewise, conspired to control local production and sale, "to prevent the markets from being over-stocked, as they commonly express it, with their own particular species of industry; which is in reality to keep it always under-stocked" (*WN* 141). Throughout *The Wealth of Nations*, Smith reserved the deeply pejorative term "sophist" for those who petition public officials for monopoly privileges: "The clamour and sophistry of merchants and manufacturers easily persuade ... [ignorant public officials] that the private interest of a part, and of a subordinate part of the society, is the general interest of the whole" (*WN* 144). British wool and cotton manufacturers casuistically convinced "the wisdom of the nation, that the safety of the commonwealth depends upon the prosperity of their particular manufacture" (*WN* 250). The "interests of the dealers ... in every particular branch of trade or manufactures, is always in some respects different from, and even opposite to, that of the publick." As a result, the "proposal of any new law or regulation of commerce which comes from this order, ought always to be listened to with great precaution." Merchants' "interest is never exactly the same with that of the publick ... [so merchants] have generally an interest to deceive and even to oppress the publick, and ... [merchants] accordingly have, upon many occasions, both deceived and oppressed it" (*WN* 267).

The ignorant parliamentarian and the deceptive merchant are the lead characters in Smith's narrative about an actual effort to repeal legal prohibitions on the export of English gold. The repeal had a "solid" basis in economic utility. Smith said, "The exportation of gold and silver in trade might frequently be advantageous to the country." He further explained that "no prohibition could prevent their exportation, when private people found any advantage in exporting them." Nevertheless, merchants supported their case with the "sophistical" argument that "the high price of exchange necessarily increased, what they called, the unfavourable balance of trade" (*WN* 433). The merchants' winning argument deserved to be called "sophistry" for two reasons. First, the "balance of trade" theory does not hold water, since a nation's wealth does not consist in its possession of precious metals. Second, the balance-of-trade argument parades a public interest in national prosperity while obscuring a private interest in facilitating trade. As Smith put it, the arguments "were addressed by merchants to parliamentarians, and to the councils of princes, to nobles and to country gentlemen; by those who were supposed to understand trade, to those who . . . knew nothing about the matter" (*WN* 434). In this case, ignorant English legislators did the right thing, though for the wrong reason. In another case, merchants' dishonesty led parliamentarians to a greater treason.

According to Smith, restrictions on trade with France hurt the British economy by cutting off a viable market for manufactured goods. "The impertinent jealousy of merchants and manufacturers" motivated spurious arguments that the "Portuguese . . . are better customers for our manufactures than the French. . . . As they give us their custom, it is pretended, we should give them ours." Merchants hid their "jealous" affection for trade restrictions behind "sneaking [rhetorical] arts." Taken in by "the interested sophistry of merchants and manufacturers," inveigled legislators overlooked "the common sense of mankind": "It always is and must be the interest of the great body of the people to buy whatever they want of those who sell it cheapest" (*WN* 493–94). Other, wrongheaded policies resulted from similarly dishonest and absurd arguments: restrictions on colonial trade (*WN* 581–84), monopoly privileges afforded trading companies (*WN* 612–13), and monopoly privileges given to textile manufacturers (*WN* 647–52). According to Smith, merchants' dishonest promulgation of discredited economic principles made Great Britain into "a nation whose government is influenced by shopkeepers" (*WN* 613). They made "the sovereign . . . an appendix to . . . the merchant" (*WN* 637).

Another section of *The Wealth of Nations* similarly suggests rhetorical probity's commercial necessity. When Smith discussed the banking industry, he presented his reader with two characters, each modeling commercially beneficial sincerity and commercially baleful dishonesty: the honest creditor and the dishonest debtor. The banker who displays genuine "probity, and prudence" will issue notes with the honest intention of repayment. According to Smith, customers reward this honesty with their "confidence" and their continued business

(*WN* 292). Smith further believed that Scotland's financial success depended on the legal enforcement of contracts and the social maintenance of trust (*WN* 309).[53] One recent economic historian, echoing Adam Smith, explains that "traders of known probity enjoyed only one real and actually very slender advantage over their weaker brethren, namely their ability to maintain their creditworthiness during a crisis."[54] As the eighteenth-century essayist Richard Steele put it, "Credit is undone in Whispers." As a result, "the Trader" is the "most unhappy of all Men, and the most exposed to the Malignity of Wantonness of the common Voice."[55] In such a world, the honest tradesman must rely on a lifetime of probity.

Next to the genuine banker, Smith presented the duplicitous creditor. The careful banker should watch out for creditors who claim to borrow for "some vast and extensive project of agriculture, commerce, or manufactures" but who, instead, speculate with their newfound capital. These activities are especially hard to spot when creditors "discount their bills sometimes with one banker, and sometimes with another" (*WN* 311). Sadly, an honest banker dealing with such a dishonest creditor might discover his role but "sometimes make . . . [the discovery] too late, and might find that he had already discounted the bills of those projectors to so great an extent, that, by refusing to discount any more, he would necessarily make them all bankrupts, and thus, by ruining them, might perhaps ruin himself" (*WN* 312). While Smith suggested that bankers exercise probity, he also suggested that they prudently evaluate people's characters to prevent overextension of credit to dishonest speculators. Smith's digression on the honest banker and the dishonest creditor, on the one hand, is a capitalist's morality tale about the personal consequences of recklessness and duplicity. But these passages lead to a wider economic lesson: the dishonest creditor who hides his true character when asking for a loan or when discounting a note harms the entire credit infrastructure. Smith contended that the Ayr Bank (opened in 1769 and collapsed in 1772) failed because it "was imprudent. . . . This bank was more liberal than any other had been both in granting cash accounts, and in discounting bills of exchange" (*WN* 313).

In *The Wealth of Nations*, Smith assured his reader that individuals' probity and their practical judgment of insincerity would set commerce aright when duplicitous individuals sought to exploit the market's weaknesses. If people discoursed with one another honestly, and if they could sniff out rhetorical duplicity, then the law's failure to protect expectation rights would not undermine commerce's stability. Smith's attention to "sophistry" and rhetorical duplicity in

The Wealth of Nations indicates that he found some commercial application for the judgment that he taught in his lectures on rhetoric and belles lettres. In *The Theory of Moral Sentiments*, Smith stated that the "rules of the other virtues," such as probity, are comparable to the "rules which critics lay down for the attainment of what is sublime and elegant in composition." Though "loose, vague, and indeterminate" (*TMS* 175), Smith's guidelines for judging ethical and pathetic probity in rhetorical style apply to commercial situations where the "strict" rules of a legal "grammar" have no bearing.

If Smith connected his rhetorical theory of probity to his legal worries about contracts or to his financial concerns about credit, then why did he not directly defend probity's utility? When lecturing on rhetorical style, why not tell students that they should study syntax and figuration so they can discern a false sentiment and judge a duplicitous character? So that they can become wealthy merchants and successful bankers? So that they can sustain a healthy free market for goods, services, and credit? There are two answers to these questions. First, Smith developed his ideas about probity's commercial utility after he composed his lectures on rhetoric, never returning to revise the lectures themselves, so the interrelation among the works will only be evidenced by analogous ideas, appearing early in the lectures on rhetoric and later in the legal and economic writings. From this perspective, the lectures on rhetoric and belles lettres look like a psychological and philosophical belletrism that Smith later justified in legal and economic arguments.

But there is a second answer to the question of why Smith never justified rhetorical probity in terms of its economic utility: he did not think utility could inspire virtue. The butcher, the baker, and the brewer may provide dinner out of a regard to their interest, but they are moved to honesty by a felt sense of its propriety. When declaiming from the economist's lectern, Smith spoke as a utilitarian. When orating from the rhetorician's rostrum, however, he spoke as a virtue ethicist.[56] He accepted Aristotle's edict: "We become just by doing just acts, temperate by doing temperate acts, brave by doing brave acts . . . [and therefore] states of character arise out of like activities."[57] As always, Smith put his own modern psychological spin on an old Greek concept. The most direct link between the lectures on rhetoric and *The Wealth of Nations* can be found in the psychological-ethical passages of Smith's *Theory of Moral Sentiments*.

Smith explained (contra Hume) that, though people's behaviors eventually must serve utility, prudent reason does not motivate these economically useful actions.[58] In the moment of decision, people neither calculate their personal interests nor consider the community's welfare. In the moment of decision, people follow their ingrained habits and their psychological impulses. Utility is the last spur to good action, the last guide to good judgment, after sympathy and propriety.[59] Similarly, people judge rhetorical style based on their feeling of its sincerity and their sense of its honesty. Since no calculation of prudence will improve or promote such judgment, no disquisitions on prudence belong among Smith's lectures on rhetoric and belles lettres. His belletrism offers exposure to and criticism of honest discourse, not reasons for or precepts behind clear language. Even if he could have revised his lectures on rhetoric to reflect his economic reflections on probity's utility, he likely would not have done so. By 1762, he had already made the most convincing apology for an honest style.

Edifying Sympathy

Smith taught rhetoric for most of his years as a university professor. He believed that learning to discern an honest style would benefit commercial society by creating trust and by exposing the untrustworthy. It seems reasonable to conclude that Smith would favor publicly funded and universally required rhetorical education, or that he would put education in service of the state—a place to cultivate civic virtue (probity) for a commercial society. However, Smith endorsed no such policy and no such association. In fact, he wanted rhetorical education to happen in civil society, benefiting the free exchange of goods and ideas without the magistrate's intervention. In *The Wealth of Nations*, he defended the barest publicly funded curriculum to enrich the minds and the lives of laborers. Since the wealthy will likely pay to educate their children, the state should only concern itself with "the education of the common people" because impoverished workers "have little time to spare for education" (*WN* 784). Smith may have been a virtue ethicist in the Aristotelian tradition, but he was no classically Greek republican clamoring for state schools to infuse citizens with civic virtue. Like others in the Scottish Enlightenment, Smith favored civil society.[60] He wanted the capitalist market and the bourgeois public sphere to emerge from the bottom up, as a naturally occurring and self-regulating process of free exchange.

His feelings about state-funded and -regulated education fed a hostility toward university faculty who siphon public money and produce lettered men: "In all christian countries, I believe, the education of the greater part of churchmen is paid for in this [public] manner." The clerisy's surfeit results in low wages and joblessness: "The long, tedious, and expensive education, therefore, of those who are [educated in publicly funded universities], will not always procure them a suitable reward, the church being crowded with people who, in order to get employment, are willing to accept of a much smaller recompence than what such an education would otherwise have entitled them to" (WN 146). Smith lamented the "unprosperous race of men commonly called men of letters" gushing from this moribund and costly system, "indigent people who have been brought up to it at the publick expense" (WN 148–49). Smith championed private educators like the ancient Greek sophists who compete for students in an unregulated market that rewards its best teachers with splendid wealth and "a degree of consideration much superior to any of the like profession in the present times" (WN 150). Because he left it largely to private actors, it is easy to conclude that Smith saw "education" as something which is good in itself, and not as a means to a distant, commercial end.[61] But such a conclusion is premature. Smith promoted "small [publicly funded] premiums, and little badges of distinction" to encourage instruction, and he recommended publicly funded licensing to foster practical learning (WN 786). Finally, as this essay argues most thoroughly, he believed that education could impart a form of bourgeois virtue: probity.

Smith's aversion to publicly funded education stems in part from his experiences at English universities and in part from his knowledge of religious education at Scottish primary schools. During the Scottish Reformation, the Kirk set up a system of popular education that promoted literacy as well as Protestant religion. By the mid-eighteenth century, this system of parish, private, and burgh schools favorably compared to the European standard-bearers of the day—namely, Holland, northern England, and Sweden.[62] Smith suggested "establishing in every parish or district a little school, where children may be taught for a reward so moderate, that even a common labourer may afford it" (WN 785). But he did not favor public direction of the curriculum. He feared that state intervention would embolden sectarian, post-Reformation parish schools. The "interested and active zeal of religious teachers can be dangerous" because their enthusiasm leads to intolerance and oppression (WN 792). John Locke placed religion in civil society's free domain to diffuse the threat of state-supported persecution. Smith added to Locke's argument, saying that "religious" instruction prepares people "for another and a better world in a life to come." Education's proper mission, however, is to fashion "good citizens in this world" (WN 788).

While state-funded and religiously directed education wastes resources on destructive or useless endeavors, the free market for ideas and artistic expressions imparts bourgeois virtue. Smith wanted the state to give "entire liberty to all those who for their own interest would attempt, without scandal or indecency, to amuse and divert the people by painting, poetry, musick, dancing; by all sorts of dramatic representations and exhibitions" (*WN* 796). In his mature years and in his economic writings, he decided that the magistrate should never appoint any rhetoric professor to the Ministry of Probity. The invisible hand of the literary market better allocates this ethical resource. In his younger days, while lecturing on rhetoric and ethics, Smith explained how liberated imaginative literature could instill bourgeois virtue. Smith believed that exposure to imaginative literature can improve a person's capacity for sympathy. The theory of sympathy, as presented in his lectures on rhetoric, does not fairly present Smith's most developed ideas on the subject. In his writings on ethics, Smith offered a sophisticated psychological model premised on the imagination's communicative role.

In his *Theory of Moral Sentiments*, Smith explained that feelings do not channel through any direct conduit. Rather, affect finds its way from one person to another by way of imagination: "Our senses . . . never did, and never can, carry us beyond our own person." The "imagination only" can "form any conception of what are . . . [another person's] sensations" (*TMS* 9). We can sympathize because: (1) We witness the external register of someone's internal condition. (A terse sentence indicates sorrow; a sublime magniloquence indicates gravity.) And (2) we notice the circumstance eliciting this internal condition. Based on external register and circumstance, we imagine the speaker's internal condition, and we judge its propriety. After this reflexive imaginative exercise, if we agree that a person's internal condition suits the external circumstance and derives from an appropriate character, then we sympathize. As Smith put it, "To approve of the passions of another, therefore, as suitable to their objects, is the same thing as to observe that we entirely sympathize with them" (*TMS* 16).

Of course, Smith never equated a judgment of probity with a judgment of propriety. An emotion may be genuinely communicated but wholly inappropriate. At numerous times in *The Theory of Moral Sentiments*, he counseled the reader to temper emotional expression in order to allow another party to imagine the circumstance and sympathize with the emotion. Because they are so unpleasant to witness, the unsocial passions, such as "hatred and resentment," cannot exceed "a bare intimation," for anything more will preclude imagination by soliciting the audience's fear and aversion (*TMS* 34–35). Furthermore, because we cannot ever fully feel what another person feels, we find maudlin displays improper to any circumstance. Smith advocated "mediocrity" in emotional expression, even when the prompting sentiment—like "violent hunger" or "intolerable" pain—warrants a paroxysm (*TMS* 27–28). Since sympathy is always "extremely imperfect" (*TMS* 11), people must improve their imaginative faculty. While the connection between the imagination and sympathy is easy to trace, the path from sympathy to probity does not present itself so readily. Smith believed that insincerity interrupts sympathy and that a developed capacity to sympathize inclines the individual toward honesty. Finally, Smith believed that critical exposure to imaginative literature could teach the imagination to appropriately sympathize. He explained literature's ability to improve sympathetic judgment when lecturing on the rhetoric of expository discourse.

In his lectures on rhetoric, shortly after explaining how best to convey sincere character and emotion in a persuasive discourse, Smith turned to exposition, particularly to historical writing. He said that the historian should avoid any effort to directly describe someone's internal character—better to indirectly present "an account of the prevailing temper and passions of the man, as soon as he is brought into the scheme of the history and afterwards to give such observations on his conduct as will open up the generall principles on which he acts" (*LRBL* 82). When indirectly describing, the writer should relate "the effects the transaction produced both on the actors and Spectators." To present the ineffable sensation of grief, one should "barely relate the circumstances the persons were in, the state of their mind before the misfortune and the causes of their passion" (*LRBL* 87). Indirect description prompts the reader imaginatively to project how he would feel or what kind of person he would be in these circumstances. Though we can never directly experience another's sentiment or inhabit her person, through the imperfect medium of literarily induced imaginative projection we can sense who she is and how she feels. Imagination fascinated and worried many Enlightenment-era intellectuals, Smith especially.[63] Despite his concerns, Smith believed in imaginative writing's ethical and pedagogical potential.[64] Indirect description, when well executed, encourages proper sympathy while teaching "those general ethical imperatives used to judge both other people and one's self."[65]

Since ethical judgment requires instruction, Smith discussed a socially developed and communicatively enacted form of emotional-ethical discourse.[66] Though imagination is universal, education informs the mores that shape a spectator's judgment. When writing of "customs and fashion," he explained that manufactured "principles . . . extend their dominion over our judgments concerning beauty of every kind" (*TMS* 194). In order to judge propriety in human conduct and art, one must develop a sense of beauty (an internal index of the prevailing customs) by "a certain practice and experience in contemplating each species of objects" (*TMS* 199). To develop good judgment in art, one must see many great works of art. Repeated exposure to great architecture leaves a residual sense of propriety, allowing one to judge "why the Doric capital should be appropriate to a pillar, whose height is equal to eight diameters; the Ionic volute to one of nine; and the Corinthian foliage to one of ten" (*TMS* 196). The same principle applies to language and literature—exposure to honest discourse inculcates a sense of probity.

Since "fashion" depends on capricious imagination, it readily changes and "may easily be altered by habit and education." Despite their stable emotional foundation, "sentiments of moral approbation and disapprobation . . . founded on the strongest and most vigorous passions of human nature" do not persist without some educational influence. Smith praised "those who have been educated in what is really good company," for their training heightens a sense of propriety founded on a stable and long-standing esteem for "justice, modesty, humanity, and good order" (*TMS* 200). Putting students in the good company of honest writers (such as Swift and Addison), Smith aimed to enforce their natural sense of stylistic probity. Encouraging students to laud a genuinely plain discourse or an ingenuously figured emotion, Smith sought to improve a reflexive and positive judgment of an honest rhetorical style.

Twentieth-century literary scholars have echoed Smith's hope for belletristic criticism when praising literature's ability to ethically educate by putting people in good company.[67] Recent psychological research confirms that exposure to literature improves our capacity to intuit other people's beliefs and our ability to judge their sincerity.[68] Present-day ethicists and political theorists return to Smith's work because he attended to the role of literary education in affective and ethical development.[69] The contemporary preoccupation with literature's ethical potential has deep roots in a variety of disciplines, both scientific and humanistic. This preoccupation points toward our sustained investment in a bourgeois public sphere populated by sympathetic and therefore sincere speakers. Though he may have left no extended treatise on education, Smith gave his students something more valuable. He exemplified the practices of sincere discourse. He publicly judged rhetorical (in)sincerity over the course of thirty lectures. He asked his students to admire stylistic excellences of good literary company. Smith's literary artist and stylistic critic are the unacknowledged ethicists of this bourgeois world.

Smith's theories about literature's psychological-imaginative effect have led some to characterize his rhetorical theory and pedagogy as individualistic and liberal (in the negative sense). Smith took the arts out of the public sphere, snatched rhetoric out of politics, pulled the citizen out of the polis. He separated bourgeois prudence from classical *phronesis*—the rhetor's ability to publicly reason from a community's shared values.[70] Many such claims should stand without contest. He certainly presaged the literary turn in humanistic education. He undoubtedly stood at an important moment when the liberal arts became "liberal" in the sense that higher education gave emancipated citizens the freedom to pursue their appreciation of equally free arts and letters in civil society. He unquestionably transformed rhetorical education from instruction in how to produce to instruction in how to appreciate discourse. He turned the language arts away from oratory and toward aesthetics.[71]

But all of these concessions do not add up to an admission that Smith or belletrism corrupted rhetorical education by removing the study of rhetoric from the practice of virtue, by discarding practical judgment, or by placing rhetorical education in the realm of civil society. In the Greek agora and the Roman senate, citizens improved their publicly realized civic virtues by debating matters of state. But Smith and his Scottish Enlightenment cohort inaugurated a new, liberal vision of civil society, a diversified layering of spaces including the parlor and the market but not parliament. According to Smith, processes of mutual recognition (such as honest exchange) cultivate an interior private virtue that holds civil society together by what Adam Seligman has called "the force of moral sentiments and natural affections."[72] The study of literature, as Charles Griswold notes, is of particular importance, because it "teaches us how ethically complex human situations can be, how to stretch the moral imagination so as to size up the relevant factors, how to carry on a conversation about the competing claims of the dramatis personae."[73]

Since he did not argue for a uniform character among citizens, and he did not promote education in service of the state, Smith may not fit within the classically republican tradition that emphasizes civic virtue. Nor does he fit in the natural-law tradition that proposes legislative efforts to suppress or direct people's desires. But, as Helena Rosenblatt points out, in the mid-eighteenth century, many discussed a third way to train character and thereby improve society:

doux commerce.[74] Smith's lifelong friend, David Hume, was among those who thought that commercial "refinement make[s] men polite . . . [and] also *moralizes* them."[75] Sweet commerce can make people's economic lives more comfortable and their ethical selves more tolerable. In the free market, people improve the economy by pursuing self-interest and by exercising honesty. In the public sphere, people improve themselves by appreciating literature and by exercising sympathy. Both the commodities exchange and the literary salon symbiotically reinforce the lessons taught by the other. Sympathy encourages probity and serves commerce. Commerce, circulating the free arts, improves sympathy.

Though they would not become good civic orators through disputation exercises, Smith hoped his students would become honest merchants by critiquing literary styles and sympathizing with historical characters. Even though the public spaces where people learn virtues and practice judgment do not feature deliberative assemblies, civil society's participants are nonetheless political. No longer the protector and distributor of republican virtue, no longer the teacher of moving orators, the liberal pedagogue models good judgment through literary criticism while encouraging a long life of free artistic appreciation. Smith trusted that individual people, given the critical tools and the literary material, can teach themselves sympathy and can learn to appreciate probity.

3

Hugh Blair on Moderation

John Locke and Adam Smith argued that capitalism promotes virtue. Contracts introduce clarity. Finance encourages sincerity. Theirs is not a common claim. More often, we hear the classical republican complaining that capitalism corrupts civic virtue or the devout Christian worrying that commerce tempts morality.[1] During the British Enlightenment, many responded to these arguments about capitalism, civic virtue, and Christian morality by claiming that capitalism relies on ethical dispositions that commerce does not sustain. A modern version of such an argument is Francis Fukuyama's suggestion that capitalism will never make people honest, but that commerce depends on the trust that honesty sustains.[2] An Enlightenment version is Hugh Blair's claim that Christian morals and republican virtue teach good habits of moderate consumption and personal savings, habits that support commerce by ensuring reinvestment and by preventing overconsumption.

Blair's discussion of rhetorical moderation exhibits the tense relationship between virtue and commerce during the British Enlightenment. In the eighteenth century, virtue and commerce seemed sometimes complementary and sometimes contradictory forces. Sometimes virtue seemed to be the soil in which capitalism could grow. Sometimes capitalism seemed to plant virtue in otherwise fallow psyches. The era's conflicted sentiments are captured in an antimetabole penned by the philosophe Montesquieu: "Everywhere there are gentle mores, there is commerce and . . . everywhere there is commerce, there are gentle mores."[3] Did capitalism make people good, or did good people make commerce possible?

Locke and Smith argued that capitalism makes people good. Drawing on Christian and classical sources, Hugh Blair saw commerce as a beneficial yet also corrupting influence. He thought virtue could preserve commerce's benefits and offset its detriments—good people make capitalism possible. Hugh Blair inherited a great deal from Adam Smith: a commitment to economic prosperity, which Blair attributed to free-market capitalism; a belief that virtue can be taught through instruction in rhetorical style; and a job as university lecturer. Blair assumed Smith's position as Professor of Rhetoric and Belles Lettres at Edinburgh, and he used Smith's lectures as a guide when preparing his own disquisitions on the subject.[4] Finally, Blair shared with Smith a commitment to belletrism because he thought that polite literature, properly studied, could morally edify.[5] Given all that the two men shared, we should not be surprised to find Blair promoting bourgeois virtue through rhetorical criticism of literary style. Blair's approach to bourgeois virtue, however, differed notably. Smith celebrated the probity that capitalism engenders, while Blair praised the moderation that capitalism needs.

Style and Probity, Literature and Tolerance

Unlike Smith, Blair was not a systematic thinker. He principally composed in three genres: essays on literary criticism, lectures on rhetorical theory, and sermons on religion and culture. But Blair made no effort at integrating his works, nor did he explain the principal exigency behind his intellectual corpus. As a result, to understand Blair's work systematically one must search for common concerns and arguments across different texts and dissimilar genres. Such a systematic analysis requires attention to mid-century circumstances and conversations. We more easily see the common themes in Blair's writing if we notice the common exigencies to which he responded.

This essay's first segment thematically analyzes Blair's writing in the context of other voices speaking on similar matters to demonstrate that Blair addressed common concerns about honesty and toleration through his lectures on rhetorical style and literature genres. I characterize this opening gambit as "suggestive" because the evidence does not conclusively prove the case. The section to follow—about Blair's treatment of bourgeois moderation—presents a conclusive case to prove that Blair was a bourgeois rhetorical stylist/ethicist. Blair *probably* worried about bourgeois honesty and toleration when lecturing on rhetorical style and literary genres. Blair *certainly* worried about bourgeois moderation when lecturing on figuration.

Smith had already defended the economic utility of honest discourse when explaining that the merchant's success depends on his "probity" since a "dealer is afraid of losing his character" (*LJ* 538). For this reason, Smith told students to use figures that sincerely express true sentiments. Though Blair did not repeat Smith's economic argument about probity, when discussing rhetorical figuration he echoed Smith's lectures on the subject. Blair directed students to prune their sentences of all "superfluities" so that the expression is "an exact copy of his idea who uses it." Precision is marred by misrepresentation. Words "may . . . not express that idea which the author intends"; "they may express that idea, but not quite fully and completely; or, they may express it, together with something more than he intends" (*Lectures* 101–2). The "figure is only the dress; the Sentiment is the body and the substance" (*Lectures* 147). Like Smith, Blair believed that a person's language should sincerely reflect her character and emotion.

When expounding on figures that affect the passions, such as hyperbole, Blair said, "the great rule with regard to the conduct of such Figures is, that the writer attend to the manner in which nature dictates to us to express any emotion or passion, and that he give his language that turn, and no other; above all, that he never affect the style of a passion which he does not feel" (*Lectures* 191). When delivering orations in popular assemblies, students learned "never to counterfeit warmth without feeling it" (*Lectures* 292). Like Smith, he thought honesty necessary to healthy public discourse in civil society. Blair's discussion of rhetorical style, set alongside Smith's economic defense of bourgeois probity, suggests that the revered belletrist, like his friend the economist, shared an appreciation for the virtue's necessity in free-market exchange.

An even stronger, though still suggestive, case can be made regarding Blair's treatment of tolerance. In Blair's day, people most often discussed the virtue (tolerance) and its practice (toleration) in religious terms. The British Enlightenment's preoccupation with tolerance stretches back to violent mid-seventeenth-century disputes between Protestants and Catholics (or between Protestants and Protestants). Like others in his era, Blair promoted rhetorical tolerance because it protects civil society from civil war. Michael Walzer aptly characterized the toleration that resulted from seventeenth-century confessional strife: "People kill one another for years and years, and then, mercifully, exhaustion sets in, and we call this toleration."[6] In addition to the benefits that such toleration offered to public discourse, many of Blair's contemporaries saw an economic boon in bourgeois tolerance.

Adam Smith, for example, believed that intolerance hampered trade. In *The Wealth of Nations*, he said that "national animosity," fueled by intolerance of the Catholic French, led to foolish trade restrictions that inhibited a potentially prosperous international commercial exchange (*WN* 495). Smith was

not alone when suggesting that tolerance paves the road for free trade and economic growth. After visiting the Royal Exchange on Threadneedle Street in
early eighteenth-century London, Joseph Addison reported hearing people and
seeing commodities from across every ocean. He stood near "an Inhabitant of
Japan and an Alderman of *London*" and next to "a Subject of the *Great Mogul.*"
He spoke to a subject of "the *Czar* of *Muscovy*"; he was affronted by "a Crowd of
Jews" and a "Groupe of *Dutch-men.*"[7] According to Addison, this workaday commodities exchange required cooperation among people of different ethnicities,
origins, and religious convictions. Smith himself observed that the merchant
must traffic promiscuously in all kinds of goods and with all kinds of people:
"He is a corn merchant this year, and wine merchant the next, and a sugar, to-
bacco, or tea merchant the year after" (*WN* 130). The eighteenth-century British
fashion boom captures the commercial importance that Smith and Addison attributed to tolerance. Without Indian calicoes and French fashion dolls, English
consumers would be neither willing nor able to buy new clothes every season.
British retailers and merchants hawked French styles in London, Indian fabrics
in Derbyshire, Scottish linens in North America.[8]

This conversation about toleration's economic utility paralleled and reinforced the conversation about religious toleration. Writing in the late seventeenth century, the English economist William Petty attributed Holland's
commercial success in part to the Dutch "Liberty of Conscience."[9] Similarly,
Voltaire commented in a journal written while traveling through England in
1726–27, "Where there is not liberty of conscience, there is seldom liberty of
trade, the same tyranny encroaching upon the commerce as upon Religion."[10]
John Locke, a strong English advocate for religious toleration, defended the
virtue's potential to promote trade in the late seventeenth-century Carolina
colonies, where he thought toleration of Jews and religious dissenters would encourage commercial success similar to what he saw in Barbados (a colony populated by prosperous Jewish merchants since 1665).[11] Long before Blair muttered
a word about rhetoric, many Enlightenment intellectuals assumed that intolerance could stall trade circuits by refusing passage to humanity's diversity.

Blair never commented directly on toleration. He did praise Adam Smith's
explication of "the whole Subject of Commerce," saying, "You have given me full
and Compleat Satisfaction and my Faith is fixed."[12] Moreover, while teaching
rhetoric, Blair promoted toleration by continually insisting that, though there
are standards of taste, these standards allow appreciation of numerous rhetorical styles. Set in the conversation about tolerance's economic utility, Blair's

lectures on literary genres sound like a discourse on diverse literary tastes delivered in order to promote an economically virtuous practice of toleration. Blair's lectures taught the norms of educated British discourse, but Blair never adhered to one aesthetic standard. In fact, Blair taught his students to recognize a variety of beauties in the world, saying, "The Tastes of men may differ very considerably as to their object, and yet none of them be wrong" (*Lectures* 16). Following Smith's lead, Blair found little merit in Lord Shaftesbury's prose (*Lectures* 103–4, 212–13). Like Smith, Blair encouraged his students to enjoy the different styles adopted by Joseph Addison and Jonathan Swift (lectures 21–24). He lauded the different but equally beautiful, styles found in Cicero and Demosthenes (lecture 26). He told his students that they should learn to appreciate various national rhetorical styles. According to Blair, there is beauty in passionate French oratory and in reserved English address (*Lectures* 93–94). Blair's celebration of stylistic variety ends with characteristically bourgeois limits to toleration, as some tastes and some styles are beyond the pale.[13] The standard of taste, improved by exposure to quality writing, ensures that this toleration will not degenerate into the corrupt notion that "all Tastes are equally good" (*Lectures* 15).

In lectures 36–47, Blair introduced students to a range of literary genres, works, and authors from England, Scotland, France, Italy, and Spain. Blair found something to praise in all these writings. The Italian Torquato Tasso exhibits "all the beauties of description, and of Poetical Style" (*Lectures* 505). The French François Fénelon "gives the Style nearly as much elevation as the French language is capable of supporting" (*Lectures* 508). The English John Milton is "most distinguished for his sublimity" (*Lectures* 512). The student listening to Blair's lectures on literature learned to adore literature from all nations, becoming, like Joseph Addison, a joyous "Citizen of the World" by consuming the diverse commodities and accompanying the diverse peoples on the cosmopolitan literary exchange.[14]

Ultimately, Blair and Smith both detested Lord Shaftesbury's prose style. Yet they shared Shaftesbury's hope for polite literature. They agreed that if people of good breeding accompany a student while exposing her to free discourse among ideologically and culturally diverse subjects, she will acquire a virtuously tolerant disposition. Shaftesbury succinctly captured the principle: "All Politeness is owing to Liberty. We polish one another, and rub off our Corners and rough Sides by a sort of *amicable Collision*."[15] The free spaces of civil society, such as the literary salon, generate people "of thorow *Good-Breeding*."[16] Civil society's denizens become "incapable of doing a rude or brutal Action"; they are "*Gentlemen of Fashion* . . . to whom a natural good Genius or the Force of good Education, has given a *Sense* of what is *naturally graceful* and *becoming*."[17] Blair's belletristic survey of literary styles confirms that he favored tolerance in bourgeois public discourse. Set in the context of a conversation about toleration's economic utility, Blair's writings on literary genres speak to a commercial exigency. But lacking testimony from the man, we cannot conclusively state that he promoted tolerance of literary styles to advance commerce. However, Blair's thoughts on another virtue, moderation, conclusively prove that he saw economic utility in rhetorical style.

Commercial Luxury and Rhetorical Moderation

Blair, like many of his compatriots, advocated stylistic moderation as a genteel habit that allows productive association through intellectual, artistic, and commercial exchange. David Hume presaged Blair: "When the tempers of men are softened as well as their knowledge improved, this humanity appears still more conspicuous. . . . [Such moderation] is the chief characteristic that distinguishes a civilized age from times of barbarity and ignorance."[18] Hume furthermore supposed that moderation in commercial exchange leads to moderation in public discourse: "This industry is much promoted by the knowledge inseparable from ages of art and refinement." Commerce conceived trade, begat knowledge, birthed civil society, and raised "mildness and moderation."[19] Hume's associations among commerce, civil society, and polite discourse support the recent scholarly consensus that bourgeois moderation led Blair and others to reject incendiary oratory in favor of polite restraint.[20] But the British Enlightenment's vague association of commerce, rhetorical moderation, and the bourgeois public sphere does not prove that anyone saw economic utility in rhetorical figuration. To see the economic implications of Blair's commitment to rhetorical moderation, we must attend to the social context of the British "consumer revolution." Marketing and distribution spurred a conversation about overconsumption. Blair responded to this economic exigency in his sermons and in his lectures on rhetoric and belles lettres. In both his religious and his rhetorical writings, he offered the bourgeois virtue of moderation as a ballast to right a commercial ship listing toward overconsumption.

It is easy to suppose that all British capitalism resembled the late eighteenth- and early nineteenth-century industrial revolutions. But at mid-century,

England's "dark satanic mills" were yet unimaginable.[21] Nonetheless, in the early eighteenth century Great Britain did witness tremendous growth in trade. Treaties and colonization allowed international markets to expand. Additionally, national markets blossomed with consumables such as pottery, clothing, watches, and furniture. Josiah Wedgwood exemplifies mid-century industry. The famous English potter turned a local Staffordshire craft into a global industry without changing the manner of production. He achieved fame and fortune by marketing and distribution.[22] Others, such as Matthew Boulton the toymaker and George Packwood the shaving supplies retailer, similarly filled the marketplace with advertisements and products galore.[23] Even Peter Laslett—who has insisted on a clear divide between the seventeenth-century preindustrial and the nineteenth-century industrial eras—conceded that "'the commercial revolution of the sixteenth and seventeenth centuries' is a . . . fairly respectable phrase."[24]

The commercial revolution came to Edinburgh in the mid-eighteenth century. The Scottish banking industry—founded to assist commerce, not to fund wars—grew considerably. Banks funded for-profit industry, especially in textile manufacture. This affair with capitalism stimulated the upper and middle economic brackets. Their pockets heavy with newfound prosperity, they bought paper, books, and nonessentials, such as elaborate textiles and carriages.[25] Thanks to these new markets, Blair fetched a high price for the first published volume of his *Sermons* (1777–1801), and he soon became one of Scotland's first clergymen to purchase and maintain a carriage.[26] In the first half of the eighteenth century, people's concerns about commerce largely focused on credit and its instability. In the second half of the century, people associated "commerce" with "the whole range of social interactions," not just the "discrete realm" of financial contracts and trade agreements.[27] Often, anxieties about commerce focused on "fashion." As Paul Keen explains, this industry quickly became "the epitome of all that was most dangerous about modernity."[28] Blair acutely followed eighteenth-century fashion, adopting modes of dress so readily that some thought him vain. His friend John Hill commented that Blair loquaciously attended to "every matter of taste, however trivial."[29] While he enjoyed the commercial revolution, he also worried about consumption's harmful potential.

Blair's sermons on fashion and luxury should be understood as a response to a long-standing conversation praising consumption for its economic benefits yet damning luxury for its moral pitfalls.[30] Bernard Mandeville—a Dutch émigré, physician, and all-around contrarian—offered the most evocative and arguably the most insightful argument about luxury's positive economic benefits.

Mandeville's *Fable of the Bees* (1705/1714/1732) defended unbridled consumption (along with a range of other vices) in both moral and economic terms. Mandeville captured his argument in a pithy couplet: "Fraud, Luxury, and Pride must live / Whilst we the Benefits receive."[31] Alarming his generation, Mandeville suggested that pride and ambition led some people to dominate others by force and then by persuasion; he furthermore claimed that this domination allowed social cohesion and advancement.[32] According to Mandeville, "wary Politicians" invented morality to convince the subordinated masses to behave themselves.[33] The moral individual satisfies his own "Self-love, whilst he is thinking on the Applause he expects of others."[34] *The Fable of the Bees* defends pride on moral grounds, yet affords luxury an economic apology. Pride maintains social order. Luxury spurs economic growth: "Frugality is . . . a mean starving Virtue, that is only fit for small Societies of good peaceable Men, who are contented to be poor so they may be easy."[35] Because the pleasures of consumption incite people to abandon their frugality and to embrace industry, luxury can best "render . . . [society] wealthy and flourishing."[36]

Mandeville's economic defense of luxury was not, in fact, *Mandeville's* economic defense of luxury. More than a decade prior (1690), Nicholas Barbon said that "Liberality" spurs industry.[37] Barbon called "Fashion . . . a great Promoter of *Trade* . . . the Spirit and Life of *Trade*."[38] He welcomed conspicuous consumption, because underconsumption (which he called "Covetousness") can lead to economic stagnation. The "Covetous Man . . . grows poor; for by not consuming the Goods that are provided for Man's Use, there ariseth a dead Stock, called Plenty; and the Value of those Goods fall. . . . And a Conspiracy of the Rich Men to be Covetous . . . would be as dangerous to a Trading State as a Forreign War."[39]

Later economists similarly emphasized luxury's utility. James Steuart, a Jacobite turned Frenchman turned mercantilist, defined luxury as "the providing of superfluity with a view to consumption." He championed luxury's ability to create industry: "No man can become luxurious, in our acceptation of the word, without giving bread to the industrious, without encouraging emulation, industry, and agriculture; and without producing the circulation of an adequate equivalent for every service. This last is the palladium of liberty, the fountain of gentle dependence, and the agreeable band of union among free societies." Steuart carefully separated economic luxury from immoral "sensuality" and "excess." "Luxury consists in providing the objects of sensuality, so far as they are superfluous. Sensuality consists in the actual enjoyment of them."[40] Ancient

Greece and Rome depended on slavery, so no amount of luxury could stimulate production. Slaves produce what they are forced to produce, regardless of demand. Ancient luxury was therefore "arbitrary" and corrupting. Modern "systematical" luxury, on the other hand, ignites demand and kindles production.[41] A short decade after Steuart published his apology for luxury, the Western world heard the most full-throated and, to date, the most celebrated defense of free-market consumerism.

Adam Smith praised "consumption" as "the sole end and purpose of all production" (WN 660). He did not worry about one overspent person infecting the population. When writing about sumptuary laws to restrict the consumption of alcohol, Smith declared, "Though individuals . . . may sometimes ruin their fortunes by an excessive consumption of fermented liquors, there seems to be no risk that a nation should do so" (WN 492). When he did grumble about unfettered consumption, Smith vented typically utilitarian anxieties. Excessive consumption might interrupt "parsimony," which Smith identified as "the immediate cause of the increase of capital." He privileged prudently investing over heedlessly spending, for "wherever capital predominates, industry prevails: wherever revenue, idleness" (WN 337).

This defense of luxury did not echo without response. While economists praised luxury's potential utility, others lamented its corrupting influence. In 1776, the same year Smith published The Wealth of Nations, John Trusler denigrated consumerism, saying that the excess visible in London's streets had tumbled England from Restorationist virtue to Augustan prodigality in one short century.[42] The opening sentences of Trusler's pamphlet drip with nostalgia for a foregone age of civic virtue: "THE great degree of luxury to which this country has arrived, within a few years, is not only astonishing but almost dreadful to think of. Time was, when those articles of indulgence, which now every mechanic aims at the possession of, were enjoyed only by the Lord or Baron of a district. Men . . . prided themselves in little but their submission and allegiance. . . . On the increase of trade . . . men began to feel new wants, they became gradually less hardy and robust, grew effeminate."[43] John Dennis insisted that Mandeville's economic defense of luxury threatened the "establish'd Religion" which was "the Foundation and Basis of the Political Constitution."[44] According to Dennis, "Moral Virtues" and "positive laws" stem from true religion and "have been introduced to restrain Vice and Luxury."[45] Eighteenth-century England drowned in a tidal flood of vanity, while Christianity fell to a "low . . . Ebb."[46] Respectively, Trusler and Dennis voiced their republican and Christian objections to commercial surfeit.

Political ideologues adopted quasi-republican and -Christian terms in their own attacks on luxury. In the late seventeenth century, Whig partisans presented themselves as the virtuous members of the "Country" party. They tarred supporters of Charles II as corrupt "Court" ministers who wallowed in royal luxury.[47] During the first decades of the eighteenth century, Tories, led by Henry St. John, 1st Viscount of Bolingbroke, turned the rhetoric of luxury and corruption against the Whigs. Bolingbroke and his followers alleged that Robert Walpole's Whig parliamentary rule depended on corrupt London financiers who lived lavishly by loaning to the government at an unsustainable rate.[48] Halfway through the century, as Steuart composed his economic defense of luxury, English aristocrats worried that consumerism would corrupt the lower orders and disrupt the social classes. Writing in 1751, Henry Fielding exclaimed that a "vast Torrent of Luxury" had introduced the English poor to "a Branch of Liberty claimed by the People to be as wicked and as profligate as their Superiors."[49] While economists sang luxury's praises, Christians, republicans, politicians, and aristocrats bemoaned its consequences.

Distilling the eighteenth-century luxury debates into a confrontation between celebratory economists and anxious moralists highlights a third perspective common among the Scottish sociologists, one that Blair himself adopted. Edinburgh's Enlightenment intellectuals charted a middle course between utilitarian joy and moralistic despair. They celebrated luxury's potential and worried about its consequences. They presented virtuous moderation as a balancing force, able to sustain commerce without courting corruption. Henry Home, Lord Kames, serves as a useful monotype of this perspective. Kames narrated the progress of civilization, heaping praise on the artistic refinement of society's commercial phase. But he worried that commercial refinement would tempt people to overconsume and to undersave: "To consider luxury in a political view, no refinement of dress, of the table, of equipage, of habitation, is luxury in those who can afford the expense; and the public gains by the encouragement that is given the arts, manufactures, and commerce. But a mode of living above a man's annual income, weakens the state, by reducing to poverty, not only the squanderers themselves, but many innocent and industrious persons connected with them. Luxury is, above all, pernicious in a commercial state."[50] Echoing Kames, Adam Ferguson said that commercial societies flirt with ruin: "Nations under a high state of commercial arts, are exposed to corruption, by their admitting wealth, unsupported by personal elevation and virtue, as the great foundation of distinction, and by having their attention turned on the side of interest, as the road to consideration and honour."[51]

David Hume, likewise, wrote that "wherever luxury ceases to be innocent, it also ceases to be beneficial; and when carried a degree too far, [it] is a quality pernicious . . . to political society."[52] Hume testified to luxury's baleful potential, especially "when it engrosses all a man's expence, and leaves no ability for such acts of duty and generosity as are required by his situation and fortune."[53] Nevertheless, while admitting its dangers, Hume believed that luxury prompted industries to develop, encouraged people to learn, and impelled communities to form: "Industry, knowledge, and humanity, are not advantageous to private life alone: They diffuse their beneficial influence on the *public*, and render the government as great and flourishing as they make individuals happy and prosperous."[54] Like Smith, Hume thought commercial luxury delectable. Yet he conceded that "luxury, when excessive, is the source of many ills." Ultimately, he concluded that luxury "is in general preferable to sloth and idleness, which would commonly succeed in its place and are more hurtful both to private persons and to the public."[55]

To preserve luxury's economic utility without courting personal ruin, Kames promoted moderation: "A person of moderation is satisfied with small profits." As paradigms of moderate consumption amid commercial plenty, Kames held up the "merchants of Amsterdam, and even of London" who enjoyed their wealth without being tempted down "the high way to perdition."[56] Like Kames, Adam Smith promoted "the temperate use" of certain luxuries—such as beer, ale, and wine—to obviate corruption. The great free-marketer went so far as to permit taxes that "dispose . . . [people] to moderate, or to refrain altogether from the use of superfluities which they can no longer easily afford" (*WN* 872). For Smith, Kames, and Hume moderation was a compass, pointing the way between the economist's celebration of consumption and the moralist's damnation of consumables.

When surveying the British Enlightenment luxury debates, as I have so far, it is tempting to repeat a common saga about the consumer's economic liberty defeating the moralist's sumptuary laws or the free-marketer's arguments trumping the mercantilist's claims.[57] But particular Enlightenment arguments trouble any story about victorious appeals to utility and defeated appeals to virtue. Often, the appeal to utility and the appeal to virtue were both applied in a single argument about luxury. For instance, English commerce's poet laureate, Daniel Defoe, confessed that "luxury" brought prosperity but courted corruption, a bind that he exemplified by contrasting "frugal Manufacturers, encourag'd by their success, [who] doubled their Industry and thrived" against "the luxurious and purse Proud Gentry, tickl'd with the happy Encrease of their Revenues, and the rising Value of their Rents." Like Defoe, the Scottish sociologists tried to reconcile the Christian's moral anxieties, the republican's civic worries, and the economist's utilitarian catechism. Hugh Blair approached this dilemma while sermonizing on religion and while lecturing on rhetoric.

Blair sympathized with the political anxieties that Henry Fielding voiced because he had witnessed the 1745 Jacobite uprising, which moderate literati like himself attributed to lower-class resentment. Much of Blair's rhetorical theory, especially his efforts at disseminating refinement and taste through literary study, has been traced to bourgeois anxiety about working-class political volatility.[58] Moreover, many of Blair's sermons discuss luxury in terms strikingly similar to those voiced by Christian moralists, such as John Dennis. Before his congregation, Blair agonized over the corrupting potential of commercial excess. He argued that material growth stunts virtue.[59] In Blair's eyes, commercializing Edinburgh looked like a hotbed of excess in "an age manifestly distinguished by a propensity to thoughtless profusion; wherein all the different ranks of men . . . vie with their superiors in every mode of luxury and ostentation; and . . . seek no farther argument for justifying extravagance, than the fashion of the times" (*Sermons* 1:340). He described people "opulent in fortune, and perhaps high in rank [who] think themselves entitled to pass their days in a careless manner, without any other object in view, than the gratification of their senses and passions" (*Sermons* 3:99). Such "persons of loose principles, or dissolute morals" infested Scottish cities. They infected others with "the contagion which is diffused by bad examples" (*Sermons* 2:355). The "licentiousness" promoted by the "wealth and luxury of the present age" disturbed Blair (*Sermons* 3:99). The "men of business" and "men of pleasure"—whose "accumulation of fortune so engrosses them as to harden their heart against every feeling of moral obligation"—bothered him (*Sermons* 3:103–4). People's pursuit of "advantages to the injury or oppression of their brethren" troubled him (*Sermons* 3:106).

But Blair's Christian worries did not foreclose his economic commitments. Like the Scottish sociologists, Blair adopted a stadial theory of history, placing commerce in the ultimate position and on the highest pedestal.[60] He testified to luxury's utility, claiming that "man derives more enjoyment from the exertion of his active powers in the midst of toils and efforts, than he could receive from a still and uniform possession of the object which he strives to gain" (*Sermons* 2:84). While luxury can morally improve the individual by inciting such "exertion," it can also corrupt. Those who simply consume are tortured by "fantastic refinements, sickly delicacy, and eager emulation" (*Sermons* 2:85). Their own fancy "has raised up the spectres which haunt them" (*Sermons* 2:86). While repeating the moralist's anxiety, the economist's enthusiasm, and the sociologist's middle course, Blair added another element to the luxury debates: a heavy dose of classical history and rhetorical theory. Like Roman rhetoricians before him, Blair associated eloquence with commerce and democracy. For this reason, he began his lectures on rhetoric with an extended historical narrative about the simultaneous ascendance of eloquence in ancient democratic republics. He explained that the republic depends on citizen virtue, which, in turn, depends on rhetorical quality.

To this long-standing association of eloquence and democracy, Blair contributed an attention to stylistic flourish. Like others, he associated figuration with luxury. (Nearly a century prior, Thomas Sprat complained that rhetorical figures corrupt language "by the luxury and redundance of *speech*.")[61] Blair further connected luxury (material and verbal) to stifling monarchy. Arbitrary French government succored "ornamental Eloquence," a public discourse, "flowery" but not "vigorous" (*Lectures* 268). According to Blair, eighteenth-century French oratory pleased the imagination but neglected to convince or to instruct. As a result, France was less virtuous than Britain, where eloquence was "much more cool and temperate . . . confined . . . almost wholly to the argumentative and rational" (*Lectures* 283). He said similar things about the quality of public discourse and the kinds of political economy found in ancient societies. In ancient Greece, when competition was the political and economic norm, fountains of eloquence spouted from virtuous teachers, such as Isocrates, and orators, such as Demosthenes. Freedom led to "serious contention for the public leading." People "put their judgment to a serious trial," refining their sensibilities and contributing to oratory's first golden era (*Lectures* 269). All this ended when commercial and political freedoms withered. The sophists, "the first corrupters of true Eloquence," principally pleased the imagination (*Lectures* 271). In ancient Rome, Blair found a similar pattern. In the early democratic commercial republic, virtuous eloquence flourished. This was Cicero's age. But as democracy and commerce atrophied, "luxury, effeminacy, and flattery overwhelmed all" (*Lectures* 280). The result was a corrupted oratory about "imaginary and fantastic subjects, such as had no reference to real life, or business" (*Lectures* 281).

Blair repeated a narrative that is central to the civic political tradition: good eloquence, freedom, and virtue all coexist and mutually support one another until luxury and monarchy corrupt this delicate balance.[62] Blair added a concern about figuration. He also apologized for moderate commercial luxury. His commitment to both the economist's celebration of consumption and the politician's worry about corruption, his affection for capitalist economy, his love of bourgeois civil society, and his worry about corrupted civic virtue place him alongside his compatriot David Hume at the limits of the civic tradition.[63] In his reflections on taste, Blair insisted that refining the critical faculty can improve the bourgeois citizen's virtue and thus protect the commercial republic against corrupting excesses. In the first of his *Lectures on Rhetoric and Belles Lettres*, Blair declared that cultivation of taste can deter people from "loose pleasures" and idleness. A developed sense of taste allows "tender and humane passions" like sympathy, and thus promotes a "public spirit." Citizens of good breeding properly display "the love of glory, contempt of external fortune, and admiration of what is truly illustrious and great." He viewed taste as an aesthetic faculty with civic potential. By fixing the imagination on great literature we are also "disposing the heart to virtue" (*Lectures* 8–9).[64]

While resolving this tension between luxury's morally corrosive effects and its commercially beneficial results, Blair echoed Kames and Hume. Kames wanted to "promote the Fine Arts in Britain" because "a flourishing commerce begets opulence; and opulence, inflaming our appetite for pleasure, is commonly vented on luxury."[65] Kames offered his reader a two-pronged solution. First, he suggested "venting opulence upon the Fine Arts." Second, he promoted literary education to instill "deep impressions of virtue."[66] Quality literature advances a "standard of taste" that refuses "voluptuousness," repudiates "beastly selfishness," and rejects an undue "appetite for superiority and respect." By honing aesthetic taste, the commercial citizen learns to forego "costly furniture, numerous attendants, a princely dwelling, [and] sumptuous feasts." According to Kames, proper literary education teaches a virtuous moderation: "simplicity, elegance, propriety."[67]

David Hume similarly suggested that a refined taste can distinguish reasonable flourish from excessive bombast.[68] Hume placed the virtuous rhetorical medium between plain-style austerity and belletristic ostentation. He warned against over-refinement because this "excess is both less beautiful, and more dangerous than" an excess of simplicity.[69] For Hume personal taste was the only bulwark against the excessive luxury that he attributed to "ASIATIC" Roman rhetoric in "the age of CLAUDIUS and NERO."[70] Like Kames and Hume, in matters personal and rhetorical Blair suggested that virtue could offset luxury's corruption. He suggested that people "enjoy the advantages of the world with propriety and decency; temperate in our pleasures; moderate in our pursuits of interest. . . . Within these limits, we may safely enjoy all the comforts which the world affords, and our station allows. But if we pass beyond these boundaries, into the regions of disorderly and vicious pleasure, of debasing covetousness or of oppressive insolence, the world will then serve only to corrupt our minds, and to accelerate our ruin" (*Sermons* 3:109). As the above passage suggests, in his sermons Blair emphasized one virtue above others—moderation.

In his *Lectures on Rhetoric*, Blair explored moderation as a virtue instilled through rhetorical judgment of style. He portrayed the languages of noncommercial and primitive peoples—Italy, France, and Amerindian nations—as excessively ornamented, overly reliant on imaginative figuration, and most prone to corrupting hyperbole. He returned to his stadial theory of history. As societies advance and commerce develops, people interact with one another more often. They cultivate taste. This causes a rhetorical "progress" toward more reserved discourse (*Lectures* 60–62). Students learned that more "refined" languages feature less figuration: "As Language makes gradual progress towards refinement, almost every object comes to have a proper name given to it, and Perspicuity and Precision are more studied" (*Lectures* 150).

But the plain style alone cannot sustain commercial vivacity. People must learn to enjoy language's imaginative flourish without indulging rhetorical excess. Blair found a moderate median between two bourgeois trends—belletrism and the plain style. Synthesizing Locke's injunctions against tropes and Smith's celebration of sentimental figures, Blair encouraged students to employ metaphor when appropriate, but to avoid its use when the situation or the subject does not warrant such a locution. He said the same of all "figures of sentiment. The excessive, or unreasonable employment of them, is mere foppery in writing" (*Lectures* 159). In lecture 16, Blair worried especially about hyperbole, personification, and apostrophe, all passionate figures. When properly adopted, Blair said the passionate figures could have beautiful and virtuous effects. When speaking of the figures that tickle the imaginative faculty, Blair likewise advised moderation: "The proper place of Comparisons lies in the middle region between the highly pathetic, and the very humble style" (*Lectures* 187).

Blair taxonomized stylistic qualities to further advance rhetorical moderation. He criticized the florid style, "too rich and gaudy in proportion to the subject." Such luxurious writing reveals nothing but "a dazzling lustre, or a false brilliancy." This description of the florid style tellingly reverberates with Blair's concerns about corrupting luxury: "Nothing can be more contemptible than that tinsel splendor of Language, which some writers perpetually affect . . . The worst is, that with those frothy writers, it is a luxuriance of words, not of fancy. . . . It has escaped these writers, that sobriety in ornament, is one great secret for rendering it pleasing; and that, without a foundation of good sense and solid thought, the most Florid Style is but a childish imposition on the Public" (*Lectures* 205). He spoke fondly of the plain and the neat styles, though he thought them deficient. Plain, unornamented writing displays a mind that lacks "great powers of fancy or genius" (*Lectures* 204). Stylistic excess degrades rhetoric. Figurative abstemiousness hinders rhetors. Commerce cannot sustain either—the one corrupts consumers, the other hinders capitalists. Therefore, Blair finally praised the moderate "elegant" style, sufficiently ornamented and resoundingly clear.

Blair gave his students a guide to rhetorical moderation: (1) study clear ideas; (2) practice composing; (3) study the best authors; (4) avoid servile imitation; (5) adapt the style to the subject and to the audience; and (6) keep attention to style from overcoming all else (*Lectures* 215–17). Furthermore, like Adam Smith, Blair condemned Lord Shaftesbury's prose. Unlike Smith, Blair largely ignored Shaftesbury's stylistic disingenuousness; rather, he attended to Shaftesbury's figurative indulgence. According to Smith, Shaftesbury violated probity. According to Blair, Shaftesbury ravaged moderation. Shaftesbury displayed his "delicacy and refinement of taste, to a degree that we may call excessive and sickly" (*Lectures* 212). While Blair found Shaftesbury's style indulgent, he thought Smith exercised rhetorical moderation. Writing about *The Wealth of Nations*, Blair told Smith, "Nothing was better suited than your Style is to the Subject; clear and distinct to the last degree, full without being too much so, and as tercly as the Subject would admit."[71]

Private Virtues and Public Benefit

Blair and Smith celebrated the consumer revolution. They believed that rhetorically instilled probity and moderation could save commerce from dishonesty and luxury, and they wanted to protect private institutions from state intervention. Smith placed literary education in civil society because he distrusted government efforts at moral education. Blair imagined two overlapping and institutions within civil society: church and university. Neither regulated by government, both housing free citizens, each instilling the genteel habits of bourgeois association.

Smith advocated privatized higher education because he thought that the state's university system had created a leeching class of ineffective and useless scholars. Blair wholeheartedly agreed with Smith's critique of publicly funded higher education: "There is so much good Sense and Truth in your [Smith's] doctrine about Universities, and it is so fit that your doctrine should be preached to the World."[72] This commitment to private higher education is revealed by Blair's testimony and by his actions. Like Smith, Blair charged two guineas to attend his lectures. (Evidence indicates that Blair often waived the minimum course fee for indigent students.) The Scottish university system, Edinburgh included, followed the civic tradition of shaping a citizenry for public service. The university's open admissions policy, its public financing, and the regular governmental intrusion in Edinburgh's curriculum were all possible because of a widespread civic ideology that placed education within the realm of public affairs.[73] In an otherwise public institution dedicated to civic virtue, Blair promoted private education for civil society.

In his sermons, Blair voiced similarly liberal inclinations. He praised the government of Great Britain for permitting freedom of religion. People should be allowed to worship as they please "as long as they infringe not the public tranquility nor disturb the state" (*Sermons* 4:177). Government "restrains the outrages and crimes which would be subversive of society, secures the property, and defends the lives of its subjects." No mandated public instruction should be allowed, since government must be restricted to "the actions of men." Government protects its citizens from "external violence" that encroaches on liberty (*Sermons* 2:144). At the beginning of his lectures on rhetoric, Blair connected religious moral edification to private literary education, saying, "The powers of Taste and Imagination are calculated to give us of the benignity of our Creator" (*Lectures* 25).

Blair told his congregation that religious reflection improves the powers of taste and imagination while tempering commercial excess. After "much commerce with the world . . . [one should become] convinced of its vanity. He has seen its most flattering hopes to be fallacious. He has felt its most boasted pleasures to be unsatisfactory" (*Sermons* 1:309). Inward piety benefits the individual soul and the public polity by infusing private virtues that yield public profits: "order, frugality, and economy." These "are the necessary supports of every personal virtue . . . the basis on which liberty, independence, and true honour, must arise" (*Sermons* 1:341). Anyone lacking such dispositions "is held in bondage to the world. . . . From the moment you have allowed yourselves to pass the line of economy, and live beyond your fortune, you have entered on the path of danger" (*Sermons* 1:342). Blair believed that people should pursue these virtues collectively in worship, where a gifted orator—like himself—could extol their advantage.

According to Blair, private religion supplements public legislation. Religion "supplies the insufficiency of law, by striking at the root of those disorders which occasion so much misery in the world. Its professed scope is to regulate, not actions alone, but the temper and inclinations" (*Sermons* 2:144). According to Blair, Scotland's commercial success required religion. Speaking to the Society for the Propagation of Christian Knowledge about their efforts to bring a moderate version of Christianity to the Scottish highlands, he said, "Religious Knowledge has a direct tendency to improve the social intercourse of men, and to assist them in co-operating for the common good. It is the great instrument of civilizing the multitude, and forming them to union.... The wisest legislators of old ... considered religion as essential to civil polity" (*Sermons* 2:271). In the barbarous Highlands, Blair promised that moderate Christianity would yield virtuous commerce and genteel public discourse.

Blair exalted religion's commercial utility, equating Christian and bourgeois virtue: "First, as private men and Christians, let us cultivate those virtues which are essential to the prosperity of our country" (*Sermons* 4:183). Since bourgeois virtue requires an artistry of moderation practiced in the finely crafted sentence, Blair concluded that both religion and rhetoric promote moderation. In many regards, like others in the civic republican tradition, Blair was "conflating political activity with the compositional techniques of public address."[74] Yet, while Cicero's republican political style advanced decorum—a flexible ability to meet circumstances with a personality suited to the audience and the situation—Blair promoted moderation—a stern capacity to resist commercial luxury and rhetorical flourish.[75] Blair blended Christianity into commerce, republican politics into bourgeois ethics, rhetoric into economics. He conscripted civic virtue in the liberal march toward civil society.

From Bourgeois Virtue to Bourgeois Belletrism

In the century after its initial appearance, Blair's *Lectures on Rhetoric and Belles Lettres* went through fifty editions in Britain, the United States, and on the Continent.[76] They were translated in French, German, Italian, Russian, and Spanish.

The *Lectures* also appeared in countless abridgments and in the works of the innumerable imitators.[77] Despite his influence, Blair receives little present-day praise. His literary preoccupations have led to charges that he was a bourgeois rhetor because he taught the *"beau monde* of *belles lettres"* to would-be merchants, lawyers, bankers, and manufacturers.[78] Without a doubt, Blair sold cultural polish to the nouveau riche.[79] However, as the above paragraphs explain, Blair offered his students much more than bourgeois distinction. He introduced economic concerns into rhetorical theory, into pedagogy, and especially into rhetorical stylistics.

The abridgments to Blair's *Lectures* account for our present-day fixation on Blair as a culturally but not politically bourgeois rhetorician. The full text of Blair's *Lectures* circulated widely, appearing in 112 complete versions (in English) between 1783 and 1911. During that same period, 110 abridgments appeared.[80] During the forty years after initial publication the abridgments outpaced the *Lectures*, appearing in fifty-four versions between 1788 and 1830; the complete *Lectures* were only printed twenty-seven times between 1784 and 1826.[81] Widely read and taught, these abridgments constitute Blair's popular legacy. They account for his transition from a rhetorician concerned with bourgeois virtue to a literary critic concerned with bourgeois belletrism.

Blair neither participated in the abridgments' production nor profited from their sale. He accepted a handsome upfront payment of £1,500 for the initial (quarto) edition of the *Lectures* (1783). Later and cheaper (octavo) editions garnered profits for the publishers but not for the author.[82] The subsequent abridgments were composed without Blair's input. It is a personal tragedy and a historical irony that wily marketers exploited the intellectual capital belonging to the British Enlightenment's great bourgeois rhetorician. It is a historical tragedy and a pedagogical irony that these marketers' principal instruments of exploitation—the abridgments—stripped Blair's work of his economic and sociological ruminations. The abridgments dropped most of Blair's reflections on the progress of civilization, his adulation of the commercial era, his anxieties concerning luxury's dangers, and his attention to stylistic moderation. These same abridgments preserved (and sometimes expanded) his discussion of polite genres, his examples of literary works, and his rules for composition.

The most marketed abridgments were (1) *Essays on Rhetoric: Abridged Chiefly from Dr. Blair's Lectures on That Science* (1784); (2) *An Abridgment of Lectures on Rhetorick: By Hugh Blair, D.D.* (1802); (3) *Lectures on Rhetoric and Belles Lettres: Chiefly from the Lectures of Dr. Blair*, edited by Abraham Mills (1832).[83]

(Hereafter I will refer to them as the *Essays*, the *Abridgment*, and the *Lectures*, respectively, and I will reserve the full title, *Lectures on Rhetoric and Belles Lettres*, for Blair's complete lectures as they were published in 1783.) During the production of all three abridgments, economic and sociological material remained on the editors' desks. Lectures 6–9 in Blair's *Lectures on Rhetoric and Belles Lettres* parallel the progress of language and the progress of civilization. Blair depicted commercial society as the apex of human achievement and moderate figuration as capitalism's rhetorical apotheosis. Blair discussed the "savage" psychology, characterized by a hyperactive imagination. The primitive prefers a syntax that forefronts the object of desire: "He would not express himself, according to our English order of construction, 'Give me fruit;' but, according to the Latin order, 'Fruit give me;' 'Fructum da mihi:'" (*Lectures* 65). As speech developed into writing, subject overtook object and rational alphabetics replaced imaginative hieroglyphics (*Lectures* 70–74). The most advanced languages convey information effectively and efficiently. English, according to Blair, is the high-water mark of clear communication (*Lectures* 94–98).

The *Essays* and the *Abridgment* preserve some discussion of language's savage beginnings, but both editions emphasize the need for language to maintain community. Consider the abbreviations of lecture 6—"Rise and Progress of Language"—in the *Essays* and the *Abridgment*. The *Essays* includes the following passage, nearly repeated verbatim, though somewhat redacted in the *Abridgment*: "One would imagine, that men must have been previously gathered together in considerable numbers, before language could be fixed and extended; and yet, on the other hand, there seems to have been an absolute necessity of speech previous to the formation of society; for, by what bond could any multitude of men be kept together, or be connected in the prosecution of any common interest, until, by the assistance of speech, they could communicate their wants and intentions to each other?"[84] Abraham Mills's *Lectures* uses nearly the exact same words to express this sentiment. Like the earlier abridgments, the *Lectures* concludes with a reflection on the divine origin of language: "But supposing language to have had a divine origin, we cannot, however, suppose, that a perfect system of it was at once given to man. It is much more natural to think, that God taught our first parents such language only, as suited their present occasions; leaving them, as he did in other things, to enlarge and improve it as their future necessities should require."[85]

Like his predecessors, Mills included discussion of inflections and onomatopoeic words—features of early language. The summary of lecture 6 in Mills's abridgment ends with three short paragraphs that mention language's imaginative and figurative qualities among the "scattered and dispersed" nomadic peoples, such as Old Testament shepherds and Amerindian hunters. The barest explanation of language's progress is offered. Stylistic development is attributed to linguistic, not social changes: "But as language, in its progress, began to grow more copious, it gradually lost that figurative style, which was its original character."[86] The *Lectures*, the *Essays*, and the *Abridgment* emphasize language's divine origin, its social purpose, and its onomatopoeic nature, but not its place in the progress of civilization.

Blair himself attributed "the first origin of all Language to Divine teaching or inspiration" (*Lectures* 55), but he quickly turned to an extended discussion of language's development from primitive and passionate utterances to imaginative ancient Greek verses (*Lectures* 56–59). He compared such primitive communities to eighteenth-century societies that had not advanced commercially. According to Blair, passionate figuration indicated a pre-commercial stage of historical development: "A Frenchman both varies his accents, and gesticulates while he speaks, much more than an Englishman. An Italian, a great deal more than either" (*Lectures* 60). Blair concluded with thoughts on modern commercial language as follows: "As Language, in its progress, began to grow more copious, it gradually lost that figurative style, which was its early character. . . . Style became more precise, and, of course, more simple." Commerce incited language's advancement: "The understanding was more exercised; the fancy, less. Intercourse among mankind becoming more extensive and frequent, clearness of style, in signifying their meaning to each other, was the chief object of attention" (*Lectures* 62). Blair's editors preserved his vocabulary of social progress, but they expunged his stadial theory of history. They discussed figuration in primitive languages but did not explain that commerce rescued rhetorical style from its primitively passionate state.

Blair's abridgers preserved the belletristic qualities of his lectures. Lectures 1 and 2, for instance, include Blair's oft-cited efforts at explaining why people should study rhetoric and why cultivation of taste matters in a commercial society. He concluded his first lecture by saying that the cultivation of taste provides "an innocent and irreproachable amusement for . . . [a person's] leisure hours." Blair maintained that such a pastime is necessary in a luxurious society that tempts a person with "many a pernicious passion" (*Lectures* 8). Proper taste leads to "contempt of external fortune, and the admiration of what is truly illustrious and great . . . reforming the corrupt propensities which too frequently prevail among mankind" (*Lectures* 9). Blair's *Lectures on Rhetoric and Belles Lettres* voice an anxiety about luxury and a hope that taste can offset commercial corruption.

The *Essays* and the *Abridgment* reduce Blair's hope for taste and his anxiety about corruption to a meaningless statement about kindness: "The improvement of Taste seems to be more or less connected with every good and virtuous disposition. By giving frequent exercise to all the tender and humane passions, a cultivated Taste increases sensibility; yet at the same time, it tends to soften the more violent and angry emotions."[87] Mills's *Lectures* tie rhetorical taste to social rank: "In an age when works of genius are so frequently the subjects of discourse . . . and when we can hardly imagine a polite society without bearing some share in such discussions; studies of [literary taste] . . . derive part of their importance from . . . furnishing materials for those fashionable topics of discourse, and thereby enabling us to support a proper rank in social life." Mills briefly explained that those who remain "entirely devoid of relish for eloquence, poetry, or any of the fine arts" may be "prone to low gratifications." But he never mentioned luxury, corruption, or the need to find a virtuous outlet in a prosperous society. According to Mills's *Lectures*, the chief advantage of studying polite literature is upward mobility, which includes a vague disposition toward "virtue" and "public spirit."[88] Gone is any discussion of taste's economic utility. In the place of bourgeois virtue is an ambiguously aestheticized morality and the promise of social distinction.

Finally, the abridgments of Blair's *Lectures on Rhetoric and Belles Lettres* subordinate moderation to prescription. Rather than telling students to practice moderate figuration, they offer strict rules. In lecture 15 ("On Metaphor"), for instance, Blair listed seven guidelines for constructing appropriately moderate metaphors, but he presented these as discussion prompts. Each "rule" precedes a lengthy (often paragraphs-long) explanation of how moderate metaphors promote virtue while luxurious ornaments corrupt discourse. Under the first rule ("that . . . [metaphors] be suited to the nature of the subject of which we treat"), Blair explained that "unseasonable employment" of metaphors results in "mere foppery in writing" (*Lectures* 159). The second rule is closer to a moral lesson than a syntactical injunction: "Beware of ever using such allusions as raise in the mind disagreeable, mean, vulgar, or dirty ideas" (*Lectures* 160). The *Essays* remove the moral quality from the first rule and they dilute it in the second: "Care must be taken not to use such allusions as raise in the mind disagreeable, mean, low, or unclean ideas." The *Abridgment* and the *Lectures* repeat this statement nearly verbatim.[89]

Blair's eighteenth lecture presents one of his strongest statements about figurative moderation. For several paragraphs, he derided the "Florid Style," which exhibits "a luxuriancy of words, not of fancy" (*Lectures* 205). The *Essays* reduce Blair's lengthy discourse to seven sentences that define the florid style as "the excess of ornament" and then reproduce one of Blair's most ornate sentences: "The tinsel splendour of language, which some writers perpetually affect, is truly contemptible." Once again, the *Abridgment* and the *Lectures* offer nearly identical treatments of the subject.[90] Blair connected youthful exuberance and florid writing in his *Lectures on Rhetoric and Belles Lettres*, but he mostly discussed the moral corruption that results from such an immoderate style. He even explained that only people of low character enjoy florid public discourse: "the mob of Readers, who are very ready to be caught, at first, with whatever is dazzling and gaudy." The poor happily consume these rhetorical gewgaws, but the "pious and benevolent heart . . . is always displeased at" such "swoln imagery" and "ornaments of a false kind" (*Lectures* 205). Every abridgment removes these moral reflections. Every abridgment attributes the florid style to the author's age, repeating Blair's explanation that the "young composer" is the provenance of immoderate figuration.

While the abridgments redact Blair's economic reflections, they enhance his literary criticism. The *Essays* and the *Abridgment* maintain, in shortened form, one of Blair's five "Critical Examination" lectures, "Lecture 20: Critical Examination of Mr. Addison's Style in No. 411 of *The Spectator*."[91] The *Essays* and the *Abridgment* abbreviate every lecture on polite genres, such as "Lecture 36: Historical Writing." They also preserve abbreviations of every lecture on a famous literary work or figure, such as "Lecture 43: Homer's *Iliad* and *Odyssey*—Virgil's *Aeneid*." Abraham Mills's early nineteenth-century *Lectures* reintroduces two of Blair's "critical examination" lectures (lectures 21 and 22). In 1854, Mills published another edition of the *Lectures*, this time adding a forty-eight-page supplement to update Blair's treatment of literary genres with new examples and analyses of nineteenth-century belles lettres.[92]

The textbook circulation of Blair's work fattened literary belletrism while starving bourgeois virtue. Recent studies of textbooks and their uses caution against drawing firm conclusions about a given rhetorical pedagogy based on the textbook assigned. Teachers employ seemingly conservative textbooks in politically liberal and even emancipatory efforts.[93] We cannot, without qualification, determine that the abridgments made Blair into a belletrist centrally preoccupied with bourgeois distinction. But, at the same time, we cannot help but suspect that these same abridgments made it difficult to teach Blair's lectures in the manner he intended. Any teacher wanting to teach bourgeois moderation with an abridgment of Blair's *Lectures on Rhetoric and Belles Lettres* would have to fill in lectures on a range of topics: how language and civilization progressed together, how aesthetic taste can protect against commercial excess, why rhetorical restraint can prevent corruption, and how the study of literature hones bourgeois virtue.

Despite all that they altered, the abridgments preserved Blair's faculty psychology. "Taste," in the *Essays*, is defined as an innate faculty, "possessed in different degrees" but capable of improvement through "culture and education."[94] The *Lectures on Rhetoric and Belles Lettres* and the *Essays* set rhetorical education on an "internal sense," defined as "the power of receiving pleasure from the beauties of nature and of art" (*Lectures* 10). Blair's faculty psychology reminds us that he belongs in the Scottish Enlightenment, in the company of Adam Smith, David Hume, and Henry Home, Lord Kames. Blair learned more than psychology from his economist friend. He adopted many of Smith's economic hopes and preoccupations, Smith's love of free commerce, and his worry about luxurious consumption. Read alongside Blair's religious writings and in the context of a mid-century British conversation about luxury, his complete *Lectures on Rhetoric and Belles Lettres* showcase his rhetorical theory's commercial application. Over 250 years after Blair first ascended the rostrum to lecture on rhetoric, we must rethink his legacy. We should set aside the abridgments and consider the social context of the commercial revolution, the intellectual context of the Scottish Enlightenment, and the conversational context of the luxury debates.

Returning to the British Enlightenment, we quickly find a label that suits the bourgeois rhetorician. Blair typified the late eighteenth-century Scottish "moderate" man, a term applied to Francis Hutcheson and David Hume alike. The firebrand Calvinist John Witherspoon criticized such men for acknowledging duties to society while ignoring duties to God. Witherspoon believed that Blair and his intellectual cohort recommended virtue "only from rational considerations, viz. the beauty and comely proportions of virtue, and its advantages in the present life, without any regard to a future state."[95] Witherspoon skewered his targets with a title that Blair would have worn proudly—"gentleman." Witherspoon derided the label and its "moderate" bearer, saying both were anathema to the more honorific "minister."[96]

Comparing Witherspoon to Blair, the minister to the gentleman, highlights the moderate man's bourgeois quality. Witherspoon's religious preoccupations led him away from Blairean worries about stylistic excess. In fact, while Blair was telling his students to avoid the florid style, Witherspoon was sailing across the Atlantic to the College of New Jersey, where he would similarly lecture on a variety of rhetorical styles. But Witherspoon never dwelled on moral degradation or excessive figuration. He said that over-figuration could easily "degenerate into bombast," but he emphasized rhetorical efficacy rather than bourgeois virtue. He discussed the plain, nervous, severe, chaste, and elegant styles, without remonstrance against florid figuration.[97] Finally, when Witherspoon discussed taste (in his closing lecture on rhetoric), he defined it as a strictly aesthetic faculty, psychologically grounded, but ethically unimportant.[98] In his writings on "moderation" and in his rhetorical lectures, Witherspoon emphasized religion over psychology, divine commandments over polite principles. Blair, as Witherspoon pointed out, was more concerned with refinement, taste, and luxury. But their contrasting preoccupations should not lead us to label Blair's rhetorical theory tragically aesthetic or Witherspoon's triumphantly civic.[99] Each man advanced an ethical mission. Witherspoon was the Calvinist and Blair the bourgeois rhetorician. Both were civically minded, but they imagined different ideal polities. Witherspoon's minister builds a shining city on a hill. Blair's merchant trades in the bustling commercial market. Witherspoon's prophet cries in the wilderness. Blair's gentleman gossips in the coffeehouse.

Early nineteenth-century editors fashioned Blair into a storehouse of cultural capital for the nouveau riche. Late twentieth-century scholars have remembered him as a derivative thinker who protected social distinction by passing knowledge of polite literature along to an ascendant commercial class. Twenty-first-century rhetorical theorists and teachers must rebrand Blair yet again, this time with a term that his contemporary critics fashioned for him. Blair was a moderate man. He pursued gentlemanly elegance though a psychologically founded and rhetorically perfected taste. He taught bourgeois virtue to offset the vice of luxury and to prevent the corruption of commerce. He celebrated civil society and its genteel rhetorical habits of honesty, tolerance, and moderation.

4

Herbert Spencer on Economy

More than twenty years after Adam Smith published *The Wealth of Nations*, Thomas Carlyle labeled Smith's beloved discipline the "dismal science." Adam Smith's brimming optimism skipped a generation of political economists because, in the late eighteenth and early nineteenth centuries, many failed to notice the rising economic tide, even as it drenched their shoes and wet their knees.[1] By the mid-nineteenth century few could deny that a century of commerce had delivered a millennium of prosperity. In 1848 Karl Marx and Frederick Engels, no fans of capitalism, grudgingly admitted its economic dynamism: "Constant revolutionizing of production, uninterrupted disturbance of all social conditions, everlasting uncertainty and agitation distinguish the bourgeois epoch from all earlier ones."[2] Writing four years earlier, Engels said the only thing worse than life as an industrial worker was life as a preindustrial farmer.[3] Engels and Marx credited capitalism for its inexpensive textiles and efficient farms, but they bemoaned its personal and social effects. People's bucolic lives were ruined, their genuine selves alienated.[4] The simultaneous celebration of capitalism's economic accomplishments and concern about its personal consequences was not confined to the radical left.

The English libertarian Herbert Spencer complements the German communists. Popularly imagined as the mid-Victorian champion of rapaciously competitive industry, Spencer harbored reservations similar to those voiced by Marx and Engels. Writing in the 1870s, he explained that industrial systems of "compound free labor" subjugated workers to cruel abuse. Reading Spencer's words, it is hard to imagine that the following passage does not preface a communist rant about alienation and exploitation:

> The wage-earning factory-hand does, indeed, exemplify entirely free labour, in so far that, making contracts at will and able to break them after short notice, he is free to engage with whomsoever he pleases and where

he pleases. But this liberty amounts in practice to little more than the ability to exchange one slavery for another; since, fit only for his particular occupation, he has rarely an opportunity of doing anything more than decide in what mill he will pass the greater part of his dreary days. The coercion of circumstances often bears more on him than the coercion of a master does on one in bondage. (*WHS* 8:516)

Of course, Spencer did not advocate transnational revolution of the proletariat. He wanted to extend freedom of contract even further through "cooperation by piece-work." Paying each worker for each screw turned and each row ploughed would make the entire system more "voluntary"; would let individuals bargain, strive, or loaf at their discretion; would expunge all exploitation and compulsion (*WHS* 8:560–63).

One word in Spencer's remarks catapults the reader out of a debate about quality of life and into a debate about rhetoric: he described cooperation by piece-work as an advanced stage in "industrial *evolution*" (*WHS* 8.562, emphasis added). According to Spencer, social evolution is a grand process requiring reformation of individual habit, political structure, and public discourse. Social evolution requires that society become more industrial, that people become more sympathetic, and that language become more economical. Economic communication facilitates sympathy, encourages honesty, elevates fairness, and advances justice. While Marx promoted political action to erase economic indignity, Spencer advocated ethical reform to purify economic liberty. While Marx advocated violent revolution to offset capitalism's cruelties, Spencer promoted rhetorical reformation to expand capitalism's excellences. Both men saw nineteenth-century English capitalism as a wildly productive but flawed political economy. One became a communist political revolutionary; the other, a bourgeois rhetorical ethicist.

Spencer's reputation as a premier Victorian bourgeois stylist/ethicist was not earned in one achievement. He first wrote "The Philosophy of Style" (1852) at a young age, while attending to politics at mid-century. This essay repeats prominent themes in his early writings, especially the *Social Statics* (1851). Later, while writing his multivolume *System of Synthetic Philosophy*, Spencer revised "The Philosophy of Style." The early Spencer followed in Smith's and Blair's footsteps, advocating bourgeois sympathy and rhetorical economy. The later Spencer continued many themes first sketched in his early writings, but his commitment to the social sciences (especially to sociobiology and psychology) led him to doubt personal agency. If genetic inheritance, psychological makeup, and social condition determine character, then people cannot purposefully teach or learn bourgeois sympathy by practicing stylistic economy. Because he took up British belletrism in his early years and then set it aside in his later years, Herbert Spencer's biography offers a representative anecdote about the decline and fall of rhetorical style and bourgeois virtue.

Early Spencer: Progress, Providence, Sympathy, and Style

In order to understand Spencer as the proper inheritor of the British Enlightenment's integration of ethics, economics, and style, we should first review his early writings on politics alongside his influential essay "The Philosophy of Style." Deeply influenced by Adam Smith's economic and moral philosophy as well as Hugh Blair's rhetorical theory, Spencer claimed that exposure to polite literature and genteel rhetorical style can enhance people's sympathy, preparing them for active participation in the public sphere and the industrial economy. He referenced utilitarian philosophy, Victorian phrenology, thermodynamics, and biology, but in so doing Spencer discoursed on the place of rhetorical style and bourgeois virtue in civil society.

Spencer's influential—and only—contribution to rhetorical theory is a twenty-four-page review article. He initially wrote "The Force of Style" in 1843 but failed to place it. For seven years, he neglected the essay while working as a civil engineer for several railroad firms. In the early 1850s, Spencer substantially revised and eventually published his article under a different title ("The Philosophy of Style") in the *Westminster Review* (October 1852), an outlet directed by John Chapman, Spencer's friend and intellectual mentor (*WHS* 20:405–6). The "Philosophy of Style" promises to survey the era's most influential textbooks, including Hugh Blair's *Lectures*, Richard Whately's *Elements of Rhetoric* (1828), George Campbell's *Philosophy of Rhetoric* (1776), and Lord Kames's *Elements of Criticism* (1762). Spencer exposed his Enlightenment roots when mentioning his sources. But he viewed Blair, Campbell, Kames, and Whately from a Victorian's perspective. He complained that no treatise on rhetoric had offered more than a series of "maxims . . . presented in an unorganized form." His essay, on the other hand, advances the science of rhetoric by reducing these rules of thumb to "some simple first principle."[5]

"The Philosophy of Style" could only have been conceived by a twenty-three-year-old engineer enthralled by "physical causation" (*WHS* 20:152); it could only have been completed by someone who also wrote for the *Civil Engineer and*

Architect's Journal (*WHS* 20:164, 200), and it could only have been colored by an autodidact devoted to phrenology (*WHS* 20:200–203). Spencer reduced all stylistic precepts to one principle—"economy." Good writing will "present ideas that may be apprehended with the least possible mental effort."[6] He described economy in mechanistic terms: "Whatever force is absorbed by the machine is deducted from the result. A reader or listener has at each moment but a limited amount of mental power available. . . . Hence the more time and attention it takes to receive and understand each sentence, the less time and attention can be given to the contained idea; and the less vividly will that idea be conceived."[7] Spencer's concern with physical causation is not restricted to the 1852 printing of "The Philosophy of Style." The first law of thermodynamics (faintly echoed above) was a grounding principle for his philosophy of evolution (developed in the late 1850s and published initially as *First Principles of a New System of Philosophy* in 1862). In the late 1760s Spencer rewrote this law as the "continuous redistribution of matter and motion" (*WHS* 1:220; italics removed). In the early 1850s he applied it to rhetorical style.

The phrenologically inclined and mechanistically obsessed Spencer discussed mental "sensibilities" or "faculties" that experience "exhaustion" and must then undertake "two processes of waste and repair."[8] Phrenology taught him that parts of the mind perform specific functions. These mental faculties can grow or atrophy with exercise or neglect. They require rest after exertion. He named several such faculties, including "reverence" and "approbation," but he focused "The Philosophy of Style" on "fatigue" and "attention."[9] Rhetorical figuration (especially climax) and arrangement engage the attention, which must be "continuously husbanded."[10] Applying the principle of physical causation and the notion of faculty psychology, Spencer reworked many precepts of British Enlightenment belletrism. He defended Anglo-Saxon over Latinate words because "increasing familiarity with such words brings greater rapidity and ease of comprehension."[11] He preferred to put the adjective before the noun: "If 'a horse black' be the arrangement used, immediately on the utterance of the word 'horse,' there arises or tends to arise, in the mind, a picture answering to that word. . . . Very likely, however, the image will be that of a brown horse."[12] Predicate-subject arrangement is similarly economical: "As the predicate determines the aspect under which the subject is to be conceived, it should be placed first."[13] Rhetorical figures should "bring the mind more easily to the desired conception."[14] Poetry "obeys all the laws of effective speech." Polite literature "imitates the natural utterances of excitement."[15] Spencer's remarks on an economic style repeat such belletristic bromides as the superiority of Anglo-Saxon over Latinate vocabulary, the belief that language should clearly convey thought and sincerely express emotion, and the contention that polite literature is the highest and most ameliorating form of language.

Because he recast British belletrism in an engineer's vocabulary, Spencer deserves his present-day reputation as a mechanistic phrenologist who defined the mind "as a processing machine in which the writer aims to reduce friction."[16] He also deserves to be remembered as one of the first technical-writing theorists. According to his friend and biographer David Duncan, Spencer acquired writing habits while working at the railroad in the early 1840s, among them "fluency and directness of composition."[17] Historians of early industrial organization notice a similar pattern among mid-century integrated corporations, railroads especially. In large integrated organizations efficient communication became very important, both horizontally among units and vertically between management and subordinates.[18] Since railroads depended on written communication, the genres and styles of industrial writing changed. Correspondence shed the prolix social niceties of eighteenth-century gentility. Railroad managers and engineers favored stylistic concision and directness (or in Spencer's terms, "economy").[19] Even today, "The Philosophy of Style" remains popular among technical-writing instructors who must explain to "efficiency-loving engineers, scientists, and managers . . . why noun stacking, jargon cramming, unrelieved abstraction, inattention to pattern, [or] excessive detail . . . is bad energy-wasting style."[20]

But the mechanistic and the phrenological attributes of Spencer's rhetorical economy are arguably its least interesting features. More interesting and more important is Spencer's adherence to the British Enlightenment faith that rhetorical style can facilitate sympathy, will ameliorate humanity, and must advance commerce. Spencer's hope that stylistic economy could improve sympathy and morality can be found in the 1852 version of "The Philosophy of Style," especially when read in the context of his early writings on politics: *Social Statics* (1851) and "The Proper Sphere of Government" (1842–43). These early political writings reveal an optimistic progressivism, a faith in individual moral improvement, and a belief that private cooperation in civil society can transform England into a just society.[21]

Some biographical information explains the origins of young Spencer's politics. This biographical information also accounts for the intellectual sources that Spencer stitched into his belletristic account of rhetorical economy. He was born to a Methodist clan marked by what he later called "the disregard of authority" (*WHS* 20:12). His father, George, and his uncle Thomas educated Spencer in the natural sciences, mechanics, and geometry (*WHS* 20:84–86). Thomas also introduced Spencer to a brand of radical Christian politics that wedded divinely guided progress to economic liberalism. (Spencer harbored early doubts about Christianity, but he remained wedded as a young man to its basic theological tenets; *WHS* 20:151–52.) As a boy, Spencer listened to his uncle fulminate against the poor laws in Malthusian terms with Christian applications.[22] As a young man, Spencer met Charles Fox, his uncle's associate, a fellow Dissenter, and a sub-engineer on the London and Birmingham Railway. In 1837, possessing an "education [that] was in but very small degree linguistic," Spencer began working under Fox (*WHS* 20:159, 104–25). Like many non-Anglican Protestants he went the capitalist way, traveling by rail.[23] Though he would not write his essay on rhetorical style for another six years, Spencer's early interest in the subject can be found in his epistolary correspondence with his father (*WHS* 20:160). At this age, he also became interested in politics. He wanted to write publicly on economic policy, including his uncle Thomas's favorite hobbyhorse, the poor laws.[24]

Spencer's Christianity waned in this period. He consorted with John Chapman's cronies, adopting their evolutionary deism. He preserved a vague faith in some higher power alongside a strong belief in progress, divinely determined yet scientifically investigated.[25] In the early 1850s, Spencer began reading in the natural sciences, where he happened upon various theories of development. He discovered Charles Lyell's *Principles of Geology* (1830–33), a work popular among those interested in evolutionary science, especially Thomas Huxley and Charles Darwin. Lyell himself remained a committed evolutionary deist. Darwin and Huxley flirted with atheism.[26] Lyell's opus describes an antique earth evolving through phases, which are recorded by a striated mantle. Spencer also discovered Karl Ernst Ritter von Baer's studies in embryology, where he found a biological "law" that he could apply to politics. In Spencer's words, "The law which holds the ascending states of each individual organism is also the law which holds of the ascending grades of organisms of all kinds" (*WHS* 20:385). An interest in the mid-century life sciences accounts for Spencer's 1852 essay "The Development Hypothesis," which champions evolutionary over creationist accounts. This early interest also explains Spencer's application of biological terms to social phenomena, such as the decision to characterize "primitive" society as a "larval" developmental stage.[27] From Smith and Blair, Spencer inherited combined interests in bourgeois political economy and belletristic rhetorical style. To these he added his budding investment in evolutionary science and his quasi-Christian deism. He cast this amalgam in two intertwined works: *Social Statics* and "The Philosophy of Style."

The *Social Statics* is a meandering tome. It supplants the utilitarian expediency principle (a Benthamite favorite) with Spencer's own "law of equal freedom": "Each man shall have the greatest freedom compatible with the like freedom of all others."[28] It rants against government efforts at improving welfare, including municipally funded sewers, publicly mandated education, commercial regulations, post offices, and poor laws.[29] It advocates women's equality. It proposes government redistribution of land through leases negotiated on the basis of merit.[30] It posits psychological mechanisms to explain social progress.[31] The *Social Statics* is, in sum, the work of an ambitious, verbose young man, raised on a diet of Christian liberalism, fascinated by politics, flirting with mid-century radicalism (including Chartism), enamored of the natural sciences, and anxious to contrive a unified philosophical system that reaches down to the most basic psychological impulses while gazing up at the most advanced economic accomplishments. While the work may fail at its proposed synthesis of all things in Spencer's mind, when analyzed alongside some of his early writings the *Social Statics* yields several important themes that reappear in "The Philosophy of Style." Attention to these themes demonstrates that Spencer's rhetorical theory belongs in and contributed to the British Enlightenment's wedding of belletristic rhetorical style and bourgeois civil society. These themes under consideration are natural teleology, individual freedom, psychological sympathy, and social striation.

From an early age, Spencer imagined that all of creation was set on a divine path. In October 1843, when first seriously contemplating politics, he wrote to a friend, saying, "I believe that every people must pass through the various phases between absolutism and democracy before they are fitted to become *permanently* free."[32] This particular missive echoes a series of short letters that Spencer published that same year in *The Nonconformist*, a radical Christian outlet.[33] Spencer's first letter reflects on the "laws" that govern the material world, the "mind," and "society."[34] Such laws originate with "the Almighty" and lead to a government that will "defend the natural rights of man—to protect person and property—to prevent the aggressions of the powerful upon the weak—in a word, to administer justice."[35] He elaborated further on this notion in the *Social Statics*: "Progress . . . is not an accident, but a necessity. Instead of civilization being artificial, it is part of nature." Furthermore, "human well-being, is in accordance with Divine will."[36] Spencer's natural teleology requires two elements—justice and morality.

Justice is the proper office of the state and should be restricted to protection of individual rights. Spencer said that justice should protect the right to liberty while ensuring that its exercise will not "*hurt* any one else." Achieved through legislative and police action, justice is best defined as "*negative beneficence.*" Like Adam Smith, Spencer did not trust the state to morally edify its citizens. Civil mandarins "lack . . . faith in natural forces." They are dissatisfied "with the ordained rate of progress." Though he insisted that human "characters are the only things not fixed," and though he proposed that "moral teaching" should mold people's characters to "hasten this process" of socialization, he removed state bureaucrats from the ethical office. He explained in a typically clunky metaphor that "social arrangements are the bones to that body, of which the national morality is the life." Once justice is established, people can individually learn what Spencer called "positive beneficence." They can learn to love liberty "from within": "Political freedom, therefore, is, as we say, an external result of an internal sentiment—is alike, in origin, practicability, and permanence, dependent on the moral sense; and it is only when this [moral sense] is supreme in its influence that so high a form of social organization as democracy can be maintained."[37]

Spencer's first theme, natural teleology, leads to his second, individual freedom. Society achieves individual freedom when "each can obtain complete happiness within his own sphere of activity, without diminishing the spheres of activity required for the acquisition of happiness by others." Liberty is the end and the means. By protecting and never impinging on freedom, the state creates the minimum conditions where people can cultivate morality. This morality, in turn, advances justice. Spencer ultimately identified moral reform as the more important goal, for "justice can be well administered only in proportion as men themselves become just." But government "partially saves us (only partially, mind) from those assaults, robberies, murders, cheatings, and kindred injuries, to which, were there no such institution, the existing immorality of men would expose us."[38] Follow the Spencerian circle: individual freedom leads to justice, which creates stability, which allows for morality, which further respects individual freedom.

Spencer owed an especially heavy debt to Adam Smith's ethics. Like Smith, Spencer separated justice from beneficence. Smith insisted that justice falls to the magistrate, who should follow a firm rule, while beneficence falls to the individual, who must follow conscience in each case (*TMS* 78–82). Paul Turpin identifies Smith's separation of justice from beneficence ("commutative" from "distributive" justice in Turpin's twenty-first-century vocabulary) as an important bourgeois development. Justice, administered by the state, ensures stability by punishing criminality. Beneficence, curated individually, allows comfort by redistributing resources. The state deserves no charitable office, just as the conscience needs no police force.[39] As Smith put it, justice is a rule that we follow, beneficence a choice that we make: "We feel ourselves to be under a stricter obligation to act according to justice, than agreeably to friendship, charity, or generosity" (*TMS* 80). Spencer elaborated on Smith's division by discussing the government's intrusion on charity. According to "The Proper Sphere of Government," national charity not only oversteps the boundary between justice and beneficence by legislatively forcing charitable support of the indigent; poor laws also "supplant the exercise of real benevolence."[40] In the *Social Statics*, Spencer explained that poor laws impinge on a person's freedom "to use such powers and opportunities as he possesses."[41] Unable to choose charity, an individual cannot grow morally. Interrupting charity stunts sympathy, which according to Spencer is the "faculty of whose growth civilization is a history."[42] These notions of beneficence and individual freedom lead to Spencer's third salient theme— sympathy—which he discovered in 1843 while reading Adam Smith's *Theory of Moral Sentiments* (*WHS* 20:228–29).

Like Smith, Spencer believed that sympathy allows people to imagine and thus experience one another's sentiments.[43] Like Smith, Spencer also contended that this innate psychological mechanism could be improved by free cooperation in civil society. Spencer remarked that Smith had overlooked an important application of his theory: "He did not perceive that the sentiment of justice is nothing but a sympathetic affection of the instinct of personal rights—a sort of reflex function of it."[44] Spencer believed that, in the progress of civilization, sympathy develops, justice increases, and liberty expands—while government contracts. At an early stage, when people behave savagely, justice must descend from authoritative law. Justice's stability allows people to exercise beneficence, to cultivate sympathy, and to respect liberty. As civil society grows, people increasingly learn to cooperate. Government becomes obsolete, since the virtues learned in civil society lead to both beneficence and justice. Spencer imagined mid-century England as a middle stage, a civilization stabilized by justice, cultivating sympathy and morality, though not free of authority. Poor laws are especially detrimental during this transitional phase because they "diminish the demands made upon . . . [sympathy], limit its exercise, check its development, and therefore retard the process of adaptation."[45] To "become fit for the so-cial state, man has not only to lose his savageness, but he has to acquire the capacities needful for civilized life."[46] "The instincts of the savage must die of inanition," and "the sentiments called forth by the social state must grow by exercise."[47]

The radical German response to emerging industrialism offers an illustra-tive comparison to Spencer's libertarian view of English civil society. Karl Marx had little hope for capitalist public discourse, for he believed that virtue could never flourish in alienated, conflict-ridden spaces like the commercial press, the literary market, or the commodities exchange. Marx wanted to overcome civil society's conflicts in a new social arrangement beyond "the existing political State" and realized in what Adam Seligman has called "some future metahis-torical entity where the 'true' essence of man would unfold."[48] Spencer similarly saw a mid-century bourgeois public sphere riddled with contradiction: author-ity versus liberty, police control versus individual conscience, evolved sympa-thy versus primitive aggression. Spencer similarly deferred resolution of civil society's conflicts. He imaginatively spun an approaching libertarian-anarchist utopia where the law resides within each person's emotionally edified breast and where benevolence emerges in every action that respects liberty and exhibits charity. In Spencer's future state, civil society's conflicts will be resolved not by a communist's order but by a capitalist's virtue, not in the mode of production but in the heart of the producer.

Spencer likely acquired his anarchistic leanings in the 1840s while chum-ming around with radical Chartists such as Thomas Hodgkin.[49] But a politi-cal elitism also surfaces in Spencer's discussion of bourgeois civil society. This sentiment points to the fourth salient theme in his early political writings—social striation. Though he believed that societies follow a divinely ordained path and though he imagined the future civil society glimmering with moral-psychological sympathy, Spencer also saw progress as uneven. Some individuals are more advanced than others, and some societies have traveled further down the road to minimal government and maximal freedom. For these reasons, Spencer described lower tiers of "aboriginal" people who "must further be de-void of sympathy, or must have but the germ of it."[50] "Savage" people lack sym-pathy, but they harbor another emotion, "reverence for authority," which leads to powerful governments that maintain order, often by inflicting the greatest "infringements of personal liberty."[51] Authority creates stability, which enables justice. In transitional societies, such as England, justice has been established, authority has been weakened, and sympathy has bloomed. People revere the law, not the lawgiver. They favor mixed governments.[52] During this middle phase Spencer forgave some authoritative social mechanisms, such as the subordination of children. (Nonetheless, he also encouraged Pestalozzian methods of education that foster children's "faculty of full self-control" to develop "the perfections of the ideal man.")[53]

Moral education to impart self-control and sympathy catapults individuals into the upper tier: "The ultimate man will be one whose private requirements coincide with public ones. He will be that manner of man, who, in spontaneously fulfilling his own nature, incidentally performs the functions of a social unit; and yet is only enabled to fulfil his own nature by all others doing the like."[54] In contrast, "savages" need slavery to develop their "industrious habits" as well as their "social sentiments."[55] While prescriptive authority might raise the savage to the middle tier of humanity, people already at this transitional phase require "an education which is emotional rather than preceptive." (Spencer insisted that such education be rescued from government control: "From all legislative attempts at emotional education may Heaven defend us!")[56] Citizens must develop emotionally before assuming their moral duties.[57]

In the *Social Statics*, Spencer said that people can improve individually and willfully by exercising sympathy and industry: "The injunctions of the moral law . . . coincide with and anticipate those of political economy."[58] An internalized capacity for sympathy defines moral law and distinguishes the civilized vanguard. By preaching this new pathetic morality, the superior person leverages "opinion [which] is the agency through which character adapts external arrangements to itself—that *his* opinion rightly forms part of this agency—is a unit of force, constituting . . . the general power which works out social changes."[59] Spencer's early political writings embody the liberal Victorian's faith that individual self-improvement ameliorates society.[60] Radical Continental thinkers such as Karl Marx dismissed cultural reform (and rhetoric), emphasized economics, and aimed to modify people's character by changing their economic environments. According to Marx, good rhetoric should transparently represent the economic truth of capitalism's contradictions, so that people can realize a future communist state.[61] Spencer saw things quite differently. In the early 1850s, Spencer emphasized cultural reform in bourgeois civil society as the proper Archimedean lever to move the economy into its next stage. Bourgeois cultural reform rests against the fulcrum of sympathy. Finally, sympathy is constituted rhetorically. Close analysis of "The Philosophy of Style" reveals rhetorical corollaries for the themes discussed in his political theory—natural teleology, individual liberty, psychological sympathy, and social striation. The corollaries between his mid-century political and rhetorical theories confirm that Spencer adopted and adapted the British Enlightenment's interweaving of rhetorical style, political economy, and bourgeois ethics.

Spencer's belief in a natural teleology correlates to his insistence that language progressively develops. He likely inherited his ideas about linguistic development from Hugh Blair, who said that language began as a passionate and imaginative expression of a primitive mind but then progressed toward a sedate "plainer and simpler style of composition, which we now call Prose" (*Lectures* 62).[62] However, Spencer deviated from Blair in some important ways. While Blair believed that passionate language tends to be figuratively wordy, Spencer contended that emotional figuration condenses expression. Though "excited persons are given to figures of speech . . . extreme brevity is one of the characteristics of passionate language."[63] Spencer elaborated on Blair's progressive view of linguistic development by applying the "law" he learned from Von Baer's embryology: "Advance from the one [primitive] stage to the other [developed] stage is from uniformity of composition to multiformity of composition" (*WHS* 20:384). In his later scientifico-philosophic evolutionary theory, published in 1862 as *First Principles of a New System of Philosophy*, he articulated a law to account for this development in societies and biological organisms: "The more homogeneous must tend ever to become less homogeneous" (*WHS* 1:328). In the early 1860s, Spencer demonstrated this law's realization across the diverse disciplinary domains of astronomy, geology, biology, and sociology. In the early 1850s, he focused on rhetoric:

> If we glance back at the past, and remember that men had once only nouns and verbs to convey their ideas with, and that from then to now the growth has been towards a greater number of implements of thought, and consequently towards a greater complexity and variety in their combinations, we may infer that we are now, in our use of sentences, much what the primitive man was in his use of words, and that a continuance of the process that has hitherto gone on must produce increasing heterogeneity in our modes of expression.[64]

This passage recalls Blair's theory of linguistic progress, but it also reinforces Spencer's theory of social evolution.

Spencer's political principle of individual freedom correlates to his rhetorical pedagogy. He saw little use in maxims and precepts. He believed that "natural aptitude," practice, and constant exposure to "well-framed sentences, will naturally ... [lead a student] to use similar" sentences. If a writer slavishly follows the principle of economy, her stylistic inflexibility will "slowly" lead to awful prose. Like Smith and Blair before him, Spencer believed that a felicitous rhetorical style requires natural expression: "These natural modes of procedure may serve as guides in writing." However, "the species of composition which the law of effect points out as the perfect one, is the one which high genius tends naturally to produce."[65] The "ultimate man" who speaks without restraint raises society by edifying the audience.

Spencer praised rhetorical economy for its efficient transfer of ideas, but he valued the stylistic virtue even more for its ability to encourage sympathy: "The predominant feelings have by use trained the intellect to represent them." Spencer described the "perfect writer" as a man of genuine emotional expression: "From his mode of expression naturally responding to his state of feeling, there will flow from his pen a composition changing to the same degree that the aspects of his subject change." Spencer further elevated sympathetically expressive (economical) rhetoric when discussing poetry, which he defined as the imitation of "the natural utterances of excitement." He said that "the matter embodied [in poetry] is idealized emotion, [and] the vehicle is the idealized language of emotion." He believed that "the poet develops from the typical expressions in which men utter passion and sentiment, those choice forms of verbal combination in which concentrated passion and sentiment may be fitly presented." Classifying poetry among the "higher forms of speech," Spencer noted its ability to "induce a preparatory sympathy." Poetic figuration and rhythm follow natural patterns "habitually found . . . in connexion with vivid mental impressions."[66] Poetry is therefore the greatest rhetorical achievement of the most civilized human being.

Finally, Spencer's notion of social striation correlates to the ranks he assigned certain stylistic patterns (and to the people exhibiting these patterns). In a memorable and often-quoted passage, Spencer described his rhetorically economical Übermensch: "A perfectly endowed man must unconsciously write in all styles." He explained further, "The kinds of sentence which are theoretically best are those generally employed by superior minds, and by inferior minds when excitement has raised them; so we shall find that the ideal form for a poem, essay, or fiction, is that which the ideal writer would evolve spontaneously." Stylistic versatility permits rhetorical economy because the "high genius" can express any sentiment. Spencer's description of the "direct" and the "indirect" styles is also a commentary on social distinction. The direct style puts qualifiers before substantives (adjectives before nouns, adverbs before verbs, and so forth). The indirect style leads with the substantive and then qualifies by introducing modifiers. Spencer thought the direct style superior because more economical. He also insisted that the direct style requires "a considerable power of concentration, and a tolerably vigorous imagination." Only the superior mind can comprehend the direct style. Since it is "easiest for undisciplined minds," the indirect style is "best fitted for the uncultivated, [which] may indeed be inferred from their habitual use of it."[67]

My analysis of common themes in young Spencer's political and rhetorical writings demonstrates that he inherited and extended the British Enlightenment's connections among rhetorical belletrism, bourgeois ethics, and social progress. His lifelong commitment to "The Philosophy of Style" further proves that through the second half of the nineteenth century, Spencer remained committed to the belletrism that he inherited from Smith and Blair. In 1858, he compiled the first (one-volume) issue of his *Essays: Scientific, Political, and Speculative*, including "The Philosophy of Style," which, in his words, had been "considerably amplified."[68] The essay appeared in subsequent editions of Spencer's *Essays* (1864, 1892) and was published as a pamphlet in the United States (1872). To prepare the 1858 edition, Spencer cut some passages and edited others.[69] He also qualified some of his claims.[70] In addition, he added examples that reflect his growing interest in political economy.[71] Spencer's later writings elaborate on his notion of the "ultimate man," put forward initially in "The Philosophy of Style" and the *Social Statics*. When writing part 8 ("Industrial Institutions") of his *Principles of Sociology* (1896), the last substantive work that he would pen before his death in 1903, Spencer discussed the next phase of social progress, the "industrial" stage, and he returned to his rhetorically gifted Übermensch: "Long studies . . . have not caused me to recede from the belief expressed nearly fifty years ago that—'The ultimate man will be one whose private requirements coincide with public ones. He will be that manner of man who, in his spontaneously fulfilling his own nature, incidentally performs the functions of a social unit; and yet is only enabled so to fulfil his own nature by all others doing the like'" (*WHS* 8:601). Spencer's later writings more fully explore the place of his belletristic notion of sympathy in bourgeois civil society and political economy. After mid-century, Spencer presented the industrial economy as the engine of an advanced society. He came to believe that sympathy leads to industry, and he kept believing that rhetorical economy leads to sympathy.

Late Spencer: Evolution, Ethics, Sympathy, and Industry

On May 20, 1844, Thomas Carlyle, the traditionalist, wrote Herbert Spencer, the radical. Never having met the man, nor read his pamphlet "On the Proper Sphere of Government," Carlyle saw "something good and salutary in all utterances of men which recognize, in any way, the eternal nature of Right and Wrong." Spencer later reflected that he was "averse" to Carlyle's "leading ideas" but appreciative of "the sympathetic feeling occasionally manifested by him" (*WHS* 20:230–31). His distaste for Carlyle's philosophy is ironic, for Spencer spent two-thirds of his life living the drama that Carlyle penned in 1833–34, *Sartor Resartus*. Spencer became a living embodiment of Carlyle's lead character, Professor Teufelsdröckh, who stitched all humanity into a philosophy of clothes. Like Teufelsdröckh, Spencer spread his interests so diversely that he could only be called a "Professor of Things in General." Then he wove all these subjects into an evolutionary tapestry.[72] Attending to Spencer's later work on evolution reveals three things. First, he continued to believe that bourgeois virtue (sympathy and rhetorical economy) contributes to social progress. Second, he reframed this belief in an elaborate sociobiological philosophy. Third, his sociobiology exalted industrial capitalism as the most advanced stage of human civilization.

In his later works, Spencer separated biological from social evolution. ("The Philosophy of Style" relates directly to social evolution and distantly to biological evolution.) He explored biological evolution in his *Principles of Biology* (1864–67) and in later essays. In the passage from his *Biology* where the reader first encounters the phrase "survival of the fittest," Spencer described creatures vying for scarce resources by adapting to the environment: "Those individuals whose functions are most out of equilibrium with the modified aggregate of external forces, will be those to die. . . . This survival of the fittest implies multiplication of the fittest" (*WHS* 2:530). Spencer went on to explain that "survival of the fittest" depends on several mechanisms. First, there is "indirect equilibration," the destruction of organisms least fitted to the environment and the preservation of those most fitted (*WHS* 2:547). Charles Darwin's theory of natural selection explores such evolutionarily indirect action. According to Spencer, however, there is also "direct equilibration," which results from a creature's habits. Progeny can inherit modification attained through direct action. As Spencer put it, "There must be a natural selection of functionally-acquired peculiarities, as well as of spontaneously-acquired peculiarities; and hence such structural changes in a species as result from changes of habit necessitated by changed circumstances, natural selection will render more rapid than they would otherwise be" (WHS 2:540). Spencer's effort to explore both direct and indirect action in speciation has led twentieth-century critics to dismiss his entire biology as pitiably Lamarckian.[73]

Nevertheless, it would be a mistake to wholly ignore Spencer's disagreement with Darwin, for this controversy illuminates Spencer's theory of social evolution. Darwin allowed some place for the inheritance of acquired characteristics, saying that "habit, or use and disuse, have, in some cases, played a considerable part in the modification of the constitution and structure [of a species]; but . . . the effects have often been largely combined with, and sometimes overmastered by, the Natural Selection of innate variations."[74] While Darwin privileged natural selection of random mutations, Spencer offered a multicausal theory that includes natural selection of random variation and inheritance of functionally produced modification. In an 1893 essay defending Spencer's view of evolution against charges made by the German biologist August Weismann (a prominent Darwinian), Spencer explained that natural selection accounts for evolution "throughout the vegetal world and throughout the lower animal world, characterized by relative passivity." But the "higher types of animals" exhibit greater volition, so they evolve by both inheritance of random mutation and acquired characteristics, "until, in animals of complex structures, inheritance of acquired characters becomes an important, if not the chief, cause of evolution" (WHS 17:45). Being the most complex animals, humans evolve primarily by habit and its inheritance.

Spencer's hybrid of natural selection and functionally acquired modification also led to a public debate with his close friend Thomas Huxley (another Darwinian). Their disagreement further sheds light on Spencer's distinction between biological and social evolution. Huxley's 1894 publication of *Evolution and Ethics* (a compilation of an 1893 lecture and a prefatory essay) is nowadays understood as a direct refutation of Spencer's evolutionary sociology. Huxley never mentioned Spencer by name, though he did pen some significantly anti-Spencerian lines, particularly his now-famous prediction that social "progress" will have to proceed independently of biological evolution through "the ethical process; the end of which is not the survival of those who may happen to be the fittest . . . but of those who are ethically the best."[75] Never one to let a polemic go unanswered, Spencer replied that social evolution involves the evolution of ethics, "for if the ethical man is not a product of the cosmic process, what is he a product of?" (*WHS* 18:113).

According to Spencer, social evolution depends on and contributes to biological evolution. Spencer's intellectual legacy, therefore, includes some openly elitist, some shockingly cruel, and some tellingly risible statements. He stated that workers are not "sufficiently provident, nor sufficiently conscientious, nor sufficiently intelligent" to "govern" themselves (*WHS* 12:246). He wanted to "let the struggle for existence bring on the unworthy the sufferings consequent on their incapacity or misconduct" (*WHS* 11:362). He believed that Irish immigrants had biologically lost their "Celtic aspect" within a generation due to functionally acquired adaptations (*WHS* 2:310). Such statements rightfully associate Spencer's work with the worst of eugenics-based racism, bourgeois elitism, and starve-the-poor social Darwinism.[76] Nevertheless, to understand Spencer's commitment to rhetorical economy, we must understand his theory of social evolution, as it was articulated in response to Darwinians such as Weismann and Huxley.

If the higher animals evolve mostly by inheritance of functionally acquired characteristics, then societies evolve mostly by habitually acquired ethics. According to Spencer, social evolution, unlike biological evolution, depends on development and preservation of justice, which connects only secondarily to innate or biologically inheritable qualities. While writing the "biological view" in his *Data of Ethics*, Spencer supposed that an "advanced social state" would eventually produce people with notable psychological and inheritable qualities: "With social evolution . . . there comes an underexercise of faculties for which the social state affords no scope, and an overtaxing of faculties required for the social state": an increased capacity for sympathy and a developed ability to defer gratification (*WHS* 9:97). Since this emotional development depends first on a "purer creed and a better government, a truer ethics belongs to a more advanced social state" (*WHS* 9:98). Justice allows social improvement, which then sanctions ethical amelioration, and finally permits emotional/biological evolution. Since social evolution toward justice precedes biological evolution of sympathy, Spencer's biology did not ground his sociology. The social organism's environment calls forth the ultimate man's biology. Sympathy's genetic quality is an adaptation to society's just circumstance.

Spencer's deep commitment to a biological view of evolution marks him as characteristically Victorian. Like John Locke and Adam Smith, Herbert Spencer divided history, though he did not call the early era "primitive" or "agrarian." Instead, he called it "militant." Moreover, he did not call the latter era "advanced" or "commercial." Rather, he called it "industrial." The militant society, according to Spencer, survives in circumstances of aggression, when other social organisms (tribes, fiefs, nations) threaten invasion: "The social type produced by the survival of the fittest, will be one in which the fighting part includes all who can bear arms . . . while the remaining part serves simply as a permanent commissariat" (*WHS* 7:570). Militant society is characterized by "compulsory cooperation" (*WHS* 7:574); government ownership and control (*WHS* 7:576–78); and a courageous, loyal people who lack compassion, creativity, or initiative (*WHS* 7:595–98). These circumstances favor "a survival of the unforgiving" (*WHS* 7:593). The industrial society thrives in circumstances of peace, when "life, liberty and property are secure, and all interests justly regarded. . . . So that by survival of the fittest must be produced a social type in which individual claims, considered as sacred, are trenched on by the State no further than is requisite to pay the cost of maintaining them, or rather, of arbitrating among them" (*WHS* 7:608). Industrial society is characterized by a "strong sense of individual freedom"; a respect for private property (*WHS* 7:628); a flourishing of "humane sentiments" including sympathy (*WHS* 7:630); "voluntary cooperation" such as that exhibited by "English and American capitalists" (*WHS* 7:635–36); and fierce "independence, resistance to coercion, honesty, truthfulness, forgiveness, kindness" (*WHS* 7:639). While military life "deadens the sympathies," industrial life allows "the sympathies free play" and thus "favours the growth of altruistic sentiments and the resulting virtues" (*WHS* 7:640).[77]

Spencer called militarism and industrialism "types" because he wanted to emphasize several points about social evolution. Though "at some time, more or less distant, the industrial type will become permanently established," he did not think late nineteenth-century England had approached pure industrialism's threshold (*WHS* 7:648). The militant and the industrial types tend to intermingle in one social organism (*WHS* 7:569). England progressed toward industrialism, yet Spencer worried that late nineteenth-century imperialism created an environment favoring the militant type. In his influential collection of essays *The Man versus the State* (1884), Spencer worried about a revitalization of militancy. He explained England's political parties by referencing the "semi-militant semi-industrial type, which now characterizes advanced nations"

(*WHS* 11:404). Toryism springs "from militancy," Liberalism, "from industrialism" (*WHS* 11:294). England's dalliances in utilitarianism and imperialism made possible a new form of Toryism that united military adventures abroad and governmental regulation at home.

Since social evolution is neither inevitable nor even, it might happen in a two-steps-forward-one-step-back rhythm. Spencer explained in his *System of Synthetic Philosophy* (1862/1904), "Rhythm results wherever there is a conflict of forces not in equilibrium" (*WHS* 1:203).[78] Important differences between Spencer's early and late theories of social evolution become evident. The young Spencer viewed social evolution as the inevitable result of some higher mandate toward human perfection. The later Spencer saw social evolution as the result of natural environmental factors, the instability of war and the stability of peace chief among them. The young Spencer imagined social evolution as a steady progress toward the "ultimate man," but the later Spencer believed the road would include many diversions, dead ends, and some regrettable backtracking.[79] Finally, the young Spencer viewed social progress as the inevitable result of good government's dedication to the law of equal freedom. The later Spencer presented social progress as a historical fact and a future possibility but no certain guarantee.

Despite these differences, an important continuity endures from the young Spencer's political pamphlets to the old Spencer's sociological tomes: the individual—not the government—is the drum major leading humanity toward industry. By developing and practicing their enlightened sensibilities (especially their respect for rights, their industrious deferment of gratification, and their sympathy for one another), citizens will shape the social organism into its more evolved form. "The characters of the units determine the character of the aggregate. . . . [So] political institutions cannot be effectively modified faster than the characters of citizens are modified" (*WHS* 7:661). In the *Study of Sociology* (1873), a collection of essays written to a popular audience, Spencer put the point more bluntly: "Forms of government are valuable only where they are products of national *character*. No cunningly-devised political arrangements will of themselves do anything" (*WHS* 12:271). In *The Man versus the State*, he worried that English people were not ready for true liberty because they had "partially emerged from the militant *régime* and . . . partially entered on that industrial *régime* to which this doctrine is proper" (*WHS* 11:408). However primitive, the popular English "belief in the authority of government" and "a political theory justifying the faith and obedience" suited the transitional circumstances (*WHS*

11:407). As he would later reflect in his *Autobiography*, Spencer's conservatism grew out of a libertarian hope interrupted by a pragmatic acknowledgment. He wanted society to evolve, but he accepted that people were still primitive. He insisted that institutions are changed by "character; and, however changed in their superficial aspects, cannot be changed in their essential natures faster than character changes" (*WHS* 21:366).

Because Spencer believed that individual character drives social change, he remained dedicated throughout his life to sympathy and rhetorical economy. In his early writings, Spencer thematically associated social progress, bourgeois sympathy, and rhetorical economy. In his evolutionary sociology, he systematically explained how style communicates sentiment and facilitates industry. More thoroughly than Smith or Locke, Spencer explained the place of rhetorical style and bourgeois virtue in capitalist political economy. "The Morals of Trade," an essay that Spencer wrote for the classically liberal *Westminster Review* (1859), provides a useful entrance into Spencer's thoughts on economics, for it grounds Spencer's ideas about social evolution in the particulars of trade, and it introduces two important binaries shaping Spencer's thoughts on sympathy: competition/community and egoism/altruism. Spencer began the essay by confessing that people at both the lower and the higher levels of trade (both the shopkeeper and the merchant) practice dishonesty and duplicity to gain a quick profit. As he explained, such "frauds are committed unblushingly, and as a matter of business" (*WHS* 15:119). Many a Victorian moralist imagined the Christian pilgrim at capitalism's Vanity Fair. Such evangelicals nonetheless respected Spencer's work and viewed commerce as a suitable Christian vocation on par with the ministry. They prayed the Christian capitalist would maintain the community's virtue despite competition's temptations.[80]

Spencer offered a different solution to the competition/community conundrum. Like Adam Smith, he suggested that competition, while encouraging a level of vice, also creates an environment where virtue survives and multiplies. Out of competition evolves an honest community. Initially, the "average character placed under special conditions" of commercial competition seizes advantage in every available manner (*WHS* 15:139). Over time, however, people develop "a social self-consciousness" that directs them away from "commercial malpractices," for they recognize that honesty improves commerce overall. In a different essay, Spencer characterized such malpractices as "commercial murder"—the "excesses committed under free competition"—but he also explained that "law" and "self-restraints" can prevent these violations of ethical exchange

(*WHS* 18:116). In fact, Spencer contended that Christian moralists were able to feel indignation at fraudulent business practices, because they had evolved social self-consciousness (*WHS* 15:141). But Spencer worried that other environmental forces might compel people away from the honest commercial community. Spencer mentioned the English admiration of nobility and the American worship of the almighty dollar as regressive forces drawing people away from properly industrial honesty and sympathy (*WHS* 15:150). He concluded the essay on a hopeful note: "By vigorous protest against adoration of mere success . . . by a stern criticism of the means through which success has been achieved, and by according honour to the higher and less selfish modes of activity," honesty can finally flourish among industrial citizens (*WHS* 15:150–51).

Spencer's vocabulary—"social evolution," "competition," "community"—was appropriate to his intellectual circumstances, for these terms derived from Victorian conversations about science and morality. This vocabulary was also appropriate to Spencer's economic circumstances, for it describes aspects of the first British railway boom (ca. 1835–50). Spencer witnessed firsthand both competition and cooperation on massive scales. The new railways had to develop new methods of internal organization, new approaches to community that would permit growth without stifling innovation. In addition, the English government had to develop new ways to regulate (or liberate) this dynamic industry.[81] (Spencer wrote about the potential for democratic, rather than managerial, government of railway firms in "Railway Morals and Railway Policy" [1854].) New railways also competed viciously with one another, leading to many defunct firms that were absorbed by their survivors. (Spencer wrote about "differentiation" and "integration" in every evolutionary process, saying that industrial societies initially demonstrate great heterogeneity of entrepreneurial activity, but that competition leads to a shift from this "incoherent heterogeneity" toward "coherent homogeneity" as less suitable firms expire and large firms coalesce in size and mission [*WHS* 1:294–95].) Little imaginative flight and less hermeneutic creativity are needed to see that Spencer's writings on evolution, community, and competition could describe biology, morality, or Victorian industry. When writing on altruism and egoism, Spencer similarly addressed the early British railway age.

The contrasting forces of egoism and altruism preoccupied the English Victorian mind as much as the competition/community binary. Though it has been common, in previous intellectual history, to paint Victorian England as a ship listing toward egoism, close analysis of the literature reveals that this era's most prolific public moralists staunchly defended altruism against the profit motive.[82] To be fair, Spencer did not exalt Christian beneficence, nor did he promote a secular surrogate. His friend John Stuart Mill may have praised "the social feelings of mankind"—that "powerful principle in human nature"—but Spencer did no such thing because he did not find any natural or biological inclination toward a universal altruism.[83] He offered his own peculiar solution to the egoism-altruism opposition. Spencer raised egoism and justice above altruism and beneficence. Justice indirectly leads to beneficence. Egoism inadvertently produces altruism.

In *The Principles of Ethics*, Spencer explained that "egoism comes before altruism" in the process of social evolution (*WHS* 9:187): "The pursuit of individual happiness within those limits prescribed by social conditions, is the first requisite to the attainment of the greatest general happiness" (*WHS* 9:190). Positive altruism (beneficence) develops naturally from familial sentiments and has great limitations. It can only be extended so far, and its exercise depletes the giver, necessitating a retreat into egoism (*WHS* 9:196, 202). As Spencer put it, "The egoistic gain from association is small; and it becomes considerable only as the recognition becomes voluntary—that is, more altruistic" (*WHS* 9:206). Negative altruism, on the other hand, has a different origin and greater potential: "The private interests of the individual are on the average better subserved . . . as he himself refrains from direct aggression . . . [and] as he succeeds in diminishing the aggressions of his fellows on one another" (*WHS* 9:207). Thus reappears a key distinction: positive and negative beneficence. Positive beneficence develops in family units and spurs us to help others; negative beneficence develops in private competition and deters us from harming others. Negative beneficence is the altruism born of egoism. Its child is honesty.

In the *Ethics*, Spencer lauded the industrial benefits of negative beneficence in free-market economies:

> As everyone knows, the larger the number of shopkeeper's bills left unpaid by some customers, the higher must be the prices which other customers pay. The more manufacturers lose by defective raw materials or by carelessness of workmen, the more must they charge for their fabrics to buyers. The less trustworthy people are, the higher rises the rate of interest, the larger becomes the amount of capital hoarded, the greater are the impediments to industry. The further traders and people in general go beyond their means, and hypothecate the property of others in speculation,

the more serious are those commercial panics which bring disasters on multitudes and injuriously affect all. (*WHS* 9:207–8)

Having found his own way through two Victorian binaries—competition/ community and egoism/altruism—Spencer arrived at the all-important notion of sympathy: "other-regarding" instead of "self-regarding." Sympathy, according to Spencer, increases with social evolution. To illustrate, he returned to polite literature as first discussed in "The Philosophy of Style." Primitive letters dealt with "the doings of the ruling classes, and found its plots in their antagonisms and deeds of violence." Yet more recent fiction "discloses a new world of interest in the everyday pleasures and pains of ordinary people." In developed societies, the arts flourish because "the pleasures which art gives increase as the fellow-feeling with these joys and sorrows strengthens" (*WHS* 9:215). At the end of *The Principles of Sociology*, he explained the underlying social etiology symptomatized by literary pathology: "By continual repression of aggressive instincts and exercise of feelings which prompt ministrations to public welfare, and on the other hand by the lapse of restraints, gradually becoming less necessary, there must be produced a kind of man so constituted that while fulfilling his own desires he fulfils also the social needs" (*WHS* 8:601).

Given Spencer's glowing comments about sympathy and its industrial role, we might expect him to rhapsodize about positive beneficence. After all, when first introducing positive beneficence in the *Ethics*, he associated the quality with sympathy (*WHS* 9:212). While Spencer did write many pages about positive beneficence, he wrote as many and he wrote initially about negative beneficence. Justice, said Spencer, initially grows out of egoistic sentiments, such as a fear of retaliation. But, once egoism establishes the rule of law, people develop greater "sympathy which makes the altruistic sense of justice possible." An altruistic sense of justice extends beyond mere egoistic gratification "by maintenance of those conditions which render achievement of satisfactions unimpeded." The altruistic sense of justice is gratified by "the ideas of those conditions" (*WHS* 10:32). We learn to love fairness and honesty not because these conditions protect us from fraud but because we see them as qualities good in themselves. Because of fear, primitive people appreciate justice's presence. Because of sympathy, advanced people adore justice's essence.

In an 1882 interview with an American journalist, Spencer explained that the U.S. "paper constitution" could not ultimately preserve liberty or advance civilization. "It is essentially a question of character."[84] "The fact is, that free institutions can be properly worked by men each of whom is jealous of his own rights, and also sympathetically jealous of the rights of others—will neither himself aggress on his neighbors, in small things or great, nor tolerate aggression on them by others."[85] Adam Smith separated justice from beneficence, saying that justice and its coercive maintenance "is the main pillar that upholds the whole edifice," while "beneficence . . . is less essential to the existence of society than justice" (*TMS* 86). Spencer balanced the whole competitive-industrial edifice atop the internal motivation toward virtue—the altruistic sense. Character alone (not the coercive force of law) protects freedom to truck and barter, contract and exchange, own and enjoy. Spencer patronizingly told his young American interviewer that the United States "would have to go back before they could go forward."[86] Americans would have to replace their paper constitutional guarantee of liberty with individual citizens who love everyone's liberty because they are sympathetic with those whose liberties get curtailed.

Spencer divided altruism into "Justice and Beneficence . . . the one needful for social equilibrium, and therefore of public concern, and the other . . . not needful for social equilibrium, and therefore only of private concern" (*WHS* 10:270). In the *Ethics*, Spencer expanded his debt to Adam Smith by placing sympathy at the root of both justice and beneficence. Sympathy leads to altruism, and altruism divides into "the primary altruism we call justice and the secondary altruism we call beneficence." Negative beneficence mandates restraint: "Passivity in deed or word, at times when egoistic advantage or pleasure might be gained by action" (*WJS* 10:275). As he explained in his "Morals of Trade" essay, people committed to altruistic justice and negative beneficence disavow fraud and honor contracts: "So long as men pay homage to those social benefactors who have grown rich honestly, they give a wholesome stimulus to industry" (*WHS* 15:149).

Spencer tied sympathy, justice, and commerce together into a neat bundle: a psychological mechanism yields an ethical advance that fosters an industrial society. However, one key element present in "The Philosophy of Style" seems to have fallen away. The ultimate man, an honest member of an industrial society, is sympathetic and therefore just. But is he rhetorically economical and therefore sympathetic? Spencer answered this question affirmatively in *The Principles of Sociology*. He explained that fraud, the bane of commercial industry, proliferates under militarism, but withers in industrial circumstances: "The love of independence joins the love of truthfulness" (*WHS* 7:220). Honesty burgeons in industrial societies where peace favors cooperation. Peaceful industry, the happy give-and-take of competition, contract, and productivity all require that people improve themselves. They must attain "higher emotions and higher intelligence." They must acquire "a stronger fellow feeling with all around." They should develop a more sophisticated language, "needful for seeing how all words and acts will tell upon their states of mind." The greatest mind perfectly communicates thought and emotion. The ultimate man possesses "an intelligence which, by each expression of face and cadence of speech, is informed what is the passing state of emotion, and how emotion has been affected by actions just committed" (*WHS* 7:225).

Ultimate Spencer: Sociology, Psychology, Education, and Style

In 1885, having published both volumes of his *Ethics* and all three of his *Sociology*, Spencer was poised to step into the pantheon of civil society's great theorists. Yet he demurred. Unlike his Scottish predecessors, Spencer never presented rhetorical education or literary criticism as the Palladia of bourgeois virtue. He never felt at home in the salon discussing the belles lettres, and he never once lectured on rhetoric, disputation, or critical appreciation. Speaking to a crowd of U.S. business moguls in 1882, Spencer anticipated a postindustrial era when humanity would finally enjoy aesthetic achievements, such as literary art, and when "life is not for learning, nor is life for working, but learning and working are for life." But in the circumstances of late nineteenth-century industrial capitalism, Spencer said that the "appropriate" personal disposition adored business, not the belles lettres.[87] In 1902, a year before he died, Spencer revisited his essay on style, confessing something that anyone who has read his prose will find evident. He never achieved an economic style. He attributed his failure to "habit": "The general traits of my style have remained unchanged, notwithstanding my wish to change some of them" (*WHS* 19.77). According to the octogenarian Spencer, "style is organic." It can only develop through natural, unconscious adaptation (*WHS* 19:78). Why would Spencer, Adam Smith's capitalist heir, civil society's liberal champion, turn away from rhetorical education and the imaginative arts? The short answer: he lost faith in the individual's ability to purposefully cultivate bourgeois virtue. The long answer requires a return to his writings on sociology, psychology, and education. This long answer further explains how British Enlightenment belletrism—a rhetorical stylistics thick with bourgeois ethics and capitalist political economy—could lose "Blair's firm connection of taste to civic virtue." How could Spencer, the British Enlightenment's intellectual heir, finally bequeath what Sharon Crowley has called "something very different from Blair's . . . [view] of taste as the cultivation of civil commitment"?[88] How could "The Philosophy of Style" ultimately endorse a schoolmarm's depoliticized and a-contextual grammar rules?

In *The Principles of Sociology*, Spencer explained that changes in character result from changes in circumstances. The social organism adapts only when the environment demands. At the end of his *Study of Sociology*, he said that "if surrounding conditions remain the same, the evolution of a society cannot be in any essential way diverted from its course." However, he assured the reader that "beliefs and actions of individuals, being natural factors that arise in the course of evolution itself, and aid in further advancing it, must be severally valued as increments of the aggregate force producing change" (*WHS* 12:396). These passages intimate a fundamental shift in Spencer's perception of individual agency. The ultimate man's rhetorical economy seems more like a sign rather than a fulcrum of social evolution. Civil society is a theater of progress, not a nursery of virtue. As Spencer aged, he inflated large social forces, such as peace and competition. Moreover, he diminished individual agency. No single person by willful effort can become more sympathetic, nor can she become more stylistically economical: "No great results can be counted upon from the study of style." A person of modest talent, regularly exposed to "well-framed speech," will exhibit "lucid" writing. That same person, diligently applying herself, may remove "defects of expression and arrangement . . . in the course of revision." But she cannot hope for anything more, for the conscious "study of style will do but little" (*WHS* 20:160). In Spencer's later writings, evolutionary sociology trumped rhetorical pedagogy, making "The Philosophy of Style" into a commentary on the ultimate man, rather than a guide to his realization.

Spencer is partly to blame for his transformation from bourgeois ethicist to psychological stylist. After completing the *Social Statics* and "The Philosophy of Style," but before 1857, the year when he committed himself to writing "a complete conception of evolution" (*WHS* 21:12), Spencer wrote *The Principles of Psychology* (1855), a work that brought him to exhaustion and illness (*WHS* 20:464–65). Like everything he wrote, the book meanders. Of immediate interest is the last chapter of his 1855 *Psychology*—on the will. Spencer unpacked a key term that appeared in the 1892 revision of "The Philosophy": "habit" is behavior both "coherent and involuntary." While voluntary action is presented to the conscious mind and can therefore be arrested or engaged, involuntary action simply happens without our deliberation. Coherent action suits the psychological and

historical circumstances to which it responds. Coherent action—like an appropriately economical style—is typically involuntary: "That Will comes into existence through the increasing complexity and imperfect coherence of automatic
changes, is most clearly seen in the converse fact, that when changes which were
once incoherent and voluntary, are very frequently repeated in experience, they
become coherent and involuntary."[89]

According to Spencer, an organism's psychological adaptation happens in
part through voluntary deliberation about actions that do not cohere with the
environment. But mostly psychological adaptation happens by habitual acquisition of coherent involuntary behaviors. An economical style, developed and
realized by force of "habit," is an unconscious and involuntary response to an
industrial environment. At the end of his *Psychology*, Spencer explained that the
popular version of "free will"—"liberty to desire or not to desire"—is simply an
"illusion" of consciousness.[90] His attention to impersonal causal forces earned
him praise from none other than Charles Darwin, who said that scientific psychology would "be securely based on the foundation already well laid by Mr.
Herbert Spencer."[91]

Spencer was not always committed to mechanistic psychology. He dithered,
at times saying that education improves the student and ameliorates society, at
times stating that education reflects the mind's habitual adaptation to its sur-
roundings. His writings on education (1854–59) exhibit this back-and-forth
between the teacher's hopeful mission and the scientist's cold description. In his
1854 essay on "Intellectual Education," Spencer postulated a relation between
"the successive systems of education, and the successive social states with which
they have co-existed," and he connected the "free-trade era" to education that
emphasizes the "natural process of mental evolution" (*WHS* 16:56–57). While
arguing that education reflects each stage of social development, he also contended that the individual teacher helps to realize a "free-trade era" by encouraging the process of "self-instruction" (*WHS* 16:100). The teacher seems to have
some agency in the course of social evolution. On the other hand, Spencer also
said that teachers should leave students to learn naturally, since the interaction
of psychological mechanisms and environmental forces leads to personal adaptation and social evolution. Teachers seem to do nothing but let impersonal
causes run their course. In an 1858 essay, Spencer wrote that optimal moral education lets children suffer the "natural consequence" of their behaviors (*WHS*
16:119). A year later, however, he insisted that conscious efforts to teach science
and engineering can advance industrial society's development (*WHS* 16:17–23).

In "The Philosophy of Style" and the *Social Statics*, Spencer expressed hope that conscious and purposeful moral development could reform the individual and improve society. For a decade thereafter, he dithered between the rhetoric teacher's exaltation of individual agency and the social scientist's emphasis on psychological and economic causes.

Spencer's commitment to the sciences eventually overrode his belief in literature's ability to exercise sympathy. He derided belletristic rhetorical pedagogy for attending to "aesthetic culture" rather than industry. Championing a scientific curriculum, Spencer said belletrism "neglects the plant for the sake of the flower. In anxiety for elegance, it forgets substance" (*WHS* 16:39). Industrial circumstances mandate a shift from "grammar and lexicons" to physics and biology (*WHS* 16:53–55). Since the economic environment causes curricular adaptation, Spencer's promotion of scientific education seems inconsistent with his belief in social evolution. In the 1850s he paradoxically advocated the inevitable. By 1882, when he published the final volume of his *Principles of Sociology*, all traces of human agency vanished. He decided that progress results from a change in circumstance. No amount of teaching science can advance industry. No effort at preaching sympathy can instill bourgeois virtue. Free-market capitalism "fundamentally depends on the cessation of war" (*WHS* 7:663). Once the environment changes, the people will adapt, and the social organism will evolve.

An enduring question for scholars of public address has been, What happened to the bourgeois public sphere? This question deserves to be parsed: Why did the British Enlightenment defense of civil society fall out of favor? Why did the spaces of eighteenth-century public discourse lose their vitality? Herbert Spencer's story offers no satisfactory reply to the latter question. It is hard to believe that the marketplace fell silent, the literary salon went empty, and the rhetoric classroom became staid because one fussy Englishman became so enamored of the social sciences that he lost faith in the individual. Twentieth-century sociologists, critical philosophers, and historians more convincingly explore the reasons for the bourgeois public sphere's demise: the welfare state's "public" encroachment on "private" arenas, the fading belief in public persona divorced from private person, the supposition of flawed and conflicting notions of "the public," and the intrusion of commercial media that entertain and obscure.[92] Spencer's story may nonetheless partially answer the first question. The philosophical defense of civil society fell out of favor in part because this apology rests on the assumption that individuals can consciously improve themselves. Bourgeois civil society depends on each person's purposeful cultivation of bourgeois virtue. The free market and the public sphere require citizens who exercise clarity, probity, moderation, and economy. The social sciences led Herbert Spencer to question and ultimately to reject this presumption. As a result, for Spencer public discourse became a sign but not a tool of social progress; bourgeois virtue, a symptom but not a means to industrialization. Two of Spencer's followers—one in the twentieth century, another in the nineteenth—recover the tension he discovered between rhetorical pedagogy and social science.

In *The Philosophy of Composition* (1977), a text that openly expresses admiration for Spencer's psychological-rhetorical efforts, E. D. Hirsch related three aesthetic qualities—unity, coherence, and emphasis—to short-term memory. Unity, coherence, and emphasis lead to a principle of "linearity" that accounts for "readability."[93] At the end of his neo-Spencerian treatment of psychology and rhetorical style, Hirsch offered four precepts to improve style: (1) Omit needless words. (2) Keep related words together. (3) Make the paragraph the unit of composition. (4) Use integrative devices between clauses and sentences.[94] Thereafter, he outlined a program for composition pedagogy, including targeted commenting and revision. Hirsch finally confessed that his pedagogical program does not relate to his psychological principles or to his stylistic precepts. He described the difference between pedagogy and psychology as that between "a mission and a subject matter."[95] His characterization best captures the tension that eventually led Spencer both as a sociologist and as a psychologist to abandon any effort at teaching rhetorical style. The social sciences record data, identify causes, and stipulate laws. Rhetorical pedagogy teaches students, assumes agency, and improves society. When Spencer became a social scientist, he lost interest in the practical effort at teaching. In his last chapters, when Hirsch discoursed on rhetorical pedagogy, he had to forget everything he said about psychology and readability. Like Spencer, Hirsch realized that he could not wear the scientist's lab coat and the professor's tweed jacket simultaneously.

George Lewes, Spencer's friend and one of his first followers on stylistic matters, similarly focused on psychology when discussing rhetoric. In his *Principles of Success in Literature* (1865), Lewes directly borrowed Spencer's notion of style, focusing on the psychology of attention.[96] He said that "literature, in its widest sense, becomes a delicate index of social evolution."[97] Like Spencer, Lewes attributed aesthetic qualities (vision, beauty, and style) to psychological mechanisms: "All Literature is founded upon psychological laws, and involves principles which are true for all peoples and for all times."[98] So have Spencer's followers proceeded since. As explained at the start of this essay, the late twentieth-century reception of Spencer's "Philosophy of Style" has emphasized its mechanistic and psychological features. Hirsch's example demonstrates how the attention to psychology removes rhetoric from politics. Lewes's example demonstrates how the emphasis on psychology removes belletrism from gentility. In both cases, rhetorical style is divorced from civil society. At mid-century, Spencer wrote a belletristic stylistic theory with implications for public discourse, but by the century's turn, partly by his doing and partly by the way he was inherited, Spencer had bequeathed the rhetorical tradition an aesthetic preoccupation with form and a psychological preoccupation with mechanism.

Focusing on the psychological aspects of Spencer's stylistic theory erases the role of bourgeois virtue and the importance of social evolution. Spencer looks like a psychological mechanist or a Victorian aesthete, not a bourgeois ethicist. This portrayal deserves reconsideration. The new story features a young Spencer hailing rhetorical economy as the engine of progress toward a free civil society and a prosperous industrial economy. The story ends with Spencer's geriatric interests in sociology and psychology eclipsing his hope for rhetorical pedagogy. At the beginning, civil society and literary study cultivate bourgeois sympathy by teaching rhetorical economy. In the end, civil society becomes civic theater. Rhetorical economy exhibits bourgeois virtue. Rhetorical pedagogy becomes irrelevant.

Conclusions and Provocations

In the late seventeenth, mid-eighteenth, and mid-nineteenth centuries, a British philosopher, a political economist, a rhetorical theorist, and a sociologist all tried to cultivate bourgeois virtue by teaching rhetorical style, each building on others' ideas and each addressing a unique stage of capitalist development. Along the way, these men incorporated a revised notion of civic virtue into their understanding of civil society. While advancing these claims, I have left one term, "rhetorical style," undefined.

As always, Hugh Blair wrote perspicuously: "It is not easy to give a precise idea of what is meant by Style. The best definition I can give of it, is, the peculiar manner in which a man expresses his conceptions, by means of Language" (*Lectures* 99). However, cursory reading in recent scholarship reveals that defining "style" is never so simple. Richard Lanham, for instance, begins in familiar Blairean territory by defining style as the "fluff" we look through to see the content (the "stuff") we look at. Then Lanham associates style with play, invention, and attention—elements that make art beautiful and marketing profitable.[1] John Muckelbauer defines style as an "orientation or inclination" toward another person.[2] A "style of engagement" enacts an ethics, underpins a social order, allows a new (or perpetuates an old) way of getting along.[3] Adding a modifier complicates things further. Jeanne Fahnestock defines rhetorical style as language "constructed to have an impact on the attitudes, beliefs, and actions of its audiences."[4]

Unfortunately, none of these definitions captures what the British Enlightenment offered to rhetorical theory. When lecturing or writing on rhetorical style, John Locke, Adam Smith, Hugh Blair, and Herbert Spencer expressed an attitude toward language. Theirs is a discourse of style, not "an ongoing process of exchange that includes the practice of deliberation," but rather "a set of acceptable statements within a discourse community . . . [that] constitute its social practices and articulate its truths . . . [and that] distinguish it as a community and legitimate its regimes of power."[5] Locke, Smith, Blair, and Spencer wrote what Richard Ohmann called an "ideology" of style,[6] or what Kathryn Flannery called "style talk."[7] The British Enlightenment sought to elevate certain kinds of language, to impart "cultural capital, a commodity differentially legitimated, controlled and distributed among members of a given society."[8]

Flannery complains that much style talk conceals ethical suppositions in a pedagogy of efficacy. By attending to universally "clear" language, style talk masks a community's beliefs about "morality, good politics, and mental hygiene."[9] What she alleges may be true of many nineteenth- and twentieth-century writers. It is certainly true of Adams Sherman Hill. However, it is not true of Locke, Smith, Blair, or Spencer, for they explicitly stated their membership in the capitalist community, their bourgeois suppositions about language, and their commitment to civil society. Locke connected his style talk to a bourgeois ethics of clarity, if not in the third book of his *Essay concerning Human Understanding*, then in his political and economic writings. In lectures and writings on jurisprudence and economics, Adam Smith explained how rhetorical probity serves commerce. Blair pondered the commercial importance of moderate consumption in his sermons, and he praised the rhetorical use of moderate figuration in his *Lectures on Rhetoric and Belles Lettres*. The most explicit of all, Spencer bellowed about the industrial importance of rhetorical economy in both "The Philosophy of Style" and *The Principles of Sociology*. For all four men, style was economics and ethics by other means.

Locke's, Smith's, Blair's, and Spencer's writings on style were not "rhetorical" in Fahnestock's sense—they were not overtly persuasive. But they were rhetorical in two other ways. As I often tell students, rhetoric is the practice, the study, and the teaching of persuasive discourse. All four men studied persuasive discourse, and they all taught others to discourse persuasively. This theorizing and teaching happened in capitalist circumstances, so it reflected capitalist mores. This theorizing and teaching aims to improve civil society, so it promotes genteel habits. The historical conclusion premised on these essays, therefore, is that style talk is rarely mere style talk. In the seventeenth, eighteenth, and nineteenth centuries, style talk was talk of bourgeois virtue.

This historical conclusion intimates a contemporary pedagogical application. Efforts at teaching style today similarly aim at molding political subjectivity, though of a different stripe. Many contemporary rhetoric teachers infuse their style talk with a progressive politics. By teaching students to play with colorful language or to be critical of sentence-level rhetorical devices, they presume to fashion "progressive," "radical," or "democratic" subjects.

T. R. Johnson, for instance, contends that standard bromides about clarity and concision "can inspire a very real form of totalitarianism."[10] In their stead, Johnson proposes a less alienating approach to "renegade rhetoric": stylistic play with figuration and rhythm.[11] Decades before Johnson, Winston Weathers proposed a "connection between democracy and style . . . [since] the study of style is a part of our democratic and free experience."[12] Following Weathers, Tom Pace advocates a stylistically attentive pedagogy, which he describes as a "revolutionary act." According to Pace, teaching students to closely criticize syntax and figuration "could lead to critical thinking against dominant forms of communication."[13] Rebecca Moore Howard wants to advance a similarly progressive politics by teaching students to analyze stylistic choices. Howard's "contextualist pedagogy" offers style as "a tool for defining, organizing, and problematizing cultural forces."[14] Laura Micciche proposes that "rhetorical grammar" in the writing classroom can simultaneously teach students sentence-level correctness alongside "critical thinking and cultural critique."[15] Min-Zhan Lu suggests that close stylistic analysis in writing classes can help students to "struggle against the voices of academic authority," to negotiate their identities amid conflicting voices, and to consider their positions "in the context of socio-political power relationships."[16] My all-too-brief presentation occludes these arguments' sophistication. I gesture toward them as representative examples of twenty-first-century teachers pursuing progressive politics by the other means of rhetorical style.

All these teachers bemoan style's demise, and they all rejoice in its resurrection. Like Robert Connors they mourn the three-decades-long "erasure" of the sentence.[17] Like Sharon Myers they celebrate its present-day return.[18] Like their British Enlightenment predecessors, they pursue ethical and political missions through the canon of style, though to different ends. British Enlightenment stylists wanted to make free, responsible denizens of bourgeois civil society. Johnson, Weathers, Pace, Moore, and Lu aim to undercut capitalist institutions by fashioning critical, democratic citizens or by releasing renegade subjectivities. To Locke and his ilk, the new progressive stylistics would seem obscure, insincere, profligate, and prolix. If British Enlightenment thinkers would think today's progressive stylistics offensive, they would find progressively renegade and critical subjectivities alarming. Therefore, this pedagogical reflection offers an epilogue to the historical argument: the rhetorical style and bourgeois ethic of clarity, probity, moderation, and economy have been countered by the progressive rhetorical pedagogy of play and critique. Such is this book's proper conclusion. The remaining paragraphs explore provocations—notions and claims that cannot be proven but are suggested by the foregoing essays. Each provocation speaks to a reader outside my primary audience of rhetoric scholar-teachers. If I cannot conclusively prove these claims, then I can at least demonstrate that the connection between rhetorical style and bourgeois virtue informs the disciplines of English literature, history, and economics.

A Literary Provocation

Some in the nineteenth century countered bourgeois stylistics by teaching a hyper-ornamented aristocratic style. Recent scholarship on Thomas De Quincey demonstrates that the Romantic Englishman's aversion to commerce spurred him to celebrate a rhetorical style quite distinct from the clear, honest, moderate, and economical prose that the bourgeois stylists adulated. Lois Agnew contends that De Quincey's "Romantic" inclination refused any "false separation between style and substance," which he attributed in part to "an emphasis on language that supports the practical needs of business."[19] De Quincey becomes the antibourgeois rhetorician, the early nineteenth-century opponent to Lockean clarity, the Romantic psychologist who refused to divide words from things. De Quincey believed that "commercial interests and a preoccupation with science may have transformed rhetoric into a tool for merely conducting business."[20] Moreover, De Quincey may not be alone in his opposition. Richard Lanham has placed Thomas Carlyle on the antibourgeois battlements, firing playful figures and ornate syntax at the bourgeoisie's clear, honest, moderate, and economical prose.[21] Reading Carlyle's purple description of style as the "Flesh-Garment, the Body of Thought" and De Quincey's celebration of rhetorical style as a "free" play "past the reach of mechanism," one cannot miss the Romantic affection for a baroque stylistics. Both men had reservations about industrial capitalism. Carlyle described bourgeois prose as "lean, adust, wiry . . . quite pallid, hunger-bitten, and dead-looking."[22] One suspects that others felt similarly. If so, then the figuratively moderate and plain stylistics of the British Enlightenment may have been countered by the aristocratic, tropically ornamented and festooned stylistics of the British Romantics.

A Rhetorical Provocation

Rhetorical style and bourgeois virtue are associated today as they were in the British Enlightenment. Needless to say, our economic circumstances do not resemble seventeenth-century England's financial revolution, eighteenth-century Britain's commercial revolution, or nineteenth-century England's industrial revolution. Furthermore, many who decry stylistic "clarity" and "honesty" make no direct connection between their approach to rhetorical style and our twenty-first-century postindustrial economy.[23] However, one champion of a new stylistics has openly and loudly insisted that the "new economy" mandates a proud stylistic versatility instead of a one-dimensional plain-style clarity. In the 2007 edition of his now-canonical *Style: An Anti-Textbook* (originally published in 1974), Richard Lanham insisted that the postindustrial effort to "improve the productivity of knowledge workers" requires "the full range of human communication; we are going to need, that is, an education in *eloquence*."[24] Later, in that same book, Lanham conceded that the knowledge economy cannot expunge the old bourgeois virtues. He also confessed to having written a textbook (*Revising Prose*, 1st ed. 1979, 5th ed. 2007) that adulates the standard bourgeois virtues of clarity and economy. (A slightly different version was published as *Revising Business Prose*, now in its 4th ed., 1999.) Lanham offered *Analyzing Prose* (2nd ed., 2003) as a counterpoint to the bourgeois emphasis on clarity and concision. Together, plain-style clarity and the analysis of literary prose cover "the whole range of prose styles."[25]

When set alongside the British Enlightenment's bourgeois rhetoric, Lanham's manuals suggest a long-standing historical association between capitalism and rhetorical style. Capitalism will always need clarity and probity, because free markets only work when all participants have perfect information. Capitalism will always demand moderation and economy, for excess is wasteful and markets are worthless if they fail to efficiently allocate resources to the most able and the most deserving producers. Capitalism will always hunger for stylistic versatility because, without innovation, free-market economies stall and stagnate. Within the discourse of the 1990s information revolution—the same discourse that inspired Lanham to hitch stylistic versatility to a postindustrial star—we can find both plain and ornamented language. The networked economy maven Kevin Kelly delighted in abundant figures, such as isocolon ("mind share . . . leads to market share"), neologism (the "fax effect"), and metaphor ("The atom is the icon of the twentieth century. The atom whirls alone. . . . The symbol for the next century is the net. The net has no center, nor orbits, no certainty. It is an in-definite web of causes").[26] In contrast, Carl Shapiro and Hal Varian, professors of business strategy and information management, opened their book *Informa-tion Rules: A Strategic Guide to the Network Economy* (1999) with a guarantee that they would not "invent any new buzzwords" or entertain needless analogies since they sought "models, not trends; concepts, not vocabulary; and analysis, not analogies."[27] Championing things over words, Shapiro and Varian echo Locke's injunction to stylistic clarity. Featuring a humble tricolon embellished by subtle alliteration, their prose exemplifies Blair's belletristic ideal.

A Historical Provocation

Rhetorical style may be fundamentally though not causally related to capitalism. I am reluctant to assert any sort of determinism when discussing humankind. Peo-ple are complex and capricious; our actions will never follow iron laws without exception. It is ultimately untenable to assert that "the windmill gives you the society with the feudal lord; the steam-mill, the society with the industrial capi-talist," just as it would be risibly absurd to declare that the microprocessor gives you the society with the eloquent entrepreneur.[28] Though the social-scientific distinction between causation and correlation may fail us, we can argue at the age-old topos of association—some things go with other things. We may never understand the mechanism tying stylistic clarity or figurative modera-tion to capitalism, but we can acknowledge the association. We can conclude that, as long as we are capitalist denizens, we will likely chatter about clarity, probity, moderation, economy, and versatility in rhetorical style. We can accept that, without changing our material circumstances—our economic "mode of production"—we may never leave the plain style or belletrism behind.

A Historiographic Provocation

Intellectual history is ethical. In this book's introduction, I defended the method of intellectual history as appropriate to the British Enlightenment. Here, I offer an ethical defense. It begins with a confession. Being a political socialist and a historical materialist, I began this study with ideological and historiographic commitments directly counter to those presented here. Putting these aside, I have followed a rhetorical principle. Scholars and teachers of rhetoric know that rhetorical invention often involves argument from all sides. In the Greek tradition, this was known as the *dissoi logoi* (contrasting words); in the Roman tradition, *argumentum in utramque partem* (argument against each side). Often presented as an exercise to help students come up with things to say (and to anticipate objections), the ancient Greeks and Romans also suggested an ethical purpose. Arguing all sides makes the rhetor more virtuous by making her more astutely aware of other perspectives and more considerate of other people's wisdom. While I am committed to the principle, I prefer another Latin locution: *audite et alteram partem*, which means "listen even to the other side." I favor this expression for a couple of reasons. It was commonly repeated as a principle of eighteenth-century justice, and it applies to twenty-first-century scholarship. Peter Abelard may have been the last scholar who argued both sides of every imaginable case. Today we are still obliged to listen to those with whom we disagree, not just to make our own arguments stronger but also to preserve the collegial ethos that permeates a healthy conversation.

The rhetorical-ethical principle—*audite et alteram partem*—enjoins those interested in the rhetoric of economics to set aside the critical bent that presently characterizes this scholarly effort[29]—to make us more informed and more considerate scholars, better and more tolerant people. In the end, we do not have to agree. But we should listen in good faith to the best possible arguments, as their believers would prefer—to preserve ideas, to teach ourselves, to practice rhetoric.

An Economic Provocation

Capitalism has always been self-consciously rhetorical. Contemporary "postindustrial" capitalism's celebrants and its critics love to characterize our economic era as peculiarly cooperative and communicative. At the new economy's iridescent dawn, Peter Drucker, post-capitalism's herald, declared that "the market" is "vastly superior" because "it organizes economic activity around *information*."[30] Building heavily on the work of new economy acolytes such as Drucker, the Italian autonomous Marxist Franco Berardi dubs ours an era of "semio-capitalism," while Paulo Virno has explained that the postindustrial laborer must be a skilled knowledge producer whose classical monotype is the orator.[31] Admittedly, in the early twentieth century Frederick Winslow Taylor, the intellectual father of industrial scientific management, did compare his pig-iron handler Schmidt to an "intelligent gorilla," a man best kept quiet and under strict control.[32] But Taylor also recognized the importance of communication in any industrial organization, saying, "This close, intimate, personal cooperation between the management and the men is of the essence of modern scientific or task management."[33] Industrial workers were silent, but their managers were not. As the above chapters demonstrate, early capitalism's participants—bankers, merchants, stockjobbers, shopkeepers—imagined themselves as a loquacious community. From its beginning to the present postindustrial era, capitalism has always been rhetorical, has always depended on communication, and has always required specifically discursive habits of cooperation. Instead of celebrating our own era as the distinctly discursive chapter in capitalism's development, we should consider rhetoric's role in past capitalist episodes. Moreover, we should further consider capitalism's role in rhetoric's development—for if capitalism has always been a rhetorical system, then, for centuries, rhetoric has been a capitalist practice.

Notes

Definitions and Introductions

1. Fukuyama, *Trust*, 11.
2. McCloskey, *Bourgeois Virtues*, 4.
3. Walker, *Genuine Teachers of This Art*, 99–100.
4. Hermogenes, *Hermogenes' "On the Types of Style,"* 90.
5. Quintilian, *Institutio Oratoria*, 215.
6. Sixteenth-century English intellectuals admired Hermogenes's writings on style for a variety of reasons, but most important is this: English Renaissance writers revisited Hermogenes's principal four subtypes of style—simple, sweet, subtle, and vehement—as expressions of character to win the audience's goodwill. The English collected these subtypes of style under a single excellence—the expression of a character appropriate to the circumstance, the audience, and the subject. Patterson, *Hermogenes and the Renaissance*, 57–64.
7. Agnew, "Rhetorical Style and the Formation of Character," 101–2.
8. Harvey, *Limits to Capital*, 24–35; Wright, *Classes*, 26–37.
9. Arrighi, *Long Twentieth Century*; Hardt and Negri, *Empire*; Poulantzas, *State, Power, Socialism*.
10. Foucault, "What Is Enlightenment?" 37.
11. Laslett, *World We Have Lost*, 211.
12. Whatley, *Scottish Society*, 75–82.
13. Balibar, *Politics and the Other Scene*, xiii. Balibar echoed the words of his teacher Louis Althusser who famously wrote, "In History, these instances, the superstructures, etc.—are never seen to step respectfully aside when their work is done or, when the Time comes, as his pure phenomena, to scatter before His Majesty the Economy as he strides along the royal road of the Dialectic. From the first moment to the last, the lonely hour of the 'last instance' never comes." Althusser, *For Marx*, 113.
14. Habermas, *Structural Transformation of the Public Sphere*, xvii.
15. Marx, *Poverty of Philosophy*, 113–14.
16. Muller, *Mind and the Market*, 154.
17. Hegel, *Elements of the Philosophy of Right*, 220.
18. Pocock, *Machiavellian Moment*, 466.
19. Hauser, *Vernacular Voices*, 21. Italics removed.
20. Havelock, *Preface to Plato*, 199.
21. Jaeger, *Archaic Greece*, 292–94.
22. Ong, *Orality and Literacy*, 42–43.
23. Skinner, *Foundations of Modern Political Thought*.
24. Sennett, *Fall of Public Man*, 4.
25. Lanham, *Style*, 26.
26. Kingwell, *Civil Tongue*, 218–19.
27. Ibid., 216–17.
28. Pocock, *Virtue, Commerce, and History*, 238.

29. Thomas Miller has complained that the "civic concerns of moral philosophy and rhetoric were redefined by a belletristic tendency to treat ethics and aesthetics as matters of personal sentiment or taste." *Formation of College English,* 9. According to Sharon Crowley, civil society's literary salons harbor a clandestine "bourgeois aesthetic desire" that will "manufacture carefully mediated responses to aesthetic experiences" without overtly acknowledging the "direct political or religious effects upon those whose taste is properly cultivated." *Composition in the University,* 44. Robert Connors contended that nineteenth-century belletristic rhetoric manuals made stylistic virtues into meaninglessly diffuse "static abstractions." The proper study of style, thereafter, became rule-bound and tendentious. *Composition-Rhetoric,* 265–79.

30. Hill, *Principles of Rhetoric and Their Application,* 64.

31. Ibid., 88–89.

32. Levine et al., *Cluetrain Manifesto,* xxiii.

33. Postrel, *Substance of Style,* 164–91.

34. Berardi, *Soul at Work,* 21.

35. Dean, *Publicity's Secret,* 4.

Chapter 1

1. This common experience of "unclear" discourse has prompted contemporary philosophers to explain the ancient pedigree and our present-day preoccupations. Jürgen Habermas has argued that, among other things, listeners engage and speakers promise semantic content realized in "constatives," speech acts that deliver propositional content and promote a validity claim of "truth." *Communication and the Evolution of Society,* 58. James Crosswhite extends Habermans's argument by saying that the existence of constatives in language indicates an ethical obligation to speak clearly. *Rhetoric of Reason,* 58–59.

2. Aristotle, *On Rhetoric,* 221.

3. Rorty, *Philosophy and the Mirror of Nature,* 139–48.

4. Woodruff, *First Democracy,* 81–107.

5. Woolhouse, *Locke,* 18.

6. Several synthetic accounts of Locke's writings on various subjects precede mine: Laslett, "Introduction"; Wood, *Politics of Locke's Philosophy*; Ashcraft, *Locke's "Two Treatises of Government"*; Schmidgen, "Politics and Philosophy of Mixture."

7. Aarsleff, "Leibniz on Locke on Language," 57.

8. Shapin and Shaffer, *Leviathan and the Air-Pump,* 51–52.

9. Bacon, *Advancement of Learning,* 26.

10. Altgoer, *Reckoning Words,* 23.

11. Sprat, *History of the Royal Society,* 40.

12. Wilkins, *Essay towards a Real Character and a Philosophical Language,* 20.

13. According to Robert Markley, Royal Society "physico-theologians" (such as Robert Boyle, John Wilkins, and Isaac Newton) imagined a "rupture between God's 'ineffable' word and the fallen languages of humankind." Through natural science these men sought to bridge that gap by finding God in nature. *Fallen Languages,* 6.

14. Howell, *Eighteenth-Century British Logic and Rhetoric,* 264–98; Conley, *Rhetoric in the European Tradition,* 191–92; Walmsley, *Locke's "Essay" and the Rhetoric of Science,* 13–15.

15. Lewis, *Language, Mind, and Nature,* 223.

16. Ibid., 224.

17. Vickers, "Royal Society and English Prose Style."

18. Stark, *Rhetoric, Science, and Magic in Seventeenth-Century England*, 53.

19. Ashcraft, *Revolutionary Politics and Locke's "Two Treatises of Government."*

20. Locke, *Draft A of Locke's "Essay,"* 42–43.

21. Locke, *Draft B of Locke's "Essay,"* 196–98.

22. Quoted in Vickers, "Royal Society and English Prose," 53.

23. Sprat, *History of the Royal Society*, 361.

24. Ashcraft, *Revolutionary Politics and Locke's "Two Treatises of Government,"* 90–91, 106.

25. Locke, *Draft A of Locke's "Essay,"* 114.

26. Thompson, *Models of Value*, 55–64.

27. Lewis, *Language, Mind, and Nature*, 11.

28. Heckscher, *Mercantilism*, 1:45–78.

29. Ibid., 1:270–301.

30. Carruthers, *City of Capital*, 27–91; Anderson, *Lineages of the Absolutist State*, 135–42.

31. Wood, *John Locke and Agrarian Capitalism*, 20–30.

32. Ashcraft, *Revolutionary Politics and Locke's "Two Treatises of Government,"* 228–29.

33. Ibid., 373–74.

34. Holmes, "John Locke's Rhetoric," 43.

35. According to C. B. Macpherson's summary of Locke, "free, equal, rational men in the state of nature" consented "to put a value on money." Civil society introduced a second level of consent to enforce property rights and commercial contracts. *Political Theory of Possessive Individualism*, 210–11. James Tully has argued to the contrary, saying that, according to Locke, money's invention signaled the end of the state of nature and the beginning of civil society. See Tully's *Discourse on Property*. What I call the "peri-social" quality of consent has troubled numerous critics because, as Richard Ashcraft pointed out, Locke believed that community preceded political society. Though he disagreed with Macpherson on many points regarding Locke's works, Ashcraft agreed that, according to Locke, in the state of nature, prior to forming political societies, people formed communities and consented to principles. Ashcraft said Locke identified a community "existing in the state of nature, despite the fact that individuals have consented to be members of a community." *Locke's "Two Treatises of Government,"* 344. When forming this community, people consented to a range of things, including a monetary equivalent and a common language.

36. Vaughn, *John Locke*, 34–35.

37. Ashcraft, *Locke's "Two Treatises of Government,"* 233–35.

38. Horsefield, *British Monetary Experiments*, 26–28.

39. Feavearyear, *Pound Sterling*, 139–40.

40. Mary Poovey's notion of a "crisis of representation" speaks to Locke's anxiety about the public faith in coins: "A system of representation [such as money] is experienced *as* problematic only when it ceases to work—that is, when something in the social context calls attention to the deferral or obfuscation of its authenticating ground." *Genres of the Credit Economy*, 6.

41. Gould, *Great Debasement*, 9–18.

42. Woolhouse, *Locke*, 333.

43. Feavearyear, *Pound Sterling*, 107–8.

44. Horsefield, *British Monetary Experiments*, 227.

45. Vogt, *John Locke and the Rhetoric of Modernity*, 44–47.

46. Locke, *Draft A of Locke's "Essay,"* 88.

47. Ibid., 34; *WJL* 2:35–36.

48. Carey, *Locke Shaftesbury, and Hutcheson*, 15–33.

49. Ashcraft, *Locke's "Two Treatises of Government,"* 40–44.

50. Ibid., 370.

51. Ashcraft defines Locke's work as "an articulate expression of the meaning of . . . [Restoration radicals'] actions and goals." *Revolutionary Politics and Locke's "Two Treatises of Government,"* xi.

52. Richard Hooker described a "law which hath been the pattern to make, and is the card to guide the world by: that law which hath been of God." *Of the Laws of Ecclesiastical Polity,* 57. Hooker furthermore contended that only the divine intellect could understand natural law; "*human law*" is derived from our imperfect intimations of natural law, as "the laws of well-doing are the dictates of right reason." Ibid., 72.

53. Hirschman, *Passions and the Interests,* 53–54.

54. According to Hobbes: (1) The "inconstancy of . . . [words'] signification" can "register for their [people's] conceptions that which they never conceived" (compare to Locke's abuses 1 and 2). (2) People can use words "metaphorically, that is, in other sense than that they are ordained for" (compare to Locke's abuses 3 and 7). (3) People falsely declare their will. (4) People use words to "grieve one another" (compare to Locke's complaints about sophists and wranglers). *Leviathan,* 17.

55. Petit, *Made with Words,* 98–100.

56. According to Hobbes, language binds people into contracts and common purposes, fashioning "speech from true principles." On the other hand, Hobbes worried that "eloquence [can be used] . . . to subvert the commonwealth." *On the Citizen,* 139–40. Hobbes directly attributed the English Revolution to university "schoolmen" who taught rhetoric and preachers who undermined "the force of true reason by verbal forks." *Behemoth,* 41.

57. Skinner, *Reason and Rhetoric in the Philosophy of Thomas Hobbes,* 250–93.

58. Hobbes, *On the Citizen,* 132.

59. Hobbes, *Leviathan,* 106–7. Brian Garsten explains that the sovereign of the *Leviathan* possesses judgment external to the people: "Instead of teaching citizens how to address one another as if each had a faculty of judgment within, Hobbes taught them to avoid such appeals and accept judgment from without." *Saving Persuasion,* 53.

60. When John Edwards accused Locke of borrowing from Hobbes's *Leviathan,* Locke insisted that he "did not know those words . . . [Edwards] quoted out of the Leviathan, were there, or any thing like them" (*WJL* 6:420).

61. Locke, *Essays on the Laws of Nature,* 181, 185.

62. Cranston, *John Locke,* 205–29.

63. Ralph Cudworth's *Treatise concerning Eternal and Immutable Morality* (1731) was not published until after Locke's death, but the Cambridge Platonist's great work circulated in manuscript during the last decades of the seventeenth century. (Cudworth died in 1688.) Many in Locke's intellectual circle knew the work; Locke befriended Ralph Cudworth's daughter, Damaris Cudworth (in 1681), with whom he maintained a lasting relationship and correspondence. Woolhouse, *Locke,* 174–75.

64. According to Cudworth, Hobbes's monarch would "affirm Justice and Injustice to be only by Law and not by Nature." *Treatise concerning Eternal and Immutable Morality,* 9.

65. Unlike Hobbes, Cudworth did not place the validity of positive law or its correlation to natural law on the sovereign's prerogative to maintain order. Positive law can command by nothing "otherwise than by Virtue of that which is *Naturally* just." Ibid., 26.

66. For a fuller explanation of how Locke believed reason could lead to knowledge of natural law, see Ashcraft, *Locke's "Two Treatises of Government,"* 73–74.

67. Atiyah, *Rise and Fall of the Freedom of Contract,* 36–37.

68. Pufendorf, *On the Duty of Man and Citizen,* 29.

69. Ibid., 97–104.

70. Grotius, *Rights of War and Peace,* 733–34.

71. Ibid., 751–64.

72. Carruthers, *City of Capital*, 123–25.

73. North and Weingast, "Constitutions and Commitment."

74. Carruthers, *City of Capital*, 128–31.

75. Grotius, *Rights of War and Peace*, 737.

76. Hooker, *Of the Laws of Ecclesiastical Polity*, 96–97.

77. Stillingfleet, *Bishop of Worcester's Answer to Mr. Locke's Second Letter*, 23.

78. Dawson, *Locke, Language and Early-Modern Philosophy*, 151–53.

79. Ibid., 210.

80. Stillingfleet, *Bishop of Worcester's Answer to Mr. Locke's Letter*, 121.

81. Stillingfleet, *Bishop of Worcester's Answer to Mr. Locke's Second Letter*, 24–25.

82. According to Aristotle, "In education practice must be used before theory, and the body be trained before the mind." *"The Politics" and "The Constitution of Athens,"* 198.

83. Ibid., 195.

84. Dierks, *In My Power*, 52–99.

85. Defoe, *Complete English Tradesman*, 1:11.

86. Ibid., 1:11, 13, 19.

87. Franklin, *Autobiography of Benjamin Franklin*, 61–64.

88. Miller, *Evolution of College English*, 61–63, 78–80.

89. Weber, *Protestant Ethic and the Spirit of Capitalism*, 48–51.

Chapter 2

1. Some scholars claim that Smith upheld what Deirdre McCloskey calls "the common claim . . . that virtues support the market." *Bourgeois Virtues*, 4. Alternatively, to put this in lay terms, Smith believed that capitalism requires virtues other than prudence. Without such virtuous people, capitalist society will be unpleasant. Skinner, *System of Social Science*, 64–65. Furthermore, without such virtuous people, capitalist society may become corrupt. Hanley, *Adam Smith and the Character of Virtue*, 52.

2. For more on probity as a component of bourgeois prudence, see ibid., 113; and McCloskey, *Bourgeois Virtues*, 295.

3. Lionel Trilling described sincerity as the performed "congruence between avowal and actual feeling," somehow central to "the state . . . of self which we call sincerity" and to the Enlightenment's "moral life." *Sincerity and Authenticity*, 2. Jürgen Habermas described sincerity as the "expressive speech acts, such as disclosing, concealing, [and] revealing," which form the basis of interpersonal trust by establishing the "truthfulness" of any discourse. *Communication and the Evolution of Society*, 58. Finally Michel Foucault described sincerity (what he called *parrhēsia*) as "the veridiction which speaks polemically about individuals and situations," one of the "four modes of truth-telling" in the Western philosophical tradition. *Courage of Truth*, 27–29.

4. Later editions expand the theory of moral judgment into a disquisition on the character of virtue. Raphael, *Impartial Spectator*, 10–11.

5. Warnick, *Sixth Canon*, 58–62.

6. Cassirer, *Philosophy of the Enlightenment*, 93–133; Gay, *Enlightenment: The Science of Freedom*, 174–86.

7. Bevilacqua, "Adam Smith and Some Philosophical Origins of Eighteenth-Century Rhetorical Theory."

8. Shaftesbury insisted that the "Pleasures of Sympathy" form the basis for morality, by making it "the *private* Interest and Good of every-one, to work towards the *general* Good." *Characteristicks of Men, Manners, Opinion, Times*, 2:62, 100. According to Hutcheson, our

attraction to good behavior begins with a "moral sense." Hutcheson explained the role of sympathy in moral judgment: "Upon this moral Sense is founded the Power of the Orator. The various Figures of Speech, are the several Manners which a lively Genius, warm'd with Passions suitable to the Occasion, naturally runs into, only a little diversify'd by Custom: and they only move the Hearers, by giving a lively Representation of the Passions of the Speaker; which are communicated to the Hearers." *Inquiry*, 171.

9. Hume opined that "no quality of human nature is more remarkable, both in itself and in its consequences, than that propensity we have to sympathize with others, and to receive by communication their inclinations and sentiments, however different from, or even contrary to our own." *Treatise of Human Nature*, 316.

10. Kames, *Elements of Criticism*, 1:17.

11. Butler, *Works of Joseph Butler*, 2:69.

12. Rivers, *Shaftesbury to Hume*, 157–73.

13. Habermas, *Structural Transformation of the Public* Sphere, 82. Following the Enlightenment's example, Habermas famously promoted an "ideal speech situation" based on revised bourgeois norms of rationality (what he called "communicative rationality"). According to Habermas, the bourgeois ideal of rational-critical debate, if revised, "on the strength of its formal properties, allows consensus only through *generalizable* interests." *Legitimation Crisis*, 110. In response to Habermas's optimistic view of liberal-rational civil society, numerous critics have alleged that this "rational-critical" public sphere excludes voices and imposes the dominant class's favored political order. Warner, *Publics and Counterpublics*, 51; Mouffe, *Democratic Paradox*, 49.

14. Cudworth, *Treatise concerning Eternal and Immutable Morality*, 145.

15. Sprat, *History of the Royal Society*, 111.

16. Sheridan, *Course of Lectures on Elocution*, vii.

17. Ibid., viii.

18. Ibid., 126.

19. Burke, *Philosophical Enquiry into the Sublime and Beautiful*, 195.

20. Himmelfarb, *Roads to Modernity*, 25–52; Israel, *Democratic Enlightenment*, 4.

21. David Hartley attributed the notion of "Word *Association*" to Locke. *Observations on Man*, 65. He further proposed that "*Words and phrases must excite Ideas in us by Association*" (268), claiming that "Words are absolutely necessary to the Art of Reasoning" (330). According to David Hume, the imagination connects ideas bearing relations of "Resemblance, Contiguity in time or place, and Cause and Effect." *Treatise of Human Nature*, 11.

22. According to Kames, "The relations by which things are linked together, have a great influence in directing the train of thought." *Elements of Criticism*, 1:21.

23. Stephen McKenna has argued that Smith inherited much more from Aristotle's theory of propriety than scholars often allow. *Adam Smith*, 44. Attention to notions such as decorum and propriety indicates Smith's classical inheritance, but Smith set such classical ideas on distinctly "psychological foundations," thus distinguishing his work as modern. Vivenza, *Adam Smith and the Classics*, 182.

24. Agnew, *Outward, Visible Propriety*, 24.

25. Ibid., 36.

26. Ibid., 83.

27. Gay, *Enlightenment: The Rise of Modern Paganism*, 31–71.

28. Shaftesbury, *Characteristicks of Men, Manners, Opinion, Times*, 1:56.

29. Reid's stoically inflected commonsense philosophy rescued ideas that skeptics like René Descartes had called into question (*Inquiry and Essays*, 109–13), including the belief in "an original power of mind" complete with "notions of right and wrong in conduct" and a

conviction that people have the ability to "perceive certain things to be right, and others to be wrong" (320). These brief quotes recall the classical phrase *sensus recti et honesti* as well as the Stoic conclusion that "understanding becomes fully realized only when common sense is seen as an ethical endeavor." Agnew, *Outward, Visible Propriety*, 57.

30. Smith, "Considerations concerning the First Formation of Languages," 223.

31. Ibid., 222.

32. Hume, *Essays, Moral, Political, and Literary*, 98.

33. Ibid., 103.

34. Shaftesbury, *Characteristicks of Men, Manners, Opinion, Times,*, 2:118. Shaftesbury often affected a disingenuous style in order to reveal his radical skepticism to a sympathetic audience while also shielding himself from charges of heresy. Rivers, *Shaftesbury to Hume*, 37–41, 107–13.

35. Other intellectual historians note Smith's belief in prudence as the chief bourgeois virtue and Smith's commitment to honesty as a facet of prudence. See Turpin, *Moral Rhetoric of Political Economy*, 38. Hanley, *Adam Smith and the Character of Virtue*, 121–23.

36. Ross, "Adam Smith and Education," 175–76.

37. Hume replaced God's laws with psychological imperatives, saying, "What necessarily arises from the exertion of . . . [the] intellectual faculties, may justly be esteemed natural." "The sentiment of justice" depends on "passions and reflections." Laws of property, according to Hume, demonstrate how "positive laws are often framed" to settle particular disputes. The result, said Hume, is a historically particular judicial system, suited to its era, whose study is "different from all the sciences . . . [because] in many of its nicer questions, there cannot properly be said to be truth or falsehood on either side." *Enquiry concerning the Principles of Morals*, 96–97. Smith's discussion of property laws (as explored in this chapter) demonstrates that he adhered to Hume's psychological-empirical approach to jurisprudence. In other areas as well, Smith showed a psychological-empirical approach that distinguishes him from the rationalism of Enlightenment natural-law theory. For instance, Smith deemphasized "natural liberty" while attending to social evolution. Minowitz, *Profits, Priests, and Princes*, 35–39.

38. Frances Hutcheson had inaugurated a more empirical approach to jurisprudence in the early eighteenth century. Whyte, *Scotland before the Industrial Revolution*, 313–14. Henry Home, Lord Kames, believed that law is rooted in moral sense, but it is historically developed. People create law when they add a "peculiar modification of duty" to a sense of "approbation or disapprobation." *Essays on the Principles of Morality and Natural Religion*, 36. Hutcheson's and Kames's psychological and empirical approaches contrast with the European natural-law tradition, which proceeded rationally from principles. Cassirer, *Philosophy of the Enlightenment*, 243. Kames's historical approach led him to trace changes in the law alongside the progress of civilization. *Sketches of the History of Man*, 57–63. Like other Scottish sociologists, Kames narrated the parallel development of morals and modes of economic production. Carey, *Locke, Shaftesbury, and Hutcheson*, 194–99.

39. Kames, *Sketches of the History of Man*, 57.

40. Ashcraft, *Revolutionary Politics and Locke's "Two Treatises of Government,"* 218–19.

41. Whatley, *Industrial Revolution in Scotland*, 64–65.

42. Smout, *History of the Scottish People*, 343–50.

43. Atiyah, *Rise and Fall of the Freedom of Contract*, 194, 205.

44. Ibid., 420–21.

45. Ibid., 455.

46. Ibid., 428. Atiyah comments that "to Adam Smith, it was the obligation not to disappoint dependence or expectations which was the source of promissory obligation" (83).

47. Brewer, "Commercialization and Politics," 210.

48. Addison, "*Spectator* No. 3," 189.

49. Ibid., 191.

50. The laws enforcing debt obligations were so draconian that creditors regularly refused to seek the full punishment afforded by the English courts. Atiyah, *Rise and Fall of the Freedom of Contract*, 100–101.

51. Ibid., 420–24.

52. Paul Turpin contends that Smith used a "language of praise and blame . . . to evaluate characters, and [to make arguments about] how that evaluation says something about the social order which these characters inhabit." *Moral Rhetoric of Political Economy*, 20; see also David Charles Gore's analysis of Smith's portrayal of merchants as nefarious sophists whose arguments deserve condemnation, "Sophists and Sophistry in the *Wealth of Nations*."

53. The Bank of Scotland was chartered in 1695, the Royal Bank in 1727, and other banks followed thereafter. Smith imagined the growing financial sector as a national boon (*WN* 297–98).

54. Brewer, "Commercialization and Politics," 212.

55. Steele, "*Spectator* No. 218," 221.

56. Straddling utilitarianism and virtue ethics, Smith troubles recent philosophical efforts at severing the two traditions. Alasdair MacIntyre, for instance, presents utilitarianism as one of many Enlightenment efforts to ground morality in teleology. See *After Virtue*, 62–63. In contrast, virtue ethicists emphasize "dispositions not only to act in particular ways, but also to feel in particular ways . . . to act from inclination formed by the cultivation of virtues" (149).

57. Aristotle, *Nicomachean Ethics*, 29. To understand Smith's debt to Aristotle, see Hanley, *Adam Smith and the Character of Virtue*, 87; and McKenna, *Adam Smith*, 44. In contrast, Alasdair MacIntyre presented Smith as an early-Enlightenment Stoic with no ethical use for passions: "On Smith's view knowledge of what the rules are, whether the rules of justice or of prudence or of benevolence, is not sufficient to enable us to follow them; to do so we need another virtue of a very different kind, the Stoic virtue of self-command, which enables us to control our passions when they distract us from what virtue requires." *After Virtue*, 235.

58. Hume argued that "the rules of equity or justice depend entirely on the particular state and condition, in which men are placed, and owe their origin and existence to that UTILITY, which results to the public from their strict and regular observance." *Enquiry concerning the Principles of Morals*, 23. Smith countered by explaining that individual behaviors derive from our judgment of individual motivation and circumstance, our sympathy with the "resentment even of an odious person" despite our "disapprobation of his ordinary character" (*TMS* 90). This comparison to Hume explains why Smith does not fit neatly into the utilitarian tradition where past legal and economic theorists place him. Rawls, *Theory of Justice*, 29–30, 49; Granovetter, "Economic Action and Social Structure," 484.

59. Raphael, *Impartial Spectator*, 47.

60. Hauser, *Vernacular Voices*, 21–23.

61. Rothschild, *Economic Sentiments*, 98.

62. Smout, *History of the Scottish People*, 420–37. Whyte, *Scotland before the Industrial Revolution*, 242–46.

63. Mitchell, "Beings That Have Existence Only in ye Minds of Men."

64. J. Michael Hogan has contended that Smith "assigned to historical writing the function of helping to establish and to certify the general principles of morality in human conduct." "Historiography and Ethics in Adam Smith's Lectures on Rhetoric," 87.

65. Ibid., 90.

66. Gross, *Secret History of Emotion*, 169–78.

67. Booth, *Company We Keep*.

68. Kidd and Castano, "Reading Literary Fiction Improves Theory of Mind."

69. Nussbaum, *Upheavals of Thought*, 361–62; Krause, *Civil Passions*, 86.

70. Thomas Miller has argued that "Smith gave less attention to producing rhetorical effects than to critiquing how such effects reveal the psychological workings of sympathetic sentiments, and he treated language not as a set of purposefully used conventions but as a transparent medium for presenting natural sentiments." *Formation of College English*, 192. Miller elaborates: "In the 'practical system of morality,' that Smith added to his last revisions of the *Theory of Moral Sentiments,* 'prudence' became the virtue of self-restraint divorced from the civic conception of practical wisdom, *phronesis* or *prudentia*" (180).

71. Court, *Institutionalizing English Literature*, 28; Miller, *Formation of College English*, 193.

72. Seligman, *Idea of Civil Society*, 33.

73. Griswold, *Adam Smith and the Virtues of Enlightenment*, 215.

74. Rosenblatt, *Rousseau and Geneva*, 52–58.

75. Ibid., 60.

Chapter 3

1. Muller, *Mind and the Market*, 4–15.

2. Fukuyama attributed this insight to Adam Smith: "As Adam Smith well understood, economic life is deeply embedded in social life, and it cannot be understood apart from the customs, morals, and habits of the society in which it occurs. In short, it cannot be divorced from culture." *Trust*, 13.

3. Montesquieu, *Spirit of the Laws*, 338.

4. Schmitz, *Hugh Blair*, 62.

5. According to John Hill, Blair's colleague and friend at Edinburgh, "It was the moral tendency of such writings, then, not the love of the amusement which they are fitted to bestow, that attracted the attention of Dr. Blair." *Account of the Life and Writings of Hugh Blair*, 203.

6. Walzer, *On Toleration*, 10.

7. Addison, "*Spectator* No. 69," 204.

8. McKendrick, "Commercialization of Fashion."

9. Petty, "Political Arithmethick," 261.

10. Quoted in Gay, *Enlightenment: The Science of Freedom*, 24.

11. Marshall, *John Locke, Toleration and Early Enlightenment Culture*, 599. Christian apologists often noted the association between commerce and toleration but questioned the virtue's merit. Jonas Proast said that Locke's proposal for toleration in England may advance "Trade and Commerce" but would not help "Christian Religion." *Argument of the Letter concerning Toleration*, 2.

12. Blair, "Letter 151," 188.

13. Blair's liberal effort to promote toleration runs into a typical difficulty. While suggesting that his students value multiple goods, he did not want to extend tolerance to morally vacuous or offensive material. In the twentieth century, the liberal rhetorical theorist Wayne Booth encountered the same difficulty while promoting a variety of literary works for the ethical stances that they endorse. Like Blair, Booth wanted to tolerate and appreciate "a plurality of goods." *Company We Keep*, 115. Nevertheless, he could not include some forms of ironic literature or open-ended literary interpretation in his variegated literary pantheon, for he found them ethically questionable. Ibid., 60–70. See also *Rhetoric of Irony*, 240–50.

14. Addison, "*Spectator* No. 69," 204.

15. Shaftesbury, *Characteristicks of Men, Manners, Opinions, Times*, 1:42.

16. Ibid., 1:81.

17. Ibid., 1:84. In our (post)modern era, we hear similar defenses of literary education (and criticism). Richard Rorty, for instance, once defended "literary criticism" because such study can provide the ethical "glue holding together the ideal liberal society . . . [which] consists in little more than a consensus that the point of social organization is to let everybody have a chance at self-creation to the best of her abilities." According to Rorty, "that goal requires, besides peace and wealth, the standard 'bourgeois freedoms.'" *Contingency, Irony, and Solidarity*, 84.

18. Hume, *Essays, Moral, Political, and Literary*, 274.

19. Ibid., 273.

20. Thomas Miller has argued that Blair told students "that civil society had become too polite to tolerate the heated oratory of ancient political rhetoric." *Formation of College English*, 235. Gerard Hauser explains the connection between the polite rhetoric that Blair taught and the toleration that bourgeois civil society required: "New conditions of social congress accompanying expanded commerce, trade, and urban growth led to an ideal of encountering diversity through tolerance and to the idea of civil society as the network of associations emerging from interactions with the other." *Vernacular Voices*, 23.

21. Estimates about the Scottish industrial revolution's beginning vary. The earliest estimates begin mid-century yet allow nothing more than a "small" and "struggling" industrial sector in late eighteenth-century Scotland. Whatley, *Industrial Revolution in Scotland*, 17; Laslett, *World We have Lost*, 165. In England, various data point to mid-century technological innovations and methods of industrial organization in a variety of industries, including brewing, food production, glass manufacture, and especially textiles. Though industrialization appears to have gained momentum from the 1730s onward, rapid acceleration in the century's last three decades may have resulted from one key technology—steam power. Bruland, "Industrialisation and Technological Change."

22. McKendrick, "Josiah Wedgwood and the Commercialization of the Potteries."

23. McKendrick, "Commercialization of Fashion," 67–77, and "George Packwood and the Commercialization of Shaving."

24. Laslett, *World We Have Lost*, 166.

25. See T. C. Smout, "Where Had the Scottish Economy Got to by the Third Quarter of the Eighteenth Century?"

26. Schmitz, *Hugh Blair*, 84.

27. Keen, *Literature, Commerce, and the Spectacle of Modernity*, 10.

28. Ibid., 29.

29. Hill, *Account of the Life and Writings of Hugh Blair*, 163.

30. See Berg and Eger, "Rise and Fall of the Luxury Debates."

31. Mandeville, *Fable of the Bees*, 23. Italics removed.

32. E. J. Hundert has argued that Mandeville's moral argument—much more than his economic contentions—rattled eighteenth-century British intellectuals. *Enlightenment's Fable*, 182–85.

33. Mandeville, *Fable of the Bees*, 37.

34. Ibid., 41.

35. Ibid., 105.

36. Ibid., 125.

37. Barbon, *Discourse of Trade*, 62.

38. Ibid., 65.

39. Ibid., 63.

40. Steuart, *Inquiry into Principles of Political Oeconomy*, 1:268. Italics removed.

41. Ibid., 1:280–81.

42. Trusler, *Way to Be Rich and Respectable*, 5–8.

43. Ibid., 5.

44. Dennis, *Vice and Luxury Publick Mischiefs*, ix.

45. Ibid., 39.

46. Ibid., 23.

47. Pocock, *Machiavellian Moment*, 406–22.

48. Kramnick, *Bolingbroke and His Circle*, 17–30.

49. Fielding, *Enquiry into the Causes of the Late Increase of Robbers*, 77. John Sekora has argued that the aristocrat's anxieties permeated English writing on luxury from the late seventeenth through the late eighteenth centuries, though this preoccupation became especially pronounced circa 1730–60. *Luxury*, 97–98.

50. Kames, *Sketches of the History of Man*, 332.

51. Ferguson, *Essay on the History of Civil Society*, 241.

52. Hume, *Essays, Moral, Political, and Literary*, 269.

53. Ibid., 279.

54. Ibid., 272.

55. Ibid., 280.

56. Kames, *Sketches of the History of Man*, 332.

57. Eli Heckscher has argued that removing restrictions on commercial traffic spurred production and allowed people to abandon the fear of scarcity that characterized medieval society. According to Heckscher, mercantilist economists soon adopted "an amoral, if not immoral, demand for stimulation of native luxury production at any price." *Mercantilism*, 2:110. Joyce Appleby contends that seventeenth-century economists defended consumerism and eventually won the argument against mercantilists who promoted trade restrictions by stoking moral anxieties about corruption and political worries about a destabilized class structure. See "Ideology and Theory."

58. Richard Sher argues that Blair's work fit a larger pattern among Scottish intellectuals who were trying to claim moral authority against Jacobin upstarts from the highlands by flouting their own possession of cultural capital. In Blair's case, this effort at political domination resulted in a centripetal construction of good rhetoric and a claim that only men of "taste"—men such as himself, able to practice tasteful delivery and composition—should be allowed political or cultural authority. See Sher's *Church and University in the Scottish Enlightenment*.

59. See, for instance, Blair's sermon "On the Influence of Religion upon Prosperity" (*Sermons* 1:41–60). See also his "Sermon on the Power of Conscience" (*Sermons* 1:264–88).

60. Blair's commitment to the stadial theory of history can best be seen in *A Critical Dissertation on the Poems of Ossian* (1765), where he explicitly differentiated among the four stages of social development that Smith discussed in his lectures on jurisprudence: hunting, pasturage, agriculture, and commerce (29). The culture and the politics of each age reflect the era and its economic base: "In the progress of society, the genius and manners of society undergo a change more favorable to accuracy than to sprightliness and sublimity" (5). Moreover, ancient languages reflect ancient people's developed imaginations and their diminished understandings, a ratio of mental faculties that inverts as humankind enters later stages, such as the agricultural and the commercial eras. For this reason, the language of antiquity is more figurative and the language of modernity more sedate, though clearer (31–32).

61. Sprat, *History of the Royal Society*, 111.

62. Pocock, *Machiavellian Moment*, 76–80.

63. Hume often returned to the topic of "good-breeding." He attributed a public value to certain privately developed virtues. For two representative moments when Hume reflected on good breeding, see *Treatise of Human Nature*, 597, and *Essays, Moral, Political, and Literary*,

132. In effect, Hume used the civic tradition to craft a cultural solution to a commercial problem. This effort has been characterized by one recent theorist as an inchoate liberal theory "at the limits of the civic tradition." Robertson, "Scottish Enlightenment at the Limits of the Civic Tradition," 177.

64. For a fuller treatment of the civic republican influence on Blair's notion of taste, see Agnew, "Civic Function of Taste."

65. Kames, *Elements of Criticism*, 1:3.

66. Ibid., 1:4.

67. Ibid., 2:726.

68. Hume, *Essays, Moral, Political, and Literary*, 3–8.

69. Ibid., 194. Italics removed.

70. Ibid., 196.

71. Blair, "Letter 151," 188.

72. Ibid.

73. Ferreira-Buckley and Halloran, "Introduction," xxiii–xxiv.

74. Hariman, *Political Style*, 102.

75. Ibid., 106.

76. Conley, *Rhetoric in the European Tradition*, 220.

77. Ferreira-Buckley and Halloran, "Introduction," xviii–xix.

78. Conley, *Rhetoric in the European Tradition*, 223. Echoing Conley, other historians present Blair as a gifted synthesizer who aptly wedded classical tradition to Enlightenment belletrism while privileging literary analysis and stylistic polish over topical invention. George Kennedy, for instance, praised Blair as one of the most influential Scottish Enlightenment rhetorical theorists, but Kennedy also lamented that "though his title was professor of 'rhetoric and belles lettres' and the title of his published lectures follows that order, 'belles lettres and rhetoric' would be a better description." *Classical Rhetoric and Its Christian and Secular Tradition*, 235. The most generous version of this narrative appears in Arthur Walzer's "Blair's Ideal Orator." According to Walzer, Blair preserved much of the classical tradition while introducing belletristic notions of politeness.

79. Thomas Miller has discussed the centripetal tendencies in Blair's rhetorical theory. *Formation of College English*, 234–35. According to Miller, while advocating a rhetorical standard through lectures on criticism and taste, Blair was also "advancing liberal tolerance" (245). Franklin Court has argued that Blair's lectures were entirely centripetal, establishing an authority about "good" discourse and insisting that students toe that line in their critical efforts. *Institutionalizing English Literature*, 31–38.

80. Carr, "Circulation of Blair's *Lectures*."

81. Ibid., 83.

82. Sher, *Enlightenment and the Book*, 246–47.

83. Carr, "Circulation of Blair's *Lectures*," 86–87.

84. Blair, *Essays on Rhetorick*, 46. In the *Abridgment*, this passage appears as follows: "One would imagine that men must have been previously gathered together in considerable numbers before language could be fixed and extended; and yet on the other hand there seems to have been an absolute necessity of speech previous to the formation of society." *Abridgment of "Lectures on Rhetorick*," 43.

85. Blair, *Lectures on Rhetoric and Belles Lettres: Chiefly from the Lectures of Dr. Blair*, 45–46.

86. Ibid., 51.

87. Blair, *Essays on Rhetorick*, xi–xii. This passage is reproduced nearly verbatim in the *Abridgment of "Lectures on Rhetorick*," 8.

88. Blair, *Lectures on Rhetoric and Belles Lettres: Chiefly from the Lectures of Dr. Blair*, 10–11.

89. Blair, *Essays on Rhetorick*, 108. In the *Abridgment of "Lectures on Rhetorick*," the passage is overwhelmingly similar: "Beware of using such allusions as raise in the mind disagreeable, mean, low, or dirty ideas" (102–3). Abraham Mills followed suit in his *Lectures on Rhetoric and Belles Lettres*: "Care must be taken not to use allusions as raise in the mind disagreeable, mean, or low ideas" (120).

90. Blair, *Essays on Rhetorick*, 134. This paragraph is nearly identical in the *Abridgment of "Lectures on Rhetorick*," 127–28, and in Abraham Mills's *Lectures on Rhetoric and Belles Lettres*, 150.

91. Blair, *Essays on Rhetorick*, 142–53.

92. Carr, "Circulation of Blair's Lectures," 86.

93. Horner, "Traditions and Professionalization"; Gold, *Rhetoric at the Margins*, 14–62; Enoch, *Refiguring Rhetorical Education*, 30–72.

94. Blair, *Essays in Rhetoric*, 14. In the original lectures, Blair said, "In the powers and pleasures of Taste, there is a more remarkable inequality among men, than is usually found, in point of common sense, reason, and judgment." Nevertheless, he insisted that "Taste is a most improveable faculty" (*Lectures* 11).

95. Witherspoon, *Ecclesiastical Characteristics*, 15. Italics removed.

96. Ibid., 15–25.

97. Witherspoon, *Lectures on Moral Philosophy and Eloquence*, 212, 229–33.

98. Ibid., 291.

99. Witherspoon's religious preoccupations, his association of civic and Christian virtue, and his refusal to define taste in anything but aesthetic terms has led Thomas Miller to characterize his rhetorical theory as civic and to label Blair a belletrist concerned primarily with the aesthetics of polite style. See "Witherspoon, Blair, and the Rhetoric of Civic Humanism."

Chapter 4

1. McCloskey, *Bourgeois Dignity*, 86–92.

2. Marx and Engels, *Communist Manifesto*, 38.

3. According to Engels, after the industrial revolution English weavers and farmers were proletarian "machines pure and simple." Despite this immiseration, they were neither illiterate nor "intellectually . . . dead," and they no longer "inherited slowness" or "inefficient methods of cultivation." *Conditions of the Working Class in England*, 52–53.

4. Engels said English industrialism was corroding "a righteous and peaceful life in all piety and probity." Ibid., 51. Karl Marx lamented, "Everything the political economist takes from you in terms of life and humanity, he restores to you in the form of *money* and *wealth*." "Economic and Philosophical Manuscripts," 361.

5. Spencer, "Philosophy of Style," 436.

6. Ibid.

7. Ibid., 437.

8. Ibid., 455.

9. In his later writings on psychology, Spencer would criticize the faculty psychology that he learned from phrenology. He still believed in a few separated mental functions, such as memory, reason, and the feelings, but he said even these develop from the same mental operations of association, reflex, and instinct found in all living creatures. *Principles of Psychology*, 527–83. See also Denton, "Early Psychological Theories of Herbert Spencer." In the early 1850s, Spencer admitted that supposing such faculties was "indefensible" psychological

science. But he found the supposition of mental faculties useful when considering rhetorical style. "Philosophy of Style," 455. The latter paragraphs of Spencer's "Philosophy of Style" exhibit a heavy psychological character. It is likely that these were added in the early 1850s as Spencer prepared to write his 1855 textbook on psychology. See Denton, "Herbert Spencer and the Rhetoricians" and "Origin and Development of Herbert Spencer's Principle of Economy."

10. Spencer, "Philosophy of Style," 457.

11. Ibid., 437–38.

12. Ibid., 440.

13. Ibid., 441.

14. Ibid., 446.

15. Ibid., 453.

16. Secor, "Legacy of Nineteenth-Century Style Theory," 81; Conley, *Rhetoric in the European Tradition*, 250–51.

17. Duncan, *Life and Letters of Herbert Spencer*, 31.

18. Alfred Chandler notes that during the first railway boom in the United States, in the 1840s, report-writing became especially important to maintaining and coordinating large and dispersed activities. *Visible Hand*, 100–104.

19. Yates, *Control through Communication*, 97–98.

20. Hirst, "Herbert Spencer's Philosophy of Style," 286.

21. Offer, *Herbert Spencer and Social Theory*, 153–55.

22. Thomas Spencer's blend of Christian morality and liberal politics reflected the Malthusian reliance on Christian principles, such as a faith that the divine order would eventually prevail by reducing population to match resource production. According to Malthus, pursuit of self-love may lead to misery in the short run, but such pursuit will eventually produce prosperity. Waterman, *Revolution, Economics, and Religion*, 34–35.

23. Many early railway proponents were Dissenters. Quakers, especially, had a notable presence on the board of management at the Birmingham line. Clapham, *Economic History of Modern Britain*, 386.

24. One of Spencer's first publications (in January 1836) parroted his uncle Thomas. Duncan, *Life and Letters of Herbert Spencer*, 19–21.

25. Taylor, *Philosophy of Herbert Spencer*, 38–39.

26. Irvine, *Apes, Angels, and Victorians*, 174–76.

27. Spencer, *Social Statics*, 419.

28. Ibid., 84–85.

29. Ibid., 274–95.

30. Ibid., 121–23, 155–71.

31. Ibid., 425–56.

32. Duncan, *Life and Letters of Herbert Spencer*, 41.

33. Though Spencer himself was no longer a practicing Christian, his work was well received by many who kept the faith, including the American evangelical preacher Henry Ward Beecher. See Beecher, "Mr. Beecher's Remarks"; see also Francis, *Herbert Spencer and the Invention of Modern Life*, 158–67; and Hofstadter, *Social Darwinism in American Thought*, 37–38.

34. Spencer, "Proper Sphere of Government," 184–85.

35. Ibid., 187.

36. Spencer, *Social Statics*, 65, 66.

37. Ibid., 78, 81, 345, 70, 239, 243.

38. Ibid., 68, 262, 266–67.

39. Turpin, *Moral Rhetoric of Political Economy*, 23.

40. Spencer, "Proper Sphere of Government," 199.

41. Spencer, *Social Statics*, 312.

42. Ibid., 321.

43. Despite his ostensible debt to Smith's moral philosophy, Spencer's treatment of sympathy more closely resembles the simplified definition offered by George Campbell, a similarity that implies Campbell's additional influence on Spencer's moral psychology. Campbell defined sympathy as "that quality of soul which renders it susceptible of almost any passion, by communication from the bosom of another." *Philosophy of Rhetoric*, 131.

44. Spencer, *Social Statics*, 97.

45. Ibid., 321.

46. Ibid., 324.

47. Ibid., 187.

48. Seligman, *Idea of Civil Society*, 60.

49. Spencer tried to distance himself from the anarchists, particularly from Pierre-Joseph Proudhon, who argued in 1840 that the best way to establish justice was to abolish property. *What Is Property?* 32–33. Spencer, in contrast, insisted on a "*right* of private property" consistent with justice. *Social Statics*, 133. Alongside the Victorian's faith in society, Spencer maintained the mid-century anarchist's opposition to government. Mark Francis explains that in "the late 1840s and early 1850s, Spencer habitually spoke of 'Society' as good, and of government as evil or bad. He was in favor of 'Society' interfering with the individual, but not of government doing so." "Herbert Spencer and the Myth of Laissez-Faire," 326.

50. Spencer, *Social Statics*, 411.

51. Ibid., 420, 422.

52. Ibid., 428.

53. Ibid., 185.

54. Ibid., 442.

55. Ibid., 418–19.

56. Ibid., 352.

57. Francis, *Herbert Spencer and the Invention of Modern Life*, 223.

58. Spencer, *Social Statics*, 459.

59. Ibid., 474.

60. Michael Taylor says that Spencer's "main political message was . . . about the efficacy of self-improvement rather than collective action in bringing about the promised future state." *Philosophy of Herbert Spencer*, 150.

61. Aune, *Rhetoric and Marxism*, 9–14.

62. Blair's theory of linguistic progress derived from Adam Smith's 1761 essay on the subject, "Considerations concerning the First Formation of Languages." Blair noted Smith's essay, among others, as influences in the published edition of his *Lectures* (62n1).

63. Spencer, "Philosophy of Style," 452.

64. Ibid., 458.

65. Ibid., 436, 458.

66. Ibid., 458, 459, 452, 453.

67. Ibid., 458, 445, 446.

68. Spencer, *Essays*, v.

69. The differences between the following sentences is typical of Spencer's efforts to increase stylistic economy between the 1852 and the 1858 versions of "The Philosophy of Style": "But whether the force of these replies be, or be not admitted, it will scarcely be denied that the right formation of a picture will be facilitated by presenting its elements in the order in

which they are wanted; and that, as in forming the image answering to—a red flower, the notion of redness is one of the components that must be used in the construction of the image, the mind, if put in possession of this notion before the specific image to be formed out of it is suggested, will more easily form it than if the order be reversed; even though it should do nothing until it has received both symbols." "The Philosophy of Style" (1852), 441. "But whether the force of these replies be or be not admitted, it will scarcely be denied that the right formation of a picture will be facilitated by presenting its elements in the order in which they are wanted; even though the mind should do nothing until it has received them all." Spencer, *Essays* (1858), 236.

70. In the 1858 version, for instance, Spencer qualified the claim that the shorter word is always more economical by explaining that the "polysyllabic word" may be preferable, especially when one seeks to convey an "emotional idea," due to the "emotional superiority of certain long words." *Essays* (1858), 232. He also qualified his discussion of the indirect and direct styles by saying that sometimes an "intermediate structure" is best, a style neither wholly direct nor wholly indirect. Ibid., 243.

71. To the 1858 version, for instance, Spencer added the following sentence to exemplify economic predication: "Were the honour now given to wealth and title given exclusively to high achievements and intrinsic worth, how immense would be the stimulus to progress!" *Essays*, 238.

72. Carlyle, *Sartor Resartus*, 14.

73. Countering nineteenth-century charges of Lamarckianism, Spencer insisted that he followed Erasmus Darwin's theory of speciation. According to Spencer, Lamarck had assumed "some indwelling tendency to develop supernaturally impressed on living matter at the outset," and this assumption of a progressive "aptitude" within an organism smacked of theology, making it "unphilosophical" (*WHS* 2:492). Spencer's charges against Lamarck are apt—Lamarck did begin his *Zoological Philosophy* by declaring his belief in a "Supreme Author of all things," and he furthermore asserted that "nature appears to carry out direct or spontaneous generations, which are incessantly renewed whenever conditions are favourable," implying a supernatural agency and guidance for mutation. *Zoological Philosophy*, 36, 103. Having shed his deistic presuppositions, the later Spencer declared that there existed "no persistent formative power inherent in organisms, and making them unfold into higher types" (*WHS* 2:492).

74. Darwin, *Origin of Species*, 120.

75. Huxley, "Evolution and Ethics" and "Science and Morals," 81.

76. Gould, *Mismeasure of Man*, 146; Hofstadter, *Social Darwinism in American Thought*, 31–51.

77. Spencer's discussion of the social types and the virtues peculiar to each echoes Adam Smith's belief that ancient societies promoted martial virtues (e.g., heroism, self-control), while commercial societies promote prudence (*TMS* 306–7). By making a distinction between ancient warlike virtues and modern sentimental virtues, Spencer followed Smith, but he also differed in an important regard. Smith worried about the loss of the ancient virtues: "Another bad effect of commerce is that it sinks the courage of mankind, and tends to extinguish martial spirit" (*LJ* 540). Spencer celebrated the waning "martial spirit" in industrial societies.

78. See also Taylor, *Philosophy of Herbert Spencer*, 65.

79. For a closer review of the non-teleological view that Spencer adopted regarding social evolution in his later years, see Offer, *Herbert Spencer and Social Theory*, 155–56.

80. Searle, *Morality and the Market in Victorian Britain*, 22–24.

81. Clapham, *Economic History of Modern Britain*, 381–424.

82. Collini, *Public Moralists*, 67–74. Collini claims that the "obvious historical comparison" to the Victorian attention to altruism is "the eighteenth century," particularly "English and Scottish moral philosophy since the time of Hobbes and certainly since Mandeville" (66–67). If Collini is right, then Spencer and many of his contemporaries extended the British Enlightenment's moral philosophy.

83. Mill, *Essays on Ethics, Religion, and Society*, 231.

84. Youmans, "Report of Mr. Spencer's Interview," 14.

85. Ibid., 18.

86. Ibid., 14.

87. Spencer, "Mr. Spencer's Address," 33–34.

88. Crowley, *Composition in the University*, 37.

89. Spencer, *Principles of Psychology*, 616.

90. Ibid., 617.

91. Darwin, *Origin of Species*, 445.

92. Habermas, *Structural Transformation of the Public Sphere*; Sennett, *Fall of Public Man*; Dean, *Publicity's Secret*; McChesney, *Problem of the Media*.

93. Hirsch, *Philosophy of Composition*, 74–82, 128–37. According to Hirsch, Spencer's essay "has never been superseded" (76).

94. Ibid., 154–55.

95. Ibid., 170.

96. Lewes, *Principles of Success in Literature*, 128–33.

97. Ibid., 19.

98. Ibid., 22.

Conclusions and Provocations

1. See Lanham's essay "Style/Substance Matrix."

2. Muckelbauer, *Future of Invention*, 42.

3. Ibid., 41–48.

4. Fahnestock, *Rhetorical Style*, 4.

5. Gerard Hauser draws this distinction between the "rhetorical" and the "ideological" definitions of "discourse." *Prisoners of Conscience*, 30–31. Though he writes about a completely different subject, his definitions apply to my argument.

6. See Ohmann's essay "Use Definite, Specific, Concrete Language."

7. Flannery, *Emperor's New Clothes*, 7.

8. Ibid., 3.

9. Ibid., 22.

10. Johnson, *Rhetoric of Pleasure*, 9.

11. Ibid., 25.

12. Weathers, "Teaching Style," 144.

13. Pace, "Style and the Renaissance of Composition Studies," 15.

14. Howard, "Contextualist Stylistics," 55.

15. Micciche, "Making a Case for Rhetorical Grammar," 717–18.

16. Lu, "Professing Multiculturalism," 448.

17. Connors, "Erasure of the Sentence."

18. Myers, "ReMembering the Sentence."

19. Agnew, *Thomas De Quincey*, 48.

20. Ibid., 63.

21. Lanham, *Style*, 64.

22. Carlyle, *Sartor Resartus*, 57; De Quincey, *Selected Essays on Rhetoric*, 193.

23. See, for instance, Butler, *Out of Style*; and Holcomb and Killingsworth, *Performing Prose*.

24. Lanham, *Style*, 67.

25. Ibid., 188–89.

26. Kelly, *New Rules for the New Economy*, 39, 9, 59.

27. Shapiro and Varian, *Information Rules*, 18.

28. Marx, *Poverty of Philosophy*, 119.

29. For an example of the "critical" nature of scholarship on the rhetoric of economics, see Joshua Hanan and Mark Hayward's edited collection *Communication and the Economy*.

30. Drucker, *Post-Capitalist Society*, 181.

31. Berardi, *Uprising*; Virno, *Grammar of the Multitude*, 55–56.

32. Taylor, *Principles of Scientific Management*, 40.

33. Ibid., 26.

Bibliography

Aarsleff, Hans. "Leibniz on Locke on Language." In *From Locke to Saussure: Essays on the Study of Language and Intellectual History*, edited by Hans Aarsleff, 42–83. Minneapolis: University of Minnesota Press, 1982.

Addison, Joseph. "*The Spectator* No. 3, Saturday, March 3, 1711." In *The Commerce of Everyday Life: Selections from "The Tatler" and "The Spectator*," edited by Erin Mackie, 188–91. New York: Bedford/St. Martin's, 1998.

———. "*The Spectator* No. 69, Saturday, May 19, 1711." In *The Commerce of Everyday Life: Selections from "The Tatler" and "The Spectator*," edited by Erin Mackie, 203–6. New York: Bedford/St. Martin's, 1998.

Agnew, Lois. "The Civic Function of Taste: A Re-assessment of Hugh Blair's Rhetorical Theory." *Rhetoric Society Quarterly* 28, no. 2 (1998): 25–36.

———. *Outward, Visible Propriety: Stoic Philosophy and Eighteenth-Century British Rhetorics*. Columbia: University of South Carolina Press, 2008.

———. "Rhetorical Style and the Formation of Character: Ciceronian Ethos in Thomas Wilson's *Arte of Rhetorique*." *Rhetoric Review* 17, no. 1 (1998): 93–106.

———. *Thomas De Quincey: British Rhetoric's Romantic Turn*. Carbondale: Southern Illinois University Press, 2012.

Altgoer, Diana. *Reckoning Words: Baconian Science and the Construction of Truth in English Renaissance Culture*. London: Associated University Press, 2000.

Althusser, Louis. *For Marx*. Translated by Ben Brewster. New York: Verso, 1996.

Anderson, Perry. *Lineages of the Absolutist State*. New York: Verso, 1979.

Appleby, Joyce. "Ideology and Theory: The Tension between Political and Economic Liberalism in Seventeenth-Century England." *American Historical Review* 81, no. 3 (1976): 499–515.

Aristotle. *The Nicomachean Ethics*. Translated and introduced by David Ross, revised by J. L. Ackrill and J. O. Urmson. Oxford, UK: Oxford University Press, 1980.

———. *On Rhetoric: A Theory of Civic Discourse*. Translated and introduced by George A. Kennedy. New York: Oxford University Press, 1991.

———. "*The Politics*" and "*The Constitution of Athens*." Edited by Stephen Everson. Cambridge, UK: Cambridge University Press, 1996.

Arrighi, Giovanni. *The Long Twentieth Century: Money, Power, and the Origins of Our Times*. New York: Verso, 2010.

Ashcraft, Richard. *Locke's "Two Treatises of Government*." New York: Routledge, 2010.

———. *Revolutionary Politics and Locke's "Two Treatises of Government*." Princeton, NJ: Princeton University Press, 1986.

Atiyah, P. S. *The Rise and Fall of the Freedom of Contract*. Oxford, UK: Clarendon Press, 1979.

Aune, James Arnt. *Rhetoric and Marxism*. Boulder, CO: Westview Press, 1994.

Bacon, Francis. *The Advancement of Learning*. Edited by Stephen Jay Gould. New York: Modern Library, 2001.

Balibar, Étienne. *Politics and the Other Scene*. Translated by Christine Jones, James Swenson, and Chris Turner. New York: Verso, 2002.

Barbon, Nicholas. *A Discourse of Trade*. London: Tho. Milbourn, 1690.

Beecher, Henry Ward. "Mr. Beecher's Remarks." In *Herbert Spencer on the Americans and the Americans on Herbert Spencer*, edited by Edward Youmans, 58–66. New York: D. Appleton and Company, 1882.

Berardi, Franco. *The Soul at Work: From Alienation to Autonomy*. Translated by Francesca Cadel and Giuseppina Mecchia, preface by Jason Smith. Los Angeles: Semiotext(e), 2009.

———. *The Uprising: On Poetry and Finance*. Los Angeles: Semiotext(e), 2012.

Berg, Maxine, and Elizabeth Eger. "The Rise and Fall of the Luxury Debates." In *Luxury in the Eighteenth Century: Debates, Desires, and Delectable Goods*, edited by Maxine Berg and Elizabeth Eger, 7–27. New York: Palgrave, 2003.

Bevilacqua, Vincent. "Adam Smith and Some Philosophical Origins of Eighteenth-Century Rhetorical Theory." *Modern Language Review* 63, no. 3 (1968): 559–68.

Blair, Hugh, D.D. *An Abridgment of "Lectures on Rhetorick."* Exeter, UK: Charles Norris, 1809.

———. *A Critical Dissertation on the Poems of Ossian, the Son of Fingal*. 3rd ed. Dublin: Peter Wilson, 1765.

———. *Essays on Rhetorick: Abridged Chiefly from Dr. Blair's Lectures on that Science. A New Edition with Additions and Improvements*. Albany, NY: Barber & Southwick, 1798.

———. *Lectures on Rhetoric and Belles Lettres: Chiefly from the Lectures of Dr. Blair*. Edited by Abraham Mills. New York: Roe Lockwood, 1842.

———. "Letter 151. From Hugh Blair, 3 Apr. 1776." In *The Correspondence of Adam Smith*, edited by Ernest Campbell Mossner and Ian Simpson Ross, 187–90. Indianapolis, IN: Liberty Fund Press, 1987.

Booth, Wayne. *The Company We Keep: An Ethics of Fiction*. Berkeley: University of California Press, 1988.

———. *A Rhetoric of Irony*. Chicago: University of Chicago Press, 1974.

Brewer, John. "Commercialization and Politics." In *The Birth of a Consumer Society: The Commercialization of Eighteenth-Century England*, by Neil McKendrick, John Brewer, and J. H Plumb, 197–262. London: Europa, 1982.

Bruland, Kristine. "Industrialisation and Technological Change." In *Industrialisation, 1700–1860*, vol. 1 of *The Cambridge Economic History of Modern Britain*, edited by Roderick Floud and Paul Johnson, 117–46. Cambridge, UK: Cambridge University Press, 2004.

Burke, Edmund. *"A Philosophical Enquiry into the Sublime and Beautiful," and Other Pre-Revolutionary Writings*. Edited by David Womersley. New York: Penguin, 1998.

Butler, Joseph. *The Works of Joseph Butler*. 2 vols. Edited by W. E. Gladstone. Oxford, UK: Clarendon Press, 1896.

Butler, Paul. *Out of Style: Reanimating Stylistic Study in Composition and Rhetoric*. Logan: Utah State University Press, 2008.

Campbell, George. *The Philosophy of Rhetoric*. Edited and introduced by Lloyd Bitzer. Carbondale: Southern Illinois University Press, 1963.

Carey, Daniel. *Locke, Shaftesbury, and Hutcheson: Contesting Diversity in the Enlightenment and Beyond*. Cambridge, UK: Cambridge University Press, 2006.

Carlyle, Thomas. *Sartor Resartus*. Edited and introduced by Kerry McSweeney and Peter Sabor. Oxford, UK: Oxford University Press, 2008.

Carr, Stephen. "The Circulation of Blair's *Lectures*." *Rhetoric Society Quarterly* 32, no. 4 (2002): 75–104.

Carruthers, Bruce G. *City of Capital: Politics and Markets in the English Financial Revolution*. Princeton, NJ: Princeton University Press, 1996.

Cassirer, Ernst. *The Philosophy of the Enlightenment*. Translated by Fritz C. A. Koelln and James P. Pettegrove, foreword by Peter Gay. Princeton, NJ: Princeton University Press, 2009.

Chandler, Alfred. *The Visible Hand: The Managerial Revolution in American Business*. Cambridge, MA: Harvard University Press, 1977.

Clapham, J. H. *An Economic History of Modern Britain: The Early Railway Age, 1820–1850*. Cambridge, UK: Cambridge University Press, 1964.

Collini, Stefan. *Public Moralists: Political Thought and Intellectual Life in Britain, 1850–1930*. Oxford, UK: Clarendon Press, 1991.

Conley, Thomas. *Rhetoric in the European Tradition*. Chicago: University of Chicago Press, 1990.

Connors, Robert. *Composition-Rhetoric: Backgrounds, Theory, and Pedagogy*. Pittsburgh, PA: Pittsburgh University Press, 1997.

———. "The Erasure of the Sentence." *College Composition and Communication* 52, no. 1 (2000): 96–128.

Court, Franklin. *Institutionalizing English Literature: The Culture and Politics of Literary Study, 1750–1900*. Stanford, CA: Stanford University Press. 1992.

Cranston, Maurice. *John Locke: A Biography*. London: Longmans, 1957.

Crosswhite, James. *The Rhetoric of Reason: Writing and the Attractions of Argument*. Madison: University of Wisconsin Press, 1996.

Crowley, Sharon. *Composition in the University: Historical and Polemical Essays*. Pittsburgh, PA: University of Pittsburgh Press, 1998.

Cudworth, Ralph. *A Treatise concerning Eternal and Immutable Morality*. Preface by Edward Chandler, Lord Bishop of Durham. London: James and John Knapton, 1731.

Darwin, Charles. *The Origin of Species, 1876*. Edited by Paul H. Barrett and R. B. Freeman. New York: New York University Press, 1988.

Dawson, Hannah. *Locke, Language and Early-Modern Philosophy*. Cambridge, UK: Cambridge University Press, 2007.

Dean, Jodie. *Publicity's Secret: How Technoculture Capitalizes on Democracy*. Ithaca, NY: Cornell University Press, 2002.

Defoe, Daniel. *The Complete English Tradesman in Two Volumes*. 2 vols. Oxford, UK: A. Talboys, 1841.

Dennis, John. *Vice and Luxury Publick Mischiefs; or, Remarks on a Book Intitled "The Fable of the Bees, or Private Vices Publick Benefits."* London: W. Mears, 1724.

Denton, George Bion. "Early Psychological Theories of Herbert Spencer." *American Journal of Psychology* 32 (1921): 5–15.

———. "Herbert Spencer and the Rhetoricians." *PMLA* 34, no. 1 (1919): 89–111.

———. "Origin and Development of Herbert Spencer's Principle of Economy." In *The Fred Newton Scott Papers*, edited by Clarence DeWitt Thorpe and Charles E. Whitmore, 55–92. Chicago: University of Chicago Press, 1929.

De Quincey, Thomas. *Selected Essays on Rhetoric*. Edited and introduced by Frederick Burwick, foreword by David Potter. Carbondale: University of Southern Illinois Press, 1967.

Dierks, Konstantin. *In My Power: Letter Writing and Communication in Early America*. Philadelphia: University of Pennsylvania Press, 2009.

Drucker, Peter. *Post-Capitalist Society*. New York: Harper Business, 1993.

Duncan, David. *The Life and Letters of Herbert Spencer*. London: Methuen, 1908.

Engels, Friedrich. *The Conditions of the Working Class in England*. Edited by Victor Kiernan. New York: Penguin, 1987.

Enoch, Jessica. *Refiguring Rhetorical Education: Women Teaching African American, Native American, and Chicano/a Students, 1865–1911*. Carbondale: Southern Illinois University Press, 2008.

Fahnestock, Jeanne. *Rhetorical Style: The Uses of Language in Persuasion*. New York: Oxford University Press, 2011.

Feavearyear, Sir Albert. *The Pound Sterling: A History of English Money*. 2nd ed. Revised by E. Victor Morgan. Oxford, UK: Clarendon Press, 1963.

Ferguson, Adam. *An Essay on the History of Civil Society*. Edited by Fania Oz-Salzberger. Cambridge, UK: Cambridge University Press, 1995.

Ferreira-Buckley, Linda, and S. Michael Halloran. "Introduction." In *Hugh Blair's Lectures on Rhetoric and Belles Lettres*, edited and introduced by Linda Ferreira-Buckley and S. Michael Halloran, xv–liv. Carbondale: Southern Illinois University Press, 2005.

Fielding, Henry. *An Enquiry into the Causes of the Late Increase of Robbers and Related Writings*. Edited by Malvin R. Zirker. Middletown, CT: Wesleyan University Press, 1988.

Flannery, Kathryn. *The Emperor's New Clothes: Literature, Literacy, and the Ideology of Style*. Pittsburgh, PA: University of Pittsburgh Press, 1995.

Foucault, Michel. *The Courage of Truth: The Government of the Self and Others II; Lectures at the Collège de France, 1983–1984*. Edited by Frédéric Fros, translated by Graham Burchell. New York: Palgrave Macmillan, 2011.

———. "What Is Enlightenment?" In *The Foucault Reader*, edited by Paul Rabinow, 32–50. New York: Pantheon Books, 1984.

Francis, Mark. *Herbert Spencer and the Invention of Modern Life*. Stocksfield, UK: Acumen, 2007.

———. "Herbert Spencer and the Myth of Laissez-Faire." *Journal of the History of Ideas* 39, no. 2 (1978): 317–28.

Franklin, Benjamin. *The Autobiography of Benjamin Franklin*. Edited by Leonard W. Labaree, Ralph L. Ketcham, Helen C. Boatfield, and Helene H. Fineman. New Haven, CT: Yale University Press, 1964.

Fukuyama, Francis. *Trust: The Social Virtues and the Creation of Prosperity*. New York: Free Press, 1995.

Garsten, Bryan. *Saving Persuasion: A Defense of Rhetoric and Judgment*. Cambridge, MA: Harvard University Press, 2006.

Gay, Peter. *The Enlightenment: The Rise of Modern Paganism*. New York: W. W. Norton, 1977.

———. *The Enlightenment: The Science of Freedom*. New York: W. W. Norton, 1969.

Gold, David. *Rhetoric at the Margins: Revising the History of Writing Instruction in American Colleges, 1873–1947*. Carbondale: Southern Illinois University Press, 2008.

Gore, David Charles. "Sophists and Sophistry in the *Wealth of Nations*." *Philosophy and Rhetoric* 44, no. 1 (2011): 1–26.

Gould, J. D. *The Great Debasement: Currency and the Economy in Mid-Tudor England*. Oxford, UK: Clarendon, 1970.

Gould, Stephen Jay. *The Mismeasure of Man*. New York: W. W. Norton, 1996.

Granovetter, Mark. "Economic Action and Social Structure: The Problem of Embeddedness." *American Journal of Sociology* 91, no. 3 (1985): 481–510.

Griswold, Charles. *Adam Smith and the Virtues of Enlightenment*. Cambridge, UK: Cambridge University Press, 1999.

Gross, Daniel. *The Secret History of Emotion: From Aristotle's "Rhetoric" to Modern Brain Science*. Chicago: University of Chicago Press, 2006.

Grotius, Hugo. *The Rights of War and Peace*. Edited and introduced by Richard Tuck. Indianapolis, IN: Liberty Fund Press, 2005.

Habermas, Jürgen. *Communication and the Evolution of Society*. Translated and introduced by Thomas McCarthy. Boston: Beacon Press, 1976.

———. *Legitimation Crisis*. Translated by Thomas McCarthy. Boston: Beacon Press, 1973.

———. *The Structural Transformation of the Public Sphere: An Inquiry into a Category of Bourgeois Society*. Translated by Thomas Burger and Frederick Lawrence. Cambridge, MA: MIT Press, 1991.

Hanan, Joshua, and Mark Hayward, eds. *Communication and the Economy: History, Value, Agency*. New York: Peter Lang, 2014.

Hanley, Ryan Patrick. *Adam Smith and the Character of Virtue*. Cambridge, UK: Cambridge University Press, 2009.

Hardt, Michael, and Antonio Negri. *Empire*. Cambridge, MA: Harvard University Press, 2000.

Hariman, Robert. *Political Style: The Artistry of Power*. Chicago: University of Chicago Press, 1995.

Hartley, David. *Observations on Man, His Frame, His Duty, and His Expectations: In Two Parts*. London: S. Richardson, 1749.

Harvey, David. *The Limits to Capital*. New York: Verso, 2006.

Hauser, Gerard A. *Prisoners of Conscience: Moral Vernaculars of Political Agency*. Columbia: University of South Carolina Press, 2012.

———. *Vernacular Voices: The Rhetoric of Publics and Public Spheres*. Columbia: University of South Carolina Press, 1999.

Havelock, Eric. *Preface to Plato*. Cambridge, MA: Harvard University Press, 1963.

Heckscher, Eli. *Mercantilism*. 2 vols. Translated by Mendel Shapiro, revised and edited by E. F. Söderlund. London: George Allen and Unwin, 1955.

Hegel, G. W. F. *Elements of the Philosophy of Right*. Edited by Allen W. Wood, translated by H. G. Nisbet. Cambridge, UK: Cambridge University Press, 1991.

Hermogenes. *Hermogenes' "On the Types of Style."* Translated by Cecil W. Wooten. Chapel Hill: University of North Carolina Press, 1987.

Hill, Adams Sherman. *The Principles of Rhetoric and Their Application*. New York: Harper and Brothers, 1882.

Hill, John. *An Account of the Life and Writings of Hugh Blair, D.D.* Edinburgh: J. Ballantyne, 1807.

Himmelfarb, Gertrude. *The Roads to Modernity: The British, French, and American Enlightenments*. New York: Vintage, 2005.

Hirsch, E. D. *The Philosophy of Composition*. Chicago: University of Chicago Press, 1977.

Hirschman, A. O. *The Passions and the Interests: Political Arguments for Capitalism before Its Triumph*. Princeton, NJ: Princeton University Press, 1977.

Hirst, Russel. "Herbert Spencer's Philosophy of Style: Conserving Mental Energy." *Journal of Technical Writing and Communication* 34, no. 4 (2004): 265–90.

Hobbes, Thomas. *Behemoth; or, The Long Parliament*. Introduced by Stephen Holmes, edited by Ferdinand Tönnies. Chicago: University of Chicago Press, 1990.

———. *"Leviathan," with Selected Variants from the Latin Edition of 1668*. Edited and introduced by Edwin Curley. Indianapolis, IN: Hackett, 1994.

———. *On the Citizen*. Edited and translated by Richard Tuck and Michael Silverthorne. Cambridge, UK: Cambridge University Press, 1998.

Hofstadter, Richard. *Social Darwinism in American Thought*. Boston: Beacon Press, 1955.

Hogan, J. Michael. "Historiography and Ethics in Adam Smith's Lectures on Rhetoric, 1762–1763." *Rhetorica* 2, no. 1 (1984): 75–91.

Holcomb, Chris, and Jimmie Killingsworth. *Performing Prose: The Study and Practice of Style in Composition*. Carbondale: Southern Illinois University Press, 2010.

Holmes, Leigh H. "John Locke's Rhetoric: Response to the Nominal Quandaries of Legitimate Communities." *Philosophy and Rhetoric* 29, no. 1 (1996): 33–50.

Hooker, Richard. *Of the Laws of Ecclesiastical Polity: Preface, Book I, Book VIII*. Edited by Arthur Stephen McGrade. Cambridge, UK: Cambridge University Press, 1989.

Horner, Bruce. "Traditions and Professionalization: Reconceiving Work in Composition." *College Composition and Communication* 51, no. 3 (2000): 366–98.

Horsefield, J. Keith. *British Monetary Experiments, 1650–1710*. Cambridge, MA: Harvard University Press, 1960.

Howard, Rebecca Moore. "Contextualist Stylistics: Breaking Down the Binaries in Sentence-Level Pedagogy." In *Refiguring Prose Style: Possibilities for Writing Pedagogy*, edited by T. R. Johnson and Tom Pace, 42–56. Logan: Utah State University Press, 2005.

Howell, Wilbur Samuel. *Eighteenth-Century British Logic and Rhetoric*. Princeton, NJ: Princeton University Press, 1971.

Hume, David. *An Enquiry concerning the Principles of Morals*. Edited and introduced by J. B. Schneewind. Indianapolis, IN: Hackett, 1983.

———. *Essays, Moral, Political, and Literary*. Edited by Eugene Miller. Indianapolis, IN: Liberty Fund Press, 1987.

———. *A Treatise of Human Nature*. Edited by L. A. Selby-Bigge and P. H. Nidditch, notes by P. H. Nidditch. Oxford, UK: Clarendon Press, 1978.

Hundert, E. J. *The Enlightenment's Fable: Bernard Mandeville and the Discovery of Society*. Cambridge, UK: Cambridge University Press, 1994.

Hutcheson, Francis. *An Inquiry into the Original of Our Ideas of Beauty and Virtue in Two Treatises*. Edited and introduced by Wolfgang Leidhold. Indianapolis, IN: Liberty Fund Press, 2004.

Huxley, Thomas. *"Evolution and Ethics" and "Science and Morals."* Amherst, NY: Prometheus Books, 2004.

Irvine, William. *Apes, Angels, and Victorians: Darwin and Huxley on Evolution*. Introduced by Sir Julian Huxley. Alexandria, VA: Time Life Books, 1963.

Israel, Jonathan I. *Democratic Enlightenment: Philosophy, Revolution, and Human Rights, 1750–1790*. New York: Oxford University Press, 2011.

Jaeger, Werner. *Archaic Greece: The Mind of Athens*. Vol. 1 of *Paideia: The Ideals of Greek Culture*. Translated by Gilbert Highet. Oxford, UK: Oxford University Press, 1945.

Johnson, T. R. *A Rhetoric of Pleasure: Prose Style and Today's Composition Classroom*. Portsmouth, NH: Heinemann, 2003.

Kames, Lord [Home, Henry]. *Elements of Criticism*. 2 vols. Edited and introduced by Peter Jones. Indianapolis, IN: Liberty Fund Press, 2005.

———. *Essays on the Principles of Morality and Natural Religion*. Edited and introduced by Mary Catherine Moran. Indianapolis, IN: Liberty Fund Press, 2005.

———. *Sketches of the History of Man, Book I*. Edited and introduced by James A. Harris. Indianapolis, IN: Liberty Fund Press, 2007.

Keen, Paul. *Literature, Commerce, and the Spectacle of Modernity, 1750–1800*. Cambridge, UK: Cambridge University Press, 2012.

Kelly, Kevin. *New Rules for the New Economy: 10 Radical Strategies for a Connected World*. New York: Penguin, 1998.

Kennedy, George. *Classical Rhetoric and Its Christian and Secular Tradition: From Ancient to Modern Times*. Chapel Hill: University of North Carolina Press, 1980.

Kidd, David Comer, and Emanuele Castano. "Reading Literary Fiction Improves Theory of Mind." *Science* 342 (October 2013): 377–80.

Kingwell, Mark. *A Civil Tongue: Justice, Dialogue, and the Politics of Pluralism*. University Park: Pennsylvania State University Press, 1995.

Kramnick, Isaac. *Bolingbroke and His Circle: The Politics of Nostalgia in the Age of Walpole.* Cambridge, MA: Harvard University Press, 1968.

Krause, Sharon. *Civil Passions: Moral Sentiment and Democratic Deliberation.* Princeton, NJ: Princeton University Press, 2008.

Lamarck, Jean Baptiste. *Zoological Philosophy: An Exposition with Regard to the Natural History of Animals.* Translated by Hugh Eliot, introduced by David Hull and Richard Burkhardt. Chicago: University of Chicago Press, 1984.

Lanham, Richard. *Style: An Anti-Textbook.* 2nd ed. Philadelphia: Paul Dry, 2007.

———. "Style/Substance Matrix." In *The Economics of Attention: Style and Substance in the Age of Information,* 157–90. Chicago: University of Chicago Press, 2006.

Laslett, Peter. "Introduction." In *John Locke: "Two Treatises of Government,"* edited and introduced by Peter Laslett, 3–137. Cambridge, UK: Cambridge University Press, 1988.

———. *The World We Have Lost.* London: Methuen, 1971.

Levine, Rick, Christopher Locke, Doc Searls, and David Weinberger. *The Cluetrain Manifesto: The End of Business as Usual.* Cambridge, MA: Perseus, 2000.

Lewes, Georg. *The Principles of Success in Literature.* Edited and introduced by Fred Newton Scott. Boston: Allyn and Bacon, 1891.

Lewis, Rhodri. *Language, Mind, and Nature: Artificial Languages in England from Bacon to Locke.* Cambridge, UK: Cambridge University Press, 2007.

Locke, John. *Draft A of Locke's "Essay concerning Human Understanding."* Edited and introduced by Peter Nidditch. London: University of Sheffield, 1980.

———. *Draft B of Locke's "Essay concerning Human Understanding."* Edited and introduced by Peter Nidditch. London: University of Sheffield, 1982.

———. *Essays on the Law of Nature.* Edited by W. von Leyden. Oxford, UK: Clarendon Press, 1954.

Lu, Min-Zhan. "Professing Multiculturalism: The Politics of Style in the Contact Zone." *College Composition and Communication* 45, no. 4 (1994): 442–58.

MacIntyre, Alasdair. *After Virtue: A Study in Moral Theory.* Notre Dame, IN: University of Notre Dame Press, 1984.

Macpherson, C. B. *The Political Theory of Possessive Individualism: Hobbes to Locke.* Oxford, UK: Oxford University Press, 1962.

Mandeville, Bernard. *The Fable of the Bees; or, Private Vices, Publick Benefits.* 2nd ed. London: Edmund Parker, 1723.

Markley, Robert. *Fallen Languages: Crises of Representation in Newtonian England, 1660–1740.* Ithaca, NY: Cornell University Press, 1993.

Marshall, John. *John Locke, Toleration and Early Enlightenment Culture: Religious Intolerance and Arguments for Religious Toleration in Early Modern and "Early Enlightenment" Europe.* Cambridge, UK: Cambridge University Press, 2006.

Marx, Karl. "Economic and Philosophical Manuscripts." In *Early Writings,* introduced by Lucio Colletti, translated by Rodney Livingstone and Gregor Benton, 279–400. New York: Penguin, 1975.

———. *The Poverty of Philosophy.* Introduced by Friedrich Engels, translated by H. Quelch. New York: Prometheus Books, 1995.

Marx, Karl, and Frederick Engels. *The Communist Manifesto.* Introduced by Eric Hobsbawm. New York: Verso, 1998.

McChesney, Robert. *The Problem of the Media: U.S. Communication Politics in the 21st Century.* New York: Monthly Review Press, 2004.

McCloskey, Deirdre. *Bourgeois Dignity: Why Economics Can't Explain the Modern World.* Chicago: University of Chicago Press, 2010.

———. *The Bourgeois Virtues: Ethics for an Age of Commerce*. Chicago: University of Chicago Press, 2006.

McKendrick, Neil. "The Commercialization of Fashion." In *The Birth of a Consumer Society: The Commercialization of Eighteenth-Century England*, 34–99. London: Europa, 1982.

———. "George Packwood and the Commercialization of Shaving: The Art of Eighteenth-Century Advertising." In *The Birth of a Consumer Society: The Commercialization of Eighteenth-Century England*, 146–94. London: Europa, 1982.

———. "Josiah Wedgwood and the Commercialization of the Potteries." In *The Birth of a Consumer Society: The Commercialization of Eighteenth-Century England*, 100–145. London: Europa, 1982.

McKenna, Stephen. *Adam Smith: The Rhetoric of Propriety*. Albany: State University of New York Press, 2006.

Micciche, Laura. "Making a Case for Rhetorical Grammar." *College Composition and Communication* 55, no. 4 (2004): 716–37.

Mill, John Stuart. *Essays on Ethics, Religion, and Society*. Edited by D. P. Dryer. Indianapolis, IN: Liberty Fund Press, 2006.

Miller, Thomas. *The Evolution of College English: Literacy Studies from the Puritans to the Postmoderns*. Pittsburgh, PA: University of Pittsburgh Press, 2011.

———. *The Formation of College English: Rhetoric and Belles Lettres in the British Cultural Provinces*. Pittsburgh, PA: University of Pittsburgh Press, 1997.

———. "Witherspoon, Blair, and the Rhetoric of Civic Humanism." In *Scotland and America in the Age of the Enlightenment*, edited by Richard Sher and Jeffrey Smitten, 242–58. Princeton, NJ: Princeton University Press, 1990.

Minowitz, Peter. *Profits, Priests, and Princes: Adam Smith's Emancipation of Economics from Politics and Religion*. Stanford, CA: Stanford University Press, 1993.

Mitchell, Robert. "'Beings That Have Existence Only in ye Minds of Men': State Finance and the Origins of the Collective Imagination." *Eighteenth Century: Theory and Interpretation* 49, no. 2 (2008): 117–39.

Montesquieu. *The Spirit of the Laws*. Edited and translated by Anne Cohler, Basia Miller, and Harold Stone. Cambridge, UK: Cambridge University Press, 1989.

Mouffe, Chantal. *The Democratic Paradox*. New York: Verso, 2000.

Muckelbauer, John. *The Future of Invention: Rhetoric, Postmodernism, and the Problem of Change*. Albany: State University of New York Press, 2008.

Muller, Jerry Z. *The Mind and the Market: Capitalism in Modern European Thought*. New York: Alfred A. Knopf, 2002.

Myers, Sharon. "ReMembering the Sentence." *College Composition and Communication* 54, no. 4 (2003): 610–28.

North, Douglas, and Barry Weingast. "Constitutions and Commitment: The Evolution of Institutions Governing Public Choice in Seventeenth-Century England." *Journal of Economic History* 49, no. 4 (1989): 803–32.

Nussbaum, Martha. *Upheavals of Thought: The Intelligence of Emotions*. Cambridge, UK: Cambridge University Press, 2001.

Offer, John. *Herbert Spencer and Social Theory*. New York: Palgrave, 2010.

Ohmann, Richard. "Use Definite, Specific, Concrete Language." In *Politics of Letters*, 241–51. Middletown, CT: Wesleyan University Press, 1987.

Ong, Walter. *Orality and Literacy: The Technologizing of the Word*. London: Methuen, 1982.

Pace, Tom. "Style and the Renaissance of Composition Studies." In *Refiguring Prose Style: Possibilities for Writing Pedagogy*, edited by T. R. Johnson and Tom Pace, 3–22. Logan: Utah State University Press, 2005.

Patterson, Annabel. *Hermogenes and the Renaissance: Seven Ideas of Style*. Princeton, NJ: Princeton University Press, 1970.

Petit, Philip. *Made with Words: Hobbes on Language, Mind, and Politics*. Princeton, NJ: Princeton University Press, 2008.

Petty, William. "Political Arithmethick." In *The Economic Writings of Sir William Petty*, vol. 1, edited by Charles Henry Hull, 232–313. Cambridge, UK: Cambridge University Press, 1899.

Pocock, J. G. A. *The Machiavellian Moment: Florentine Political Thought and the Atlantic Republican Tradition*. Princeton, NJ: Princeton University Press, 1975.

———. *Virtue, Commerce, and History: Essays on Political Thought and History, Chiefly in the Eighteenth Century*. Cambridge, UK: Cambridge University Press, 1985.

Poovey, Mary. *Genres of the Credit Economy: Mediating Value in Eighteenth- and Nineteenth-Century Britain*. Chicago: University of Chicago Press, 2008.

Postrel, Virginia. *The Substance of Style: How the Rise of Aesthetic Value Is Remaking Commerce, Culture, and Consciousness*. New York: HarperCollins, 2003.

Poulantzas, Nicos. *State, Power, Socialism*. Introduced by Stuart Hall, translated by Patrick Camiller. New York: Verso, 2000.

Proast, Jonas. *The Argument of the "Letter concerning Toleration," Briefly Consider'd and Answer'd*. Oxford, UK: George West and Henry Clements, 1690.

Proudhon, Pierre-Joseph. *What Is Property?* Edited and translated by Donald R. Kelley and Bonnie Smith. Cambridge, UK: Cambridge University Press, 1994.

Pufendorf, Samuel. *On the Duty of Man and Citizen according to Natural Law*. Edited by James Tully and translated by Michael Silverthorne. Cambridge, UK: Cambridge University Press, 1991.

Quintilian. *Institutio Oratoria, Books VII–IX*. Translated by H. E. Butler. Cambridge, MA: Harvard University Press, 1921.

Raphael, D. D. *The Impartial Spectator: Adam Smith's Moral Philosophy*. Oxford, UK: Oxford University Press, 2007.

Rawls, John. *A Theory of Justice*. Rev. ed. Cambridge, MA: Harvard University Press, 1999.

Reid, Thomas. *Inquiry and Essays*. Edited by Ronald Beanblossom and Keith Lehrer. Indianapolis, IN: Hackett, 1983.

Rivers, Isabel. *Shaftesbury to Hume*. Vol. 2 of *Reason, Grace, and Sentiment: A Study of the Language of Religion and Ethics in England, 1660–1780*. Cambridge, UK: Cambridge University Press, 2000.

Robertson, John. "The Scottish Enlightenment at the Limits of the Civic Tradition." In *Wealth and Virtue: The Shaping of Political Economy in the Scottish Enlightenment*, edited by István Hont and Michael Ignatieff, 137–78. Cambridge, UK: Cambridge University Press, 1983.

Rorty, Richard. *Contingency, Irony, and Solidarity*. Cambridge, UK: Cambridge University Press, 1989.

———. *Philosophy and the Mirror of Nature*. Princeton, NJ: Princeton University Press, 1979.

Rosenblatt, Helena. *Rousseau and Geneva: From the "First Discourse" to the "Social Contract," 1749–1762*. Cambridge, UK: Cambridge University Press 1997.

Ross, Ian. "Adam Smith and Education." In *Studies in Eighteenth-Century Culture*, vol. 13, edited by O. M. Brack, 173–87. Madison: University of Wisconsin Press, 1984.

Rothschild, Emma. *Economic Sentiments: Adam Smith, Condorcet, and the Enlightenment*. Cambridge, MA: Harvard University Press, 2001.

Schmidgen, Wolfram. "The Politics and Philosophy of Mixture: John Locke Recomposed." *Eighteenth Century: Theory and Interpretation* 48, no. 3 (2007): 205–23.

Schmitz, Robert Morell. *Hugh Blair*. New York: King's Crown Press, 1948.

Searle, G. R. *Morality and the Market in Victorian Britain*. Oxford, UK: Clarendon Press, 1998.

Secor, Marie. "The Legacy of Nineteenth-Century Style Theory." *Rhetoric Society Quarterly* 12, no. 2 (1982): 76–94.

Sekora, John. *Luxury: The Concept in Western Thought, Eden to Smollett*. Baltimore, MD: Johns Hopkins University Press, 1977.

Seligman, Adam. *The Idea of Civil Society*. New York: Free Press, 1992.

Sennett, Richard. *The Fall of Public Man*. New York: W. W. Norton, 1976.

Shaftesbury, 3rd Earl of [Cooper, Anthony Ashley]. *Characteristicks of Men, Manners, Opinions, Times*. 3 vols. Foreword by Douglas Den Uyl. Indianapolis, IN: Liberty Fund Press, 2001.

Shapin, Steven, and Simon Shaffer. *Leviathan and the Air-Pump: Hobbes, Boyle, and the Experimental Life*. Princeton, NJ: Princeton University Press, 1985.

Shapiro, Carl, and Hal. R. Varian. *Information Rules: A Strategic Guide to the Network Economy*. Boston: Harvard Business School Press, 1999.

Sher, Richard. *Church and University in the Scottish Enlightenment: The Moderate Literati of Edinburgh*. Princeton, NJ: Princeton University Press, 1985.

———. *The Enlightenment and the Book: Scottish Authors and Their Publishers in Eighteenth-Century Britain, Ireland, and America*. Chicago: University of Chicago Press, 2006.

Sheridan, Thomas. *A Course of Lectures on Elocution*. New ed. Providence, UK: Carter and Wilkinson, 1796.

Skinner, Andrew. *A System of Social Science: Papers Relating to Adam Smith*. Oxford, UK: Clarendon Press, 1979.

Skinner, Quentin. *The Foundations of Modern Political Thought*. 2 vols. Cambridge, UK: Cambridge University Press, 1978.

———. *Reason and Rhetoric in the Philosophy of Thomas Hobbes*. Cambridge, UK: Cambridge University Press, 1996.

Smith, Adam. "Considerations concerning the First Formation of Languages." In *Lectures on Rhetoric and Belles Lettres*, edited by J. C. Bryce, 201–31. Indianapolis, IN: Liberty Fund Press, 1985.

Smout, T. C. *A History of the Scottish People, 1560–1830*. London: Fontana, 1969.

———. "Where Had the Scottish Economy Got to by the Third Quarter of the Eighteenth Century?" In *Wealth and Virtue: The Shaping of Political Economy in the Scottish Enlightenment*, edited by István Hont and Michael Ignatieff, 45–72. Cambridge, UK: Cambridge University Press, 1983.

Spencer, Herbert. *Essays: Scientific, Political, and Speculative*. London: Longman, Brown, Green, Longmans and Roberts, 1858.

———. "Mr. Spencer's Address." In *Herbert Spencer on the Americans and the Americans on Herbert Spencer*, edited by Edward Youmans, 28–34. New York: D. Appleton and Company, 1882.

———. "The Philosophy of Style." *Westminster Review* 114 (October 1852): 435–59.

———. *The Principles of Psychology*. London: Longman, Brown, Green and Longmans, 1855.

———. "The Proper Sphere of Government." In *The Man versus the State, with Six Essays on Government, Society, and Freedom*, 181–264. Introduced by Albert Jay Nock, foreword by Eric Mack. Indianapolis, IN: Liberty Fund Press, 1982.

———. *Social Statics; or, The Conditions Essential to Human Happiness Specified, and the First of Them Developed*. London: John Chapman, 1851.

Sprat, Thomas. *The History of the Royal Society of London for the Improving of Natural Knowledge*. London: J. Martyn, 1667.

Stark, Ryan. *Rhetoric, Science, and Magic in Seventeenth-Century England*. Washington, DC: Catholic University Press, 2009.

Steele, Richard. "*The Spectator* No. 218, Friday, November 9, 1711." In *The Commerce of Everyday Life: Selections from "The Tatler" and "The Spectator*," edited by Erin Mackie, 220–22. New York: Bedford/St. Martin's, 1998.

Steuart, Sir James. *An Inquiry into Principles of Political Oeconomy*. 2 vols. Edited and introduced by Andrew S. Skinner. Chicago: University of Chicago Press, 1966.

Stillingfleet, Edward. *The Bishop of Worcester's Answer to Mr. Locke's Letter concerning Some Passages Relating to His "Essay of Humane Understanding*." London: J.H. for Henry Mortlock, 1697.

———. *The Bishop of Worcester's Answer to Mr. Locke's Second Letter; Wherein His Notions of Ideas Is Prov'd to Be Inconsistent with It Self, and with the Articles of the Christian Faith*. London: J.H. for Henry Mortlock, 1698.

Taylor, Frederick Winslow. *The Principles of Scientific Management*. New York: W. W. Norton, 1967.

Taylor, Michael. *The Philosophy of Herbert Spencer*. New York: Continuum, 2007.

Thompson, James. *Models of Value: Eighteenth-Century Political Economy and the Novel*. Durham, NC: Duke University Press, 1996.

Trilling, Lionel. *Sincerity and Authenticity: The Charles Norton Eliot Lectures, 1969–1970*. Cambridge, MA: Harvard University Press, 1972.

Trusler, John. *The Way to Be Rich and Respectable, Addressed to Men of Small Fortune*. London: R. Baldwin, 1776.

Tully, James. *A Discourse on Property: John Locke and His Adversaries*. Cambridge, UK: Cambridge University Press, 1980.

Turpin, Paul. *The Moral Rhetoric of Political Economy: Justice and Modern Economic Thought*. New York: Routledge, 2011.

Vaughn, Karen. *John Locke: Economist and Social Scientist*. Chicago: University of Chicago Press, 1980.

Vickers, Brian. "The Royal Society and English Prose Style: A Reassessment." In *Rhetoric and the Pursuit of Truth: Language Change in the Seventeenth and Eighteenth Centuries, Papers Read at a Clark Library Seminar 8 March 1980 by Brian Vickers and Nancy Struever*, 3–76. Introduced by Thomas Wright. Los Angeles: William Andrews Clark Memorial Library, 1985.

Virno, Paolo. *A Grammar of the Multitude*. Translated by Isabella Bertoletti, James Cascaito, and Andrea Casson. Los Angeles: Semiotext(e), 2004.

Vivenza, Gloria. *Adam Smith and the Classics: The Classical Heritage in Adam Smith's Thoughts*. Oxford, UK: Oxford University Press, 2001.

Vogt, Philip. *John Locke and the Rhetoric of Modernity*. Lanham, MD: Lexington, 2008.

Walker, Jeffrey. *The Genuine Teachers of This Art: Rhetorical Education in Antiquity*. Columbia: University of South Carolina Press, 2011.

Walmsley, Peter. *Locke's "Essay" and the Rhetoric of Science*. Lewisburg, PA: Bucknell University Press, 2003.

Walzer, Arthur. "Blair's Ideal Orator: Civic Rhetoric and Christian Politeness in Lectures 25–34." *Rhetorica* 25, no. 3 (2007): 269–95.

———. *On Toleration*. New Haven, CT: Yale University Press, 1997.

Warner, Michael. *Publics and Counterpublics*. New York: Zone Books, 2002.

Warnick, Barbara. *The Sixth Canon: Belletristic Rhetorical Theory and Its French Antecedents*. Columbia: University of South Carolina Press, 1993.

Waterman, A. M. C. *Revolution, Economics, and Religion: Christian Political Economy, 1798–1833*. Cambridge, UK: Cambridge University Press, 1991.

Weathers, Winston. "Teaching Style: A Possible Anatomy." *College Composition and Communication* 21, no. 2 (1970): 144–49.

Weber, Max. *The Protestant Ethic and the Spirit of Capitalism.* Translated by Talcott Parsons, introduced by Anthony Giddens. New York: Routledge, 1992.

Whatley, Christopher. *The Industrial Revolution in Scotland.* Cambridge, UK: Cambridge University Press, 1997.

———. *Scottish Society, 1707–1830: Beyond Jacobinism, towards Industrialization.* Manchester, UK: Manchester University Press, 2000.

Whyte, Ian. *Scotland before the Industrial Revolution: An Economic and Social History, c. 1050–c. 1750.* London: Longman, 1995.

Wilkins, John. *An Essay towards a Real Character and a Philosophical Language.* London: 1668.

Witherspoon, John. *Ecclesiastical Characteristics; or, The Arcana of Church Policy: Being an Humble Attempt to Open Up the Mystery of Moderation.* Glasgow, 1753.

———. *Lectures on Moral Philosophy and Eloquence.* Philadelphia: William W. Woodward, 1810.

Wood, Neal. *John Locke and Agrarian Capitalism.* Berkeley: University of California Press, 1984.

———. *The Politics of Locke's Philosophy: A Social Study of "An Essay concerning Human Understanding."* Berkeley: University of California Press, 1983.

Woodruff, Paul. *First Democracy: The Challenge of an Ancient Idea.* Oxford, UK: Oxford University Press, 2005.

Woolhouse, Roger. *Locke: A Biography.* Cambridge, UK: Cambridge University Press, 2007.

Wright, Erik Olin. *Classes.* New York: Verso, 1997.

Yates, JoAnne. *Control through Communication: The Rise of System in American Management.* Baltimore, MD: Johns Hopkins University Press, 1989.

Youmans, Edward. "Report of Mr. Spencer's Interview." In *Herbert Spencer on the Americans and the Americans on Herbert Spencer,* edited by Edward Youmans, 9–20. New York: D. Appleton and Company, 1882.

Index

Typeset by
BOOKCOMP

Printed and bound by
SHERIDAN BOOKS

Composed in
ADOBE JENSON PRO, BERLING NOVA SANS PRO

Printed on
NATURES NATURAL

Bound in
ARRESTOX